GIVE US YOUR BEST AND BRIGHTEST

THE GLOBAL HUNT FOR TALENT AND ITS IMPACT ON THE DEVELOPING WORLD

DEVESH KAPUR
and
JOHN McHALE

Center for Global Development
Washington, D.C.

Copyright © 2005
CENTER FOR GLOBAL DEVELOPMENT
1776 Massachusetts Avenue, N.W.
Washington, D.C. 20036
www.cgdev.org

*Give Us Your Best and Brightest: The Global Hunt for Talent
and Its Impact on the Developing World* may be ordered from:
BROOKINGS INSTITUTION PRESS
c/o HFS
P.O. Box 50370
Baltimore, MD 21211-4370
Tel.: 800/537-5487
410/516-6956
Fax: 410/516-6998
Internet: www.brookings.edu

Library of Congress Cataloging-in-Publication data

Kapur, Devesh, 1959–
    Give us your best and brightest : the global hunt for talent and its impact on
    the developing world / Devesh Kapur.
        p.   cm.
    Summary: "Examines the political and economic implications of migrant
    flows from a development perspective"—Provided by publisher.
    Includes bibliographical references and index.
    ISBN-13: 978-1-933286-03-7 (isbn-13, paper : alk. paper)
    ISBN-10: 1-933286-03-2 (isbn-10, paper : alk. paper)
    1. Professional employees—Developing countries. 2. Brain drain—Developing
countries. 3. Human capital—Developing countries. 4. Skilled labor—Developing
countries. 5. Developing countries—Emigration and immigration. 6. Developed
countries—Emigration and immigration. I. McHale, John. II. Title.
    HD8038.D44K36 2005
    331.12'791—dc22   2005018132

9 8 7 6 5 4 3 2 1

The paper used in this publication meets minimum requirements of the
American National Standard for Information Sciences—Permanence of Paper for
Printed Library Materials: ANSI Z39.48-1992.

Typeset in Sabon and Myriad

Composition by Cynthia Stock
Silver Spring, Maryland

Printed by Versa Press
East Peoria, Illinois

Center for Global Development

The Center for Global Development is an independent, nonprofit policy research organization dedicated to reducing global poverty and inequality and to making globalization work for the poor. Through a combination of research and strategic outreach, the Center actively engages policymakers and the public to influence the policies of the United States, other rich countries, and such institutions as the World Bank, the IMF, and the World Trade Organization to improve the economic and social development prospects in poor countries. The Center's Board of Directors bears overall responsibility for the Center and includes distinguished leaders of nongovernmental organizations, former officials, business executives, and some of the world's leading scholars of development. The Center receives advice on its research and policy programs from the Board and from an Advisory Committee that comprises respected development specialists and advocates.

The Center's president works with the Board, the Advisory Committee, and the Center's senior staff in setting the research and program priorities, and approves all formal publications. The Center is supported by an initial significant financial contribution from Edward W. Scott Jr. and by funding from philanthropic foundations and other organizations.

Contents

Preface

International migration is a development issue. In the last half-century, cross-border trade and financial flows transformed the global economic and political landscape and created new opportunities and new challenges for the developing world. In this century, cross-border flows of people—whether as permanent migrants or temporary workers, and irrespective of legal status—are bound to be equally transformative.

This book is about one aspect of this phenomenon—the movement from poor to rich countries of people with skills: the once-named "brain drain." The economic and social consequences of substantial immigrant inflows for the receiving countries have prompted considerable debate and rich analysis. The welfare and human rights of migrants—whether their movement is provoked by income gaps, ethnic cleansing, economic instability, or human trafficking—is an issue attracting increasing international attention. This book addresses a third subject heretofore largely neglected: how immigration policies of the rich countries matter to those nations sending immigrants.

For the Center for Global Development, publication of this book marks the start of a broader investigation into cross-border flows of people and their causes and consequences for developing countries. The Center's mission is to reduce global poverty and inequality, including and especially through research that inspires better policy in the rich world. A key question for us is whether, how much, and in what form immigration and labor mobility policies of rich countries matter for the "brain drain"—and whether and how they interact with developing country policies and constraints to affect "brain gain," that is, the return of human capital and of complementary investment from rich to poor countries. This book suggests immigration policy does matter—and could matter more in the future, though often with unintended and surprising effects. It also sets out how immigration policies could be more development friendly—benefiting rich as well as developing economies.

Concerns about migration of human capital from developing countries have undergone a sea change in recent years. The sentiment and the language have switched from alarm ("brain drain") to hope for remittances, for "brain gain" arising from the greater incentives to acquire human capital when emigration is a possibility, and for the network effects of enriched and savvy diasporas ("brain trust"). In fact, neither view in the extreme is warranted. But to understand why and the implications, we need to understand the mechanisms through which these flows can affect sending countries, and why those effects are likely to differ depending on characteristics of the sending country.

Devesh Kapur and John McHale begin by surveying the magnitude of the poor to rich country flows, as well as the rich country policies that are driving them. They then provide detailed study of the multiple channels through which skilled migration affects development. Although they stress that the balance of effects will vary by country and by sector, they draw attention to the potential harm that can be done when a poor country loses a substantial fraction of its already scarce talent.

At a time when institutional quality is front and center in the development debate, they emphasize the impact of internationally mobile human capital on building effective institutions. Finally, they provide a rich discussion of the available policy options, outlining those that avoid the worst losses to poor countries, while maintaining the most liberal feasible international migration regime.

There is a growing awareness in the development community that the movement of people is potentially as important to development outcomes as the movement of goods and capital. Yet little is known about the recent and likely future course of policies in rich countries that will affect movement of people. And in comparison to the breadth and depth of analysis of the development impacts of trade and financial flows, almost nothing is known about the development impact of international migration. This timely and thoughtful volume advances tremendously our understanding of the issues and sets a high standard for future contributions to this important new area of development policy research. Without more knowledge, there can be no basis for consensus on what set of migration policies would be pro-development. I believe this book will ultimately be seen as the key first step in building a more development friendly policy consensus.

Nancy Birdsall
President
Center for Global Development
Washington, D.C.

Acknowledgments

We have acquired significant debts to a number of people in preparing this monograph. Our greatest debt is to Nancy Birdsall at the Center for Global Development (CGD) for supporting the work throughout its too-long gestation. We are very grateful both for her insights on migration and development and for her willingness to put up with two procrastinating authors.

We are also very thankful to the participants in two workshops organized by CGD to discuss, first, the original plan for the monograph and then, later, a working draft. At CGD, Noora-Lisa Aberman and Lawrence McDonald have been invaluable in shepherding the manuscript through to publication. We have also been fortunate to have had the skilled editorial assistance of Janet Walker and Vicky Macintyre at Brookings.

Jorge Domínguez, director of the Weatherhead Centre for International Affairs at Harvard, has been a bedrock of support for research on migration. Jagdish Bhagwati, Dani Rodrik, and Alan Winters have been especially generous with their time and support. We owe a particular debt to Ajay Agrawal, Iain Cockburn, and Mihir Desai, our coauthors on related projects, for their influence on our thinking on international migration, though of course they are in no way responsible for any misuse of their ideas here. Megan Crowley, David Doyle, Mike Murakami, Radoslav Raykov, Anjali Salooja, Radu Tatucu, and Edward Young have provided truly outstanding research assistance along the way, for which we are very grateful.

In addition, Devesh Kapur would like to acknowledge the strong financial support of Diego Hidalgo, which helped jump-start his work on international migration.

CHAPTER 1

Introduction

For many poor countries, the share of their skilled nationals residing in rich countries is staggeringly high. The emigration rate among their tertiary-educated population has been conservatively estimated at 41 percent for the Caribbean region, 27 percent for Western Africa, 18.4 percent for Eastern Africa, and 16 percent for Central America.[1] There is growing concern that such outflows help trap countries in poverty. Yet departures from vulnerable regions have increased in response to reduced immigration restrictions for—and at times active recruitment of—skilled workers from poorer countries.

These selective reductions have aroused surprisingly muted criticism compared with other rich-country policies affecting development, such as the protection and subsidization of agricultural sectors, restrictions on access to cheaper medicines under trade-related intellectual property rights (TRIPS), and the austerity imposed on crisis-hit countries as part of bailout packages. The ambivalence surrounding targeted immigration is due in part to the fact that policy of this kind helps break down artificial barriers to freedom of movement—if only for a subset of the population. There is also some question as to whether skilled emigration is truly detrimental to development. Although the loss of a doctor serving

---

1. These estimates are from Docquier and Marfouk (2004), who conducted a massive survey of census and other data from all countries of the Organization for Economic Cooperation and Development (OECD) to estimate the size of the immigrant populations in each by education level and country of birth. Their findings are reviewed in chapter 2.

hundreds or even thousands of patients in rural Africa clearly depresses living standards for those remaining behind, does the emergence of tightly networked Chinese and Indian diasporas in Silicon Valley really harm their home country's domestic high-tech sectors? Since the 1960s, the pendulum seems to have swung from concern about the "brain drain" sapping development to a celebration of "brain circulation." This book is in part an effort to push the pendulum a bit of the way back.

This might seem like an odd moment to fret about talent being poached from the developing world. For one thing, the high-tech boom largely responsible for the rich-country immigration reforms of the 1990s recently came to an end, putting the liberalization drive into reverse in the United States (although it seems to be continuing to increase elsewhere).[2] For another, the terrorist attacks of 2001 and after have focused attention on security, with the result that potential migrants are coming under greater scrutiny and their applications taking longer to process. Although fallen from the front pages, international human capital flows will undoubtedly be an important development issue in the coming decades. Three powerful long-term trends are likely to rekindle the international competition for talent.[3]

2. Most notably, the United States has again capped H-1B visas at 65,000, lowering the level from 195,000, and made it more difficult for foreign students to obtain visas. The H-1B is a temporary visa used to attract large numbers of highly skilled workers. It often serves as a way station for workers waiting for employment-based permanent residency. The U.S. response has been more the exception than the rule. Australia has continued to accept close to record levels of skilled workers. Canada, meanwhile, has lowered the points cutoff on its revamped skilled-worker program to counter falling acceptance rates. Similarly, the United Kingdom has lowered the points cutoff on its Highly Skilled Worker Programme but increased the points for younger workers and workers with qualified partners. A somewhat unheralded development on the U.S. liberalization front is the recent removal of the severe restrictions on the availability of North American Free Trade Agreement–related (or TN) temporary visas for skilled Mexican workers. These visas have been available to Canadians in unrestricted numbers since the early 1990s, and they appear to have facilitated a substantial movement of skilled professionals from Canada to the United States.

3. Even the United States is becoming concerned about the barriers to talented foreigners. In a companion to its Science and Engineering Indicators for 2004, the National Science Board set off an alarm in "An Emerging and Critical Problem of the Science and Engineering Labor Force," stating that "the number of U.S. citizens prepared for [science and engineering] jobs will, at best, be level; and the availability of people from other countries who have science and engineering training will decline, either because of limits imposed by U.S. national security restrictions or because of intense global competition for people with these skills" (National Science Board, 2004, p. 1). The issue of demand-driven human capital outflows from poorer countries is likely to be with us for some time.

First, the skill bias of recent technological advancements is leading governments to strive for a competitive advantage in emerging knowledge-based industries. With a continuing high demand for skill, industry is likely to lobby for more liberal immigration policies to ease cost pressures, and strong skilled-wage growth will once again dampen domestic worker opposition. Although nothing fuels the desire for protection quite like deteriorating labor market conditions, skilled workers have enjoyed absolute and relative wage gains for several decades now and thus remain relatively relaxed about immigration. At the same time, even highly skilled workers are not immune to protectionist turns, as indicated by their mounting complaints about the outsourcing of some skilled service sector jobs. But cost-focused outsourcing is more likely to strengthen the high-tech sectors of rich countries than it is to weaken them and hence will probably bolster the confidence of the skilled workforce.

Second, international competition for skilled labor will be abetted by the aging of rich-country populations together with the ever-expanding technical possibilities for costly (and often highly beneficial) health care. On the labor market side, this trend is likely to increase the demand for less-skilled care and other services needed by an older population. But because the fiscal costs of population aging are huge, targeted attempts will also be made to attract higher-earning foreign workers to help pay for pension and health care benefits for the domestic population. The harsh reality is that, given the size of the tax increases that will be necessary to pay promised benefits for older citizens, these promises are at extreme risk of being broken by future politicians and electorates. The baby boom generation in particular will want to backfill the taxpaying workforce behind it to stave off the worst of this risk. As we show in later chapters, however, immigration is far from being a "silver bullet" for rich-country aging. Many of the immigrants being recruited as taxpayers to help pay for these overburdened systems will themselves acquire entitlements to future benefits to be paid for by future taxpayers, making immigration only a temporary fix to the long-term costs of an aging population. Despite this, with the alternatives of even greater tax increases for the working population or even greater benefit cuts for the retired population, there will be strong pressures to "import" taxpayers at the margin.

Third, international competition for talent is bound to increase because of the broader globalization of production and trade. Although in theory international product and capital market integration can substitute for international labor market integration, in practice they tend to evolve together. Multinational companies, for example, want to be able to move their staff between locations and sometimes use the threat of moving jobs to win more flexibility to hire foreign workers domestically. Familiarity with foreign cultures also makes people more willing to move and destination country populations more willing to accept them. Looking forward, as trade in services becomes more liberal, the lines between trade and migration become blurred. Perhaps most important, as product market competition intensifies, governments will be pressed to ease immigration restrictions so as to provide domestic firms, especially those in innovation-intensive sectors of the economy, with a source of competitive advantage through improved and cheaper access to a diverse set of skills.

How will this increased competition for talent affect the development prospects of poor countries? Our admittedly unsatisfying answer is that the benefits and costs will vary, depending on the country and sector. The direct costs of absent human capital can be substantial, as demonstrated by the shortages of skilled labor in key areas such as pediatrics in Africa or by the significant net fiscal losses due to disproportionate emigration of the highly skilled in India. But countries can also obtain substantial benefits from the international mobility of their human capital. To cite a few examples, the Chinese and Indian diasporas in Silicon Valley have facilitated international business for domestic high-tech firms, remittances to Latin America have been buffering consumption there, and Irish emigrants who left in the 1980s and subsequently returned were instrumental in sustaining the "Celtic Tiger" economy of the 1990s.

The effects of skilled emigration on poor countries occur through four basic channels. The *prospect* channel refers to the way the prospect or option of emigrating alters the level and form of human, social, and financial capital accumulated by forward-looking individuals. Having an emigration option can also affect domestic institutions and policies such as the progressivity of the tax system and the financing of higher education. The *absence* channel refers to the way the absence of such capital from the home economy affects domestic factor markets and institutions. In this case, standard measures of emigration costs that do not take into account the heterogeneity of skills are likely to underestimate the costs of lost specialized skills, with a key absence-related loss stemming from missing institution builders. The *diaspora* channel denotes the impact of emigrants on the home economy from afar. In addition to being a source of trade, investment, remittances, and knowledge, a successful diaspora can play a critical role in reducing barriers to international business through its role as "reputational intermediary" and thus help poor countries integrate into global production chains and international trade. The last channel, *return,* represents the impact of emigrants returning with augmented skills, social networks, and wealth, now better equipped to contribute to their home economies than if they had never left.

As is increasingly recognized, the massive gap in living standards between the developing and the developed world reflects vast differences in the soundness of their institutional foundations. These foundations include security of property and person, scope for trusting trading partners, and honesty and capability of the providers of public services. They are weakest in truly failed states. But weak institutions also hold back growth in functioning but still predatory states. Of course, people are the ones who build institutions; and talented people are most likely to be the targets of rich-country recruiters. Moreover, the places that potential institutional builders are most likely to leave are those where institutional quality is worst.

If one assumes that people of exceptional talent and drive are essential to institutional reform, it is easy to see that the loss of institution builders—hospital managers, university department heads, political reformers, to name just a few—can help trap countries in poverty. At the same time, other channels of skilled emigration may have some positive effects on institutional development. The prospect of exit via emigration, for example, can increase the bargaining power of productive citizens compared with their more predatory brethren, in effect forcing the latter to give value creators better deals in such forms as lower taxes, smaller bribes, and better public sector working conditions. Also, members of the diaspora—especially returnees with a deep knowledge of successful institutional structures—can be important forces for reform. In sum, mobile talent can play a complex role in institutional development.

To best understand that role in poorer countries, one should perhaps first consider how the absence of highly talented individuals affects institutional development, meaning both the supply of institution builders and the demand for better institutions. The *supply* side is the more straightforward. Countries have limited supplies of people willing and able to take on entrenched interests in order to reform schools, establish clinics, and fight for the rule of law. However, the individuals most likely to be institution builders by talent and temperament are also those most likely to be internationally marketable. Furthermore, the incomes of noncorrupt but talented individuals working in public institutions with compressed wage scales are likely to compare unfavorably with foreign alternatives. Such people are highly susceptible to giving up and starting over in an environment where they are more valued. To compound the potential loss of institution-building supply, the *demand* for improved institutions may go down when the most productive leave, for they are the very individuals who are capable of being successful in high-quality institutional environments and thus have the strongest interest in seeing that these institutions are built.

Our discussion of the four channels of influence—prospect, absence, diaspora, and return—focuses on their effects on the welfare of "those remaining behind" (TRBs) in the home country. This is not to imply that the welfare of TRBs is all that matters. Emigration obviously has important welfare effects on the emigrants themselves. Presumably, these effects will generally be positive—otherwise they would not leave. However, the welfare effects on TRBs are less well understood. Of course, skilled emigration also affects destination countries and their skilled workers, who must compete directly in the job market with the emigrants. Although much still needs to be learned about the costs and benefits of skilled immigration, this aspect of the migration experience has been comparatively well studied.[4]

We also omit unskilled emigration from the discussion, though clearly an important phenomenon that will continue to occur (much of it illegally) as long as there are large gaps in living standards between countries. In view of these gaps, unskilled emigrants are likely to experience even larger welfare gains from emigration than are skilled workers, for whom international factor markets are more integrated. Even so, official immigration policy of rich countries has been focusing more on the need for skilled workers, portending a future of increased human capital outflows from developing countries. The causes and consequences of this phenomenon are the central concern of this book.

The reader might also wonder about likely developments on the supply side of the international skill market. Will the world's skilled workers continue to uproot themselves in great numbers in pursuit of the living standards available to them in rich countries? The answer, of course, depends on the success of poorer countries in closing the now-large income gaps between themselves and rich countries. China's (and more recently India's) rapid growth is a positive sign that these income gaps have the potential to close, and that people may not be forced to

---

4. For surveys, see Borjas (1994, 1995) and National Research Council (1997).

seek prosperity through often highly disruptive international moves. Unfortunately, despite the possibility illustrated by the Chinese and Indian examples, extreme inequalities are likely to persist between the developed and developing parts of the world, providing a deep vein of potential emigrants for some time to come, with the prospects for Africa looking particularly bleak. In the chapters that follow, then, we assume that there is a willing (though not unlimited) supply of internationally mobile skilled labor and focus on the effects on flows of the selective demand-side removal of migration barriers.

So what should be done? We discuss the policy responses under four headings: control, compensation, creation, and connections. At the risk of oversimplifying a complex policy challenge, we offer the following formulation: control when absolutely necessary; compensation when it is feasible; creation and connections whenever possible. By *control* we mean efforts to curb the flow of skilled immigrants or emigrants. Even though "brain drains" can be damaging, we do not think the solution is to try to put the barriers back up. International migration is already too restricted and stands awkwardly as the missing element of globalization.[5] As they seek economic advantage, rich countries are tilting their immigration policies more and more toward skilled workers for whom they anticipate easy assimilation. Although more balanced immigration would be fairer and better for development, even selective liberalization of immigration barriers that follows the path of least political resistance is better than no liberalization at all. At times, however, selective recruitment (or "poaching") of talent will be so damaging—not least in enticing doctors and nurses from countries experiencing health crises—that rich countries should "just say no." But rather than remove emigration options for those lucky enough to have them, we think it is generally better to look for ways to make sure that everyone shares in the spoils when those options are exercised.

This leads us to consider ways of *compensating* those remaining behind.[6] The numerous mechanisms for this purpose differ in the degree

---

5. See the excellent discussions in Bhagwati (2004) and Wolf (2004).

6. We thank Jagdish Bhagwati for pointing out that compensation may be interpreted as making up for losses to "those remaining behind." As he rightly notes, the case for emigrant taxation need not depend on whether TRBs are harmed by the emigration. The taxation could be viewed as compensation for the source country's past investments in the emigrant's human capital, or for the ongoing benefits of citizenship. We thus use compensation in the broad sense of payments in money or in kind to the source country and do not limit the case for such payments to situations in which the source country is harmed.

to which the compensation is paid by the rich-country governments, rich-country employers, or the emigrants themselves. They also differ in the agency that enforces the compensation. The options include tying development aid to human capital recruitment, arranging for rich-country personnel to act as replacements, sharing payroll and income tax revenues with poor-country providers of human capital, having countries of origin impose ongoing tax obligations on their emigrants (the Bhagwati tax), providing conditional education grants that are repayable on emigration, and sharing the proceeds of visa fees or the revenues of visa auctions. All of these mechanisms pose practical difficulties. And almost all require the cooperation of rich-country governments.

We also look at rich- and poor-country policies designed to *create* human capital and thereby address the skill imbalances that are both the cause and consequence of emigration. On the rich-country side, systematic underinvestment in sectors such as health care and education (especially for public systems) has led to almost permanent skill shortages and ongoing "crisis" recruitment from poorer countries. When such crises recur in sectors clearly being damaged by emigration, rich countries have an obligation to correct the problems with their own policies for creating human capital rather than continually relying on poor countries to fill the gaps. They are deterred from doing so, however, by the costs of investing in the necessary manpower, which must often be borne years before the benefits are realized. Also, governments have an obligation to use well what human capital they do recruit. To this end, Canada, for one, has pushed immigration policy in a more skill-focused direction. Nevertheless, when professionals such as doctors actually arrive, their credentials are not always recognized. Although all countries have the right—indeed an obligation—to regulate quality in professions with large asymmetries of information between sellers and buyers, such concerns sometimes seem to be a screen for the protection of domestic competitors or may simply be the result of too few resources being devoted to immigrant integration. Poor countries also need to respond to inevitable outflows with reforms of their own human capital–creation policies. Where substantial skill outflows are foreseeable, forward-looking poor-country governments need to "overinvest" in skill creation, possibly in association with policies that put a greater burden of the costs of those investments on the recipients of the education—especially if they ultimately decide to leave. In addition, poor countries need to improve the quality of their educational institutions, not least because weak institutions themselves drive out the talented educators on whom successful domestic skill creation depends.

A less controversial approach is to ensure that emigrants remain economically and socially *connected* to their former homes, which include policies that affect the probability of return. The purpose here is to maximize the benefits from having a well-connected diaspora and the capital-augmented return. Receiving and sending countries can make it easier for emigrants to travel, send remittances, and make investments. They can also help in solving the collective action problems inherent in organizing a diaspora and cooperate with groups that do form. One way to increase the probability of return is to make visas temporary without the possibility of leading to permanent status. The idea is that young people build skills, savings, and social networks while abroad and then return to use their accumulated human, financial, and social capital to the benefit of the home country. Such policies seem fair if the migrants understand the terms of their visa from the outset. Indeed, time limitations are perfectly legitimate for short stays. But seeing that many people quickly put down roots in their adopted countries, we think that medium- to long-term temporary and nonconvertible visas are not humane policy. A better approach is to create *incentives* to return as opposed to prohibitions on staying. For instance, governments could allow emigrants to return again at a later time if things do not work out, make social security entitlements portable, sponsor the return of people with badly needed skills, put money in special accounts during the migrant's stay that can only be accessed on return, or ask the country of origin to provide information on opportunities at home.

Our analysis is structured in three parts. We set the scene in part I with a review of what is known about the extent of skilled emigration and about rich-country policies facilitating it. In chapter 2 we piece together a rough statistical portrait of international human capital stocks and flows that highlights emigration rates by education level, the incidence of the disproportionate losses of the very highly skilled, and the return patterns of students from developing countries who acquire their education in rich countries. In chapter 3, we document policy developments relating to skilled emigration in five leading recipient countries—Australia, Canada, Germany, the United Kingdom, and the United States—policies that are largely responsible for changes in emigrant stocks and flows. In chapter 4, we reflect on the long-term forces that are driving these policy evolutions and on whether the skill-focused trend is likely to continue. Part II turns to the various channels through which these stocks and flows have affected the source countries, with a chapter on each of the prospect, absence, and return channels and two chapters on the poorly understood disapora channel. In reviewing the limited evidence on the strength of these channels, we use boxes to outline their various effects in certain countries and sectors. The picture that emerges is quite complex. No broad statement about overall desirability is possible, though we can make stronger statements at the sectoral level and can also identify certain channels of influence that are detrimental and others that are beneficial (or could be made so). Part III provides some policy options for both rich (destination) countries and poor (source) countries that would help international skill mobility become more beneficial for poorer nations without making the international migration system even more illiberal than it is today.

CHAPTER 2

Absent Human Capital: What Do We Know?

The data on international migration are so poor that it is difficult to estimate simple migrant stocks and flows, let alone their human capital content.[1] By contrast, considerable effort has been put into amassing, refining, and updating data on international financial flows. Several international agencies have taken charge of maintaining these data, most notably the World Bank, International Monetary Fund, Bureau of International Statistics, and the Organization for Economic Cooperation and Development (OECD). To date, no comparable interest has been shown in human capital outflows, perhaps because their consequences are less visible and take longer to reveal themselves than the impacts of financial crises. A good analogy is the response to crises resulting from severe drought versus endemic malnutrition due to poverty: the international community tends to tolerate the latter condition to a much greater degree, even though in the long term its human costs may greatly exceed those due to occasional droughts.

Unfortunately, developing countries, which have the most to gain from compiling and maintaining data on human capital flows, lack the capabilities to do so. In some cases, they are not interested because those leaving are part of the governing elites. The disaggregated and individual nature of these outflows compounds the problem. Nonetheless,

---

1. For example, some countries report the sizes of their foreign-born populations, while others report the size of their noncitizen populations.

these movements are no more complex than financial outflows, and some means already exist to collect data on them. Censuses, population surveys where they exist, consular offices of embassies, visa applications, in some cases tax authorities—all can provide pertinent information on flows from developing to industrial countries. The first hurdle, of course, is that databases are not geared to compiling this information, and no international standards exist on census or visa information that would match the infrastructure for collecting data on financial flows. In addition, heightened national security concerns have reduced the possibility of open access to data from many of these sources, although developing countries could do more to make their collective interest in this regard known to international organizations.

Another impediment, perhaps the most difficult to overcome, is that the principal measures of human capital flows used to date—years of schooling or level of education—say little about quality. Hence the most that is known concerns the stock of foreign-born tertiary-educated people from some developed countries.[2] This says nothing about the quality of the group, particularly whether it is from the tail end of the distribution, which may be affected by the more varying quality of educational institutions in developing countries. Furthermore, the number of years of education says little about areas of study and how serious the loss of skilled personnel may be in important areas such as science and technology, or what political and economic effects are induced by factors such as emigrants' religion, ethnicity, and region of origin. Notwithstanding these limitations, we draw on a number of sources in this chapter to provide a rough statistical portrait of the relevant human capital stocks and flows.

UN Estimates of Migrant Stocks and Flows

The United Nations estimates that in 2000, 175 million people were living outside their country of birth. This figure is just less than 3 percent of the world's population and considerably more than the 120 million estimated in 1990. About 104 million of these people were living in what the United Nations considers "more developed regions" than their home countries; this group represented close to 9 percent of the home population. Among countries with migrant stocks of more than 1 million people (table 2-1), the United States, with close to 35 million immigrants,

2. See Adams (2003).

Table 2-1. Migrant Stocks of More than One Million in 2000[a]

Country	Thousands	Percent of total population
United States	34,988	12.4
Russia	13,259	9.1
Germany	7,349	9.0
Ukraine	6,947	14.0
France	6,277	10.6
India	6,271	0.6
Canada	5,826	18.9
Saudi Arabia	5,255	25.8
Australia	4,705	24.6
Pakistan	4,243	3.0
United Kingdom	4,029	6.8
Kazakhstan	3,028	18.7
China, Hong Kong	2,701	39.4
Côte d'Ivoire	2,336	14.6
Iran	2,321	3.3
Israel	2,256	37.5
Moldova	2,088	5.4
Jordan	1,945	39.6
United Arab Emirates	1,922	73.8
Switzerland	1,801	25.1
Italy	1,634	2.8
Japan	1,620	1.3
Netherlands	1,576	9.9
Turkey	1,503	2.3
Argentina	1,419	3.8
Malaysia	1,392	6.3
Singapore	1,352	33.6
South Africa	1,303	3.0
Belarus	1,284	12.6
Burkina Faso	1,124	9.7
Kuwait	1,108	57.9
Venezuela	1,006	4.2

Source: United Nations Population Division (UNPD) (2002).

a. For most countries, the migrant stock number is a midyear estimate of the number of foreign-born. Estimates of the number of noncitizens are used where data on nativity are not available (Japan, Iran, Jordan, Kuwait, and Germany).

has by far the largest foreign-born population.[3] (Recently released estimates from the 2000 census put the figure somewhat lower, at just over 31 million.) The large stocks of foreign-born residents in second-ranked Russia and fourth-ranked Ukraine are largely driven by mobility—restricted even as it was—within the former Soviet Union. Among developed countries, Germany, France, Canada, Australia, and the United Kingdom also have large foreign-born populations. Indeed, when measured as a share of the domestic population, the foreign-born populations of Canada (18.9 percent) and Australia (24.6 percent) are substantially larger than that in the United States (12.4 percent).[4] Another striking feature of foreign-born populations is their large presence (both in terms of absolute numbers and especially as a share of the population) in the oil-exporting Arab countries, in Israel (due to the immigration of the Jewish diaspora), and in poor African countries such as Côte d'Ivoire and Burkina Faso (with neighbor countries with severe civil unrest).

In the second half of the 1990s, the annual net outflow in a number of countries averaged more than 2 people per 1,000 (table 2-2). Not surprisingly, departure figures were highest for countries experiencing civil or regional wars. In war-tornTimor, the rate was 41 per 1,000, and in Burundi, 13 per 1,000. Elsewhere, economic factors presumably played the predominant role in pushing people out, as was the case in Estonia (8 per 1,000), Bulgaria (5 per 1,000), the Philippines (3 per 1,000), and Jamaica (3 per 1,000).

Estimated Emigration Rates by Education Level

The raw numbers do not indicate *who* is leaving. Development impacts—both positive and negative—are highly contingent on this aspect of emigration, on whether it is poor laborers with less than a primary education or the educated elite who are leaving. Depending on the questions asked, census data for developed countries may shed some light on the human capital characteristics of the foreign-born populations by country of origin. Until recently, the only cross-country comparison of human capital loss from developing countries has been done for U.S. census data. Two directly comparative studies have been completed

3. Where estimates of the size of the foreign-born population are not available, the table records estimates of the noncitizen or foreign population (see note to table 2-1 for the countries with noncitizen population estimates).

4. Recent census estimates put the foreign-born shares slightly lower: 21.9 percent in Australia, 18.4 percent in Canada, and 11.1 percent in the United States.

Table 2-2. Countries with Estimated Net Emigration of More than Two per
1,000 of Population, Annual Average, 1995–2000

Country	Net emigration per 1,000	Net emigration (thousands)
Timor Leste, Democratic Republic of	40.6	32
Samoa	22.8	4
Burundi	12.9	80
Kazakhstan	12.2	200
Guyana	10.6	8
Tajikistan	10.3	61
Suriname	10.3	4
Fiji	8.8	7
Estonia	8.0	12
Sierra Leone	7.8	33
Haiti	7.4	19
Congo, Democratic Republic of	7.1	340
Saint Lucia	7.0	1
Mongolia	6.5	16
Guinea	6.2	48
Georgia	5.7	30
Burkina Faso	5.5	60
Bulgaria	4.9	40
Mali	4.7	50
Lesotho	3.4	7
Mexico	3.3	310
Benin	3.2	19
Trinidad and Tobago	3.1	4
Guatemala	2.8	30
Sudan	2.6	77
Philippines	2.6	190
Jamaica	2.6	1
Cape Verde	2.5	1
Armenia	2.5	9
Nicaragua	2.5	12
Belize	2.3	1
Guadeloupe	2.2	1
Mauritius	2.0	2
Latvia	2.0	5

Source: UNPD (2002).

using data from the 1990 census and subsequently the 2000 census.[5] In a recent massive data-gathering exercise, Frédéric Docquier and Abdeslam Marfouk extended this line of inquiry to almost the entire OECD, using national census and survey data.[6]

The methodology used in these earlier studies consists of two key steps. First, residents in the United States aged 25 and older who emigrated from specified developing countries were assigned to one of three educational categories: primary or less (0 to 8 years of education), secondary (9 to 12 years of education), and tertiary (more than 12 years of education). Second, the stock of individuals at each level of education was compared with domestic stocks.[7]

While revealing, this methodology has a number of obvious drawbacks. First, the educational categories are broad and imprecise. For instance, a graduate from one of India's elite institutes of technology would be placed in the same category as a graduate from a low-quality private college. Second, it is not clear whether individuals received their educations in their home country or abroad. Concern about human capital loss obviously differs for a person educated in the home country at the expense of home-country taxpayers as opposed to people who studied in their adopted country at their own or their adopted country's expense. Third, no mention is made of the age at which people left their home country. The difference between individuals who left with their parents as infants and those who left immediately after graduation from university to take a high-paying job abroad is self-evident.

Table 2-3 records some salient characteristics of certain developing-country populations residing in the United States in 2000. By far the largest number of emigrants, more than 9 million, were from Mexico. Roughly half of this group (52 percent) came before 1990, and roughly half (48 percent) came afterward. Of the more than 6 million Mexicans aged 25 or older living in the United States, nearly half possess a primary education or less, and only 14 percent have some form of tertiary education. The educational composition is very different for the next two largest groups of nationals, from the Philippines and India. A relatively high share of Filipinos (65 percent) came before 1990, but the share with some tertiary education is much higher than for Mexicans, standing at 73 percent. By contrast, Indians are newcomers, with

5. Carrington and Detragiache (1998); Adams (2003).
6. Docquier and Marfouk (2004).
7. Estimates of domestic stocks are from Barro and Lee (1993, 2000).

Table 2-3. Foreign-Born Population in the United States in 2000: Entry Year and Education Level, Selected Developing Countries

Country of birth	Total 2000	Entry year (percent)		Total 25 or older	Education 25 or older (percent) [a]		
		1990– 2000	Pre- 1990		Primary	Secondary	Tertiary
Mexico	9,177,485	48	52	6,374,825	48	38	14
Philippines	1,369,070	35	65	1,163,555	8	20	73
India	1,022,550	55	45	836,780	5	15	80
China	988,785	49	51	846,780	20	26	54
El Salvador	817,340	40	60	619,185	41	42	17
Dominican Republic	687,680	43	57	527,520	30	43	29
Jamaica	553,825	31	69	449,795	8	47	45
Colombia	509,875	45	55	402,935	13	41	46
Guatemala	480,665	49	51	341,590	43	37	20
Peru	278,185	47	53	220,815	8	39	53
Pakistan	223,475	57	43	165,425	7	26	67
Brazil	212,430	66	34	154,250	9	36	55
Nigeria	134,940	53	47	109,160	2	15	83
Egypt	113,400	41	59	96,660	4	19	78
Bangladesh	95,295	70	30	69,180	9	29	62
Turkey	78,380	47	53	64,780	14	28	58
Indonesia	72,550	50	50	53,170	3	23	75
Armenia	65,280	57	43	44,380	9	41	51
Croatia	40,910	33	67	35,455	19	40	41
Albania	38,660	83	17	25,785	14	48	38
Morocco	34,685	53	47	29,670	5	30	65
Sri Lanka	25,265	50	50	21,820	2	26	72
Sudan	19,790	76	24	12,730	8	29	63
Tunisia	9,110	32	68	5,555	7	29	64

Source: U.S. Census 2000; Adams (2003), based on special tabulations from U.S. Census 2000.

a. Primary corresponds to 0–8 years of schooling, secondary to 9–12 years, and tertiary to more than 12 years.

55 percent coming after 1990; however, the share with tertiary education is 80 percent, which is even higher than for Filipinos. Among the other groups on the list, only those from El Salvador and Guatemala exhibit the same low levels of education as do Mexican emigrants.

As a crude measure of the significance of absent human capital, we look at the number of tertiary-educated individuals (aged 25 and older) residing in the United States as a percentage of the total tertiary-educated population (domestically resident and emigrant) of that country (table 2-4). Following William Carrington and Enrica Detragiache,

Table 2-4. Absent Human Capital: Emigration Rates by Education Level, Population 25 or Older, 1990 and 2000[a]

Percent

a. Rates to the United States[b]

Country of birth	U.S. resident population (≥ 25)				1990				2000			
	1990	2000	Change	Percent change	Total	Pri-mary	Second-ary	Terti-ary	Total	Pri-mary	Second-ary	Terti-ary
Mexico	2,743,638	6,374,825	3,631,187	132	7.1	1.7	20.9	10.3	11.7	9.7	14.7	14.2
Philippines	728,454	1,163,555	435,101	60	2.2	0.1	4.4	6.6	3.5	0.6	2.2	10.5
India	304,030	836,780	532,750	175	0.1	0.1	0.1	1.1	0.2	0.1	0.2	2.7
China	404,579	846,780	442,201	109	0.1	0.1	0.1	1.4	0.1	0.1	0.2	2.2
El Salvador	263,625	619,185	355,560	135	10.2	1.6	66.6	26.1	19.5	11.0	53.4	28.3
Dominican Republic	187,871	527,520	339,649	181	5.9	0.6	29.7	14.2	11.4	5.0	29.8	19.9
Jamaica	159,913	449,795	289,882	181	11.8	0.4	23.4	67.5	25.0	4.5	29.0	78.6
Colombia	162,739	402,935	240,196	148	1.1	0.1	3.7	5.6	2.1	0.4	3.8	9.0
Guatemala	127,346	341,590	214,244	168	3.3	0.4	29.1	13.5	7.1	3.7	23.0	20.5
Peru	86,323	220,815	134,492	156	0.9	0.1	2.3	3.0	1.8	0.3	2.4	4.0
Pakistan	52,717	165,425	112,708	214	0.1	0.1	0.2	2.4	0.3	0.1	0.5	6.0
Brazil	53,904	154,250	100,346	186	0.1	0.1	0.7	0.6	0.2	0.1	0.5	1.1
Egypt	53,261	96,660	43,399	81	0.3	0.1	0.4	2.5	0.3	0.1	0.2	2.2
Bangladesh	12,385	69,180	56,795	459	0.1	0.1	0.1	0.6	0.1	0.1	0.3	2.2
Turkey	43,605	64,780	21,175	49	0.2	0.1	0.7	1.5	0.2	0.1	0.4	1.3
Indonesia	32,172	53,170	20,998	65	0.1	0.1	0.1	1.4	0.1	0.1	0.1	0.7
Sri Lanka	8,715	21,820	13,105	150	0.1	0.1	0.1	3.8	0.2	0.1	0.1	5.3
Sudan	2,496	12,730	10,234	410	0.1	0.1	0.1	1.8	0.1	0.1	0.3	3.3
Tunisia	2,816	5,555	2,739	97	0.1	0.1	0.3	1.6	0.1	0.1	0.2	1.3

b. Rates to all OECD countries[c]

Country of birth	1990				2000			
	Total	Pri-mary	Second-ary	Terti-ary	Total	Pri-mary	Second-ary	Terti-ary
Mexico	7.4	6.5	8.9	10.4	11.5	9.5	14.3	14.3
Philippines	4.1	1.1	3.1	12.8	5.2	1.4	3.1	14.8
India	0.2	0.1	0.2	2.6	0.3	0.1	0.3	4.2
China	0.2	0.1	0.1	3.1	0.2	0.1	0.2	4.2
El Salvador	14.4	8.2	38.5	32.9	20.2	11.2	53.6	31.5
Dominican Republic	7.9	3.8	23.6	17.9	12.5	5.8	30.9	21.7
Jamaica	25.6	11.0	28.9	84.1	29.0	8.3	30.0	82.5
Colombia	1.8	0.5	3.9	9.2	2.7	0.8	4.6	11.0
Guatemala	4.3	2.1	18.9	18.2	6.9	3.5	22.8	21.5
Peru	1.6	0.3	2.6	5.6	2.8	0.7	3.6	6.3
Pakistan	0.4	0.2	0.6	6.1	0.7	0.3	1.1	9.2
Brazil	0.3	0.1	0.9	1.7	0.6	0.1	1.5	3.3
Egypt	0.7	0.2	1.0	5.3	0.8	0.2	0.7	4.2
Bangladesh	0.1	0.1	0.2	2.3	0.3	0.1	0.7	4.7
Turkey	4.9	4.2	9.3	6.3	5.0	4.6	7.5	4.6
Indonesia	0.3	0.1	0.4	6.2	0.2	0.1	0.3	2.0
Sri Lanka	1.6	0.8	1.5	24.8	2.8	1.9	1.8	27.5
Sudan	0.1	0.0	0.4	5.0	0.2	0.1	0.7	5.6
Tunisia	4.7	4.6	3.4	12.3	4.3	4.2	3.0	9.6

c. Tertiary rates to OECD countries, by region[d]

Region	1990	2000	Difference	2000/1990
Caribbean	41.4	40.9	−0.5	0.99
Western Africa	20.7	26.7	6.0	1.29
Eastern Africa	15.5	18.4	2.9	1.19
Central America	12.9	16.1	3.2	1.25
Central Africa	9.8	13.3	3.5	1.36
Southeastern Asia	10.3	9.8	−0.5	0.95
Northern Africa	6.8	6.2	−0.6	0.91
Western Asia	6.9	5.8	−1.1	0.84
South America	4.7	5.7	1.0	1.21
Southern Africa	6.9	5.3	−1.6	0.77
South-Central Asia	4.0	5.1	1.1	1.28
Eastern Europe	2.3	4.5	2.2	1.96
Eastern Asia	4.1	4.3	0.2	1.05

a. For each education category, the emigration rate equals the number of emigrants divided by the domestically resident population plus the number of emigrants.

b. Sources: For 1990, Carrington and Detragiache (1998); for 2000, Adams (2003). Both sources combine U.S. Census data with data on human capital stock from Barro and Lee (1993, 2000).

c. Sources: Docquier and Marfouk (2004) and authors' calculations.

d. Source: Docquier and Marfouk (2004).

we call this measure the *emigration rate*.[8] To the extent that emigrants are included in the measure of the domestically resident population arrived at by Robert Barro and Jong-Wha Lee, this calculation will underestimate the true emigration rate, and so it can reasonably be viewed as a lower bound.[9]

Rates at which the tertiary-educated immigrate to the United States vary greatly across countries. In 2000 the figures ranged from 2.7 percent for tertiary-educated Indians (notwithstanding the fact that 80 percent of U.S. resident Indians have a tertiary education) to 78.6 percent for Jamaicans. Here, whatever the relative quality, the raw numbers suggest a staggering absence of scarce human capital from the home country. Although only 14 percent of the Mexican-born population in the United States has a tertiary education, that population is so large that the tertiary emigration rate is still 14.2 percent—which is far higher than the Indian rate, which, however, may be hiding a large amount of absent Indian human capital given the high human capital intensity of Indian emigrant graduates.

8. Carrington and Detragiache (1998).
9. Barro and Lee (1993).

It is also interesting to compare changes in these foreign-born populations (aged 25 and older) over the course of the 1990s. Most striking is the tremendous increase in size. The Indian-born population, for example, increased by almost 534,000, or 175 percent. Emigration rates jumped too, as illustrated by figures for China, which rose from 1.4 percent in 1990 to 2.2 percent in 2000.[10] All these increases reflect large increases in the underlying absent stocks.

What overall conclusions can one draw about U.S.-bound skilled emigration? First, for a number of countries—notably Mexico and countries in Central America and the Caribbean—a substantial fraction of their educated populations are residing in the United States when measured by the crude tertiary emigration rate. Second, excepting those from Mexico and Central America, the foreign-born populations residing in the United States tend to have a fairly high education. And third, when measured as a percentage of total tertiary-educated stocks, the stocks of absent human capital in many countries increased substantially over the 1990s.

Table 2-4 also uses the recently available data from Docquier and Marfouk to calculate country-specific emigration rates to the entire OECD for the same set of countries. For countries in Central and South America and the Caribbean, the emigration rates to the entire OECD are not that much higher than the emigration rates solely to the United States. This obviously reflects the fact that the United States is the destination of choice for most emigrants from these regions. Elsewhere, however, geography and historical ties make other OECD countries attractive destinations. For example, the emigration rate of tertiary-educated individuals from Tunisia to the United States is just 1.3 percent compared with 9.6 percent to the OECD as a whole—most of which is accounted for by nearby European countries. For the two most populous countries in the world, China and India, expanding the focus to the entire OECD also leads to a substantial increase in the estimated tertiary emigration rate. In 2000 the Chinese and Indian emigration rates to the United States were 2.2 and 2.7 percent, respectively, but reached 4.2 percent in the entire OECD.[11] To get a better overall picture, the table also shows emigration rates by broad region for the tertiary-educated. The rates from some regions are shockingly high. In 2000 the tertiary

10. Tertiary-educated stocks residing within many developing countries also increased during the 1990s. China's stock increased from just under 12 million to almost 21 million.
11. Adams (2003).

rate for the Caribbean region was in excess of 40 percent. The figure for Western Africa was 27 percent. Moreover, for a number of very poor regions the rate rose substantially over the 1990s. It climbed almost 30 percent for Western Africa (or 6 percentage points, the highest percentage point increase of all regions), 36 percent for Central Africa, and 96 percent for Eastern Europe.

"Quality"as Reflected in Indian Immigration to the United States

The foregoing analysis raises a key question: to what extent are the "best and brightest" disproportionately emigrating? Put in terms of a concrete example, does the fact that the tertiary-educated Indians in the United States equal just 2.7 percent of tertiary-educated Indians in India mean that India is losing just a small and nonthreatening fraction of its human capital to the United States—or are the Indians that leave of disproportionately high "quality"?

The evidence, particularly from studies of graduates of the six branches of the Indian Institute of Technology (IIT), strongly suggests that those Indians who leave are not drawn randomly from the population of graduates, let alone the population at large. The acceptance rate at these institutes is between 1 and 2 percent from an already highly selective pool. According to an analysis of the "brain drain" from IIT Mumbai in the 1970s, 31 percent of its graduates settled abroad, while the estimated migration rate of engineers for the country as a whole was 7.3 percent.[12] Furthermore, the migration was significantly higher in those branches of engineering in which IIT entrants had the highest scholastic ranking: thus the percentage abroad in electrical engineering (which had higher entrance requirements in those years) was nearly 43 percent, whereas in metallurgical engineering (with lower requirements) it was about 20 percent. Similarly, the top quartile of the graduating class had 43 percent abroad but the rest of the class only 27 percent.

Other disciplines in India have also experienced this type of severe selection bias in emigration. In medicine, the migration rates for doctors in general was about 3 percent during the 1980s, but for graduates of the All India Institute for Medical Sciences, India's most prestigious

12. See Sukhatme (1994). The survey, conducted in 1986, covered students who graduated from IIT Mumbai between 1973 and 1977. Students taking the entrance exam for the IITs are ranked on their performance in a written exam. Students with higher rankings have greater choice of institute and branch of engineering, and once these places are filled, the lower-ranked students choose from the remaining disciplines.

medical training establishment, the rate was 56 percent between 1956 and 1980, and it stood at 49 percent in the 1990s.[13] (The next section examines the outflows from this sector more generally.) A recent analysis of graduates of India's premier management school in February 2000 found that the grades of typical recruits in the international sector are "significantly higher" than those of their counterparts in the domestic sector.[14]

Selection bias is also reflected in the wage and income attainment of the Indian-born population residing in the United States compared with that of Indians born there and non-Indian foreign nationals.[15] Drawing on U.S. census figures for 1990 and Current Population Survey (CPS) data for 1994–2001 (see tables 2-5 and 2-6), we find that the Indian-born population in the United States is indeed very highly skilled. Focusing on the March 2001 CPS results, we see that 78 percent of this population (aged 25 to 64) has a bachelor's degree or better, and almost half of this group has a postgraduate degree: 28 percent has a master's degree, 6 percent a professional degree, and 4 percent a Ph.D. By contrast, only 9 percent of the native-born population has a postgraduate degree. Interestingly, the share with a postgraduate degree in the "other" foreign-born category is also 9 percent. This figure reflects the relatively low educational attainment and high immigrant numbers from Mexico and Central American countries. A striking feature of this last group is that a very high share did not complete high school (32 percent in 2001 compared with 9 percent for the native-born), and also a relatively high share had Ph.D.s (2 percent versus 1 percent).

An even more direct way to gauge the relative skill level of the Indian-born population is to look at their incomes in relation to those of U.S.-born Indians and non-Indian foreign nationals (table 2-6).[16] In March 2001, for example, the median income of the native-born population was $23,925, and 4 percent of this group earned more than $95,700, or more than four times the native-born median. By contrast, 12 percent of the Indian-born population—three times the percentage of the native-born—had incomes greater than this level.

13. For figures between 1956 and 1980, see Khadria (1999). Data on the 1990s are based on submissions by the Comptroller and Auditor General to the Indian Parliament. See Synopses of Debates, Rajya Sabha, Proceedings Other than Questions and Answers, August 22, 2001 (http://parliamentofindia.nic.in/rs/rsdebate/synopsis/193/22082001.html).

14. See Bhattacharjee, Krishna, and Karve (2001).

15. For detailed discussion of this type of selection bias, see Desai, Kapur, and McHale (2003).

16. We restrict our attention to the working-age population (18 to 64).

Table 2-5. Educational Attainment for Native-, Indian-, and Other Foreign-Born, Aged 25–64, 1990 and 1994–2001[a]
Percent

Year	Population share					Graduate breakdown		
	Below high school	High school graduate	Some college	Bachelor's degree	Graduate level	Master's	Profes-sional	Ph.D.
Native-born								
1990	17	32	28	15	8	5	2	1
1994	13	36	27	16	8	6	1	1
1995	12	35	28	17	8	6	2	1
1996	12	35	28	18	8	6	1	1
1997	11	35	28	18	8	6	1	1
1998	11	35	28	18	8	6	1	1
1999	10	34	28	19	9	6	1	1
2000	10	34	29	19	9	7	1	1
2001	9	33	29	19	9	7	1	1
Indian-born								
1990	12	11	14	27	36	21	9	6
1994	8	9	15	35	32	17	11	4
1995	8	10	12	26	44	24	13	7
1996	8	13	12	30	38	27	7	4
1997	7	16	10	34	33	23	6	4
1998	6	14	15	35	31	22	5	3
1999	6	10	10	36	38	25	7	6
2000	6	8	9	35	41	27	6	8
2001	3	9	10	40	38	28	6	4
Other foreign-born								
1990	38	20	20	13	9	5	2	1
1994	34	25	17	16	8	5	2	2
1995	35	25	17	15	8	5	2	2
1996	35	23	18	15	8	5	2	2
1997	34	24	18	16	9	5	2	2
1998	33	25	16	17	9	6	2	2
1999	33	25	17	16	9	6	2	2
2000	32	26	17	16	9	5	2	2
2001	32	25	17	17	9	5	2	2

Source: For 1990, U.S. Census Bureau (1990); for 1994–2001, March Current Population Survey.

a. The five columns under "population share" show the percentage living in the United States who have attained various levels of education for the specified years. The remaining three columns provide a further breakdown by degree type for those who have attained graduate-level education.

Table 2-6. Income Distribution for Native-, Indian-, and Other Foreign-Born, Aged 18–64, 1990 and 1994–2001[a]

Year	Median (2001 U.S. dollars)	Population share (as percent of median)				
		0–50	50–100	100–200	200–400	>400
Native-born						
1990	20,293	33	17	27	18	4
1994	19,836	31	19	28	18	4
1995	20,100	30	20	28	18	5
1996	20,626	30	20	29	17	4
1997	21,418	30	20	29	17	4
1998	21,580	30	20	29	16	4
1999	22,826	30	20	30	16	4
2000	23,126	30	20	29	16	5
2001	23,925	29	21	30	16	4
Indian-born						
1990	20,670	35	14	21	20	10
1994	21,943	32	14	24	21	9
1995	24,980	28	14	26	22	11
1996	25,145	31	16	25	19	10
1997	24,301	29	18	24	21	8
1998	27,915	29	15	23	24	9
1999	31,715	30	11	24	26	9
2000	29,986	35	9	18	24	14
2001	28,121	34	11	18	25	12
Other foreign-born						
1990	14,483	39	21	23	13	4
1994	13,053	42	23	21	11	3
1995	13,803	41	24	21	11	4
1996	13,562	42	24	22	10	3
1997	13,729	41	24	22	10	3
1998	14,443	40	25	21	10	4
1999	14,816	41	26	21	9	3
2000	15,510	40	26	21	11	3
2001	16,084	37	26	23	10	3

Source: For 1990, U.S. Census Bureau (1990); for 1994–2001, March Current Population Survey.

a. The five columns under "population share" show the percentage living in the United States who lie between various fractions and multiples of the median native-born income for the specified years.

As table 2-6 also shows, the median for the Indian-born group is well above the median for the native-born, which in turn is well above the median for the "other" foreign-born. This again reflects the low average human capital of immigrants from Mexico and Central America (see table 2-3). Even so, the share with very high incomes—again defined as four times the native-born median—is just slightly less in the other foreign-born category than that for the native-born population. Thus although the Indian-born population is undoubtedly an outlier in terms of its human capital intensity (again, see table 2-3), these data are consistent with substantial numbers of very skilled individuals residing in the United States.

The Example of Medical Outflows

Of all the talent lost from developing countries, medical professionals are perhaps of the greatest concern—all the more so in the wake of the AIDS pandemic. To appreciate how scarce medical professionals are in some poorer countries, consider that net importers of health professionals such as Australia and Canada have more than 200 physicians and 800 nurses per 100,000 people, whereas Ghana, a net exporter of health professionals, has only 6.2 physicians and 72 nurses per 100,000—which translates to 16,129 people per physician and 1,389 people per nurse (table 2-7).

Although fragmentary, trends in health professional flows can be pieced together from destination- and source-country data.[17] Driven by domestic nursing shortages, in 2001–02 the United Kingdom for the first time listed more overseas additions to its nurse register than home-country additions: 735 nurses were from the Philippines, 2,114 from South Africa, and 1,342 from Australia. Recruitments from other countries such as India and Zimbabwe were also up sharply over the previous three years. The Code of Practice put in place in 1999 (extended to private recruitment agencies in 2001) prohibited recruiting in South Africa and the West Indies because of the severe shortages in these regions. However, noncompliance by recruitment agencies is reportedly widespread.

According to the U.S. Department of Health and Human Services, the United States suffered a shortage of 111,000 registered nurses in 2000. Foreign recruitment has thus far played a limited role in easing the

---

17. Here, we draw heavily on an excellent recent survey for the World Health Organization by Buchan and Poz (2002).

Table 2-7. WHO Estimates of Population per Health Professional, Selected Countries and Years

Countries in table 2-4	Population per physician	Year	Population per nurse	Year
Mexico	536.5	1990	1,156.1	1995
Philippines	813.0	1996	239.2	1996
India	2,083.3	1992	2,222.2	1992
China	618.4	1998	1,014.2	1998
El Salvador	933.7	1997	2,865.3	1997
Dominican Republic	463.8	1997	3,344.5	1997
Jamaica	713.8	1996	1,550.4	1996
Colombia	862.1	1997	2,070.4	1994
Guatemala	1,071.8	1997	3,703.7	1997
Peru	1,073.0	1997	869.6	1997
Pakistan	1,754.4	1997	2,941.2	1996
Brazil	786.2	1996	2,421.3	1996
Egypt	495.0	1996	429.2	1996
Bangladesh	5,000.0	1997	9,090.9	1997
Turkey	826.4	1998	917.4	1998
Indonesia	6,250.0	1994	2,000.0	1994
Sri Lanka	2,739.7	1999	973.7	1999
Sudan	11,111.1	1996	1,724.1	1996
Tunisia	1,428.6	1997	349.7	1997
Additional countries				
Australia	416.7	1998	120.5	1998
Canada	436.7	1995	111.5	1996
Germany	285.7	1998	104.5	1998
Ghana	16,129.0	1996	1,388.9	1996
Nigeria	5,405.4	1992	1,512.9	1992
Russia	237.5	1998	121.8	1998
South Africa	1,776.2	1996	212.0	1996
United Kingdom	609.8	1993	201.2	1989
United States	358.4	1995	102.9	1996

Source: World Health Organization (2002).

shortages because of restrictions imposed by U.S. immigration laws. Between 1997 and 2000, just 506 foreign nurses applied for licensure, with 32.6 percent of applications coming from the Philippines, 22 percent from Canada, and 7.4 percent from Africa (mainly Nigeria and South Africa). But lobbying by health care employers (and possibly even overburdened employees) is sure to build as shortages increase.

On the sending side, approximately 85 percent of Filipino nurses—some 150,000 individuals—are working overseas. In 2001 some 5,353 were thought to have left to work in the United Kingdom, 5,045 went to Saudi Arabia, 1,529 to Ireland, and 413 to Singapore. Filipinos are also prominent as domestic helpers and on the crews of the world's commercial ships. Overall, an estimated 7 million Filipinos are working abroad, which is equal to more than 20 percent of the domestic labor force.[18]

Given the importance of remittances to the domestic economy—they amount to roughly 10 percent of gross domestic product (GDP) a year—the Philippine government has initiated deliberate policies to encourage nurses to emigrate.[19] For other poor countries, however, the emigration of nurses is an unwanted hemorrhage that is worsening. Despite health care needs due to AIDS, the number of nurses in South Africa applying to work in another country rose from 500 in the early 1990s to more than 3,500 by the end of the decade. Those remaining behind are frustrated and demoralized by the deteriorating quality of care and staff shortages.[20]

Like most other sub-Saharan countries, Ghana is a country coping with an extreme shortage of physicians. Although low per capita income is a major factor behind the scarcity, physician emigration appears to have exacerbated preexisting shortages. Interviews with graduates from Ghana's medical schools suggest that about half of the physician graduates between 1985 and 1994 had left the country within 4.5 years, and three-quarters had left within 9.5 years.[21] The resulting loss has put a tremendous strain on the capacity to provide care, with the vacancy rate for physicians in 1998 standing at almost 50 percent. The clear factor pulling doctors away is the huge salary gap between Ghana and rich countries: in January 1999, a junior doctor (with five years or less of experience) earned an average of $200 a month, while a senior doctor earned just $272.

Elsewhere in Africa the situation is not much better. Since 1996 more than 100 doctors and 1,800 nurses have left Zimbabwe, most moving to English-speaking countries where they can earn a higher salary. Of the 1,200 doctors trained in Zimbabwe during the 1990s, only 360 were still practicing in 2001.[22] In 2001 doctors in Kenya earned the equivalent of

18. Martin and Widgren (2002).
19. Martin and Widgren (2002).
20. Buchan, Parkin, and Sochalski (2003).
21. Dolvo and Nyonator (1999).
22. Physicians for Human Rights (2004).

US$414 a month for working in the public domain. Low salary combined with the disparity in potential earnings has led to an exodus of doctors from Kenya—which the Kenya Medical Association estimates to be 20 doctors a month, an alarming rate given that the country has only 600 doctors in the public sector. The situation is equally serious in Nigeria, which has lost 21,000 doctors to the United States. According to American Medical Association records, however, the number of Nigerian doctors licensed to practice medicine in the United States is much smaller—fewer than 2,000.[23] This suggests that the majority may be working in positions that do not require a license or may have left medicine altogether. Either way, the outflow represents a considerable loss to the Nigerian health system.

Portuguese-speaking African countries have been losing sizable fractions of their health professionals to Portugal.[24] War-ravaged Angola, for example, has sent 820 doctors to Portugal, which is close to the 961 doctors remaining there. Guinea-Bissau has suffered an even more dramatic loss of 358 doctors to Portugal, compared with fewer than 200 remaining. Because a substantial fraction of these emigrant doctors received all or part of their medical training in Portugal, care should be taken in interpreting these numbers as a "brain drain." However, the fact remains that these African doctors are practicing in a relatively rich Western country rather than in Africa.

The shortage of health professionals also shows up in vacancy rates for established posts in the public sector.[25] In Malawi, for example, only 28 percent of established nursing posts were filled in 2003, down from 47 percent in 1998. The situation was worse for specialists in central hospitals, where only 9.3 percent of posts were filled—including just 1 surgeon out of 24 positions. Also in 1993, South Africa's Department of Health estimated that 4,000 doctor positions and 32,000 nursing positions were unfilled in the public sector. These vacancy numbers compare with a public sector workforce of 11,500 doctors and 86,000 nurses.

It is easy to become dulled to this litany of numbers. The human stakes in the medical brain drain and the paradox of poor-to-rich country flows are poignantly captured in a recent *New York Times* article:

23. Physicians for Human Rights (2004).
24. Stillwell and others (2004).
25. Physicians for Human Rights (2004).

The result of the nursing crisis—the neglect of the sick—is starkly apparent here on the dilapidated wards of Lilongwe Central Hospital [in Malawi], where a single nurse often looks after 50 or more desperately ill people. What is equally visible is the boon to Britain, where Lilongwe Central's former nurses minister to the elderly in the carpeted lounges of nursing homes and to patients in hushed private hospital rooms.

It is the poor subsidizing the rich, since African governments paid to educate many of the health workers who are leaving. At Lilongwe Central, an 830-bed hospital, there are supposed to be 532 nurses. Only 183 are left. That is about half as many as there were just six years ago. And only about 30 of those are registered nurses, the highly skilled cadre that is most sought abroad.[26]

Foreign Populations in Other OECD Countries

Even though the United States has by far the largest population of skilled emigrants, it is certainly not the only important receiving country. OECD estimates for 1990 and 2000 show 4.1 million foreign-born residents in Australia and 5.5 million in Canada (table 2-8). Although these numbers are well below the 31.1 million foreign-born counted in the 2000 U.S. census, as a fraction of the population (21.9 percent in Australia and 18.4 percent in Canada) they both exceed the U.S. fraction of 11.1 percent. Because immigration policies in Canada and Australia focus on skill, the educational attainment is relatively high in both countries.[27]

The OECD countries listed in tables 2-8 and 2-9 show great diversity in both the size and educational attainment of their foreign populations. Germany has the largest foreign-born population in the group: 7.34 million in 2000, or 8.9 percent of the total population. By far the largest contributor is Turkey, which accounted for more than 28 percent of the

26. Celia Dugger, "An Exodus of African Nurses Puts Infants and the Ill in Peril," *New York Times*, July 12, 2004.

27. Across all immigration streams to Canada in 2000, 44 percent of all principal applicants and dependents aged 15 or older had a bachelor's degree or better. Focusing on just the skilled (points-based) stream, 82 percent of principal applicants had a bachelor's or better (27 percent with a master's or doctorate degree). Even for dependents (15 or older), 69 percent had a bachelor's or higher degree. Moreover, the leading source countries for immigrants to Canada are developing countries. In 2000, for example, the top five sending countries were China, India, Pakistan, the Philippines, and Korea.

Table 2-8. Estimates of Foreign-Born Participants, circa 1990 and 2000

Estimate source	Circa 1990			Circa 2000		
	Foreign or foreign-born (millions)	Percent of population	Year	Foreign or foreign-born (millions)	Percent of population	Year
Census						
Australia	3.8	22.3	1991	4.1	21.9	2001
Canada	4.3	16.1	1991	5.5	18.4	2001
United States	19.8	7.9	1990	31.1	11.1	2000
OECD						
Austria	0.46	5.9	1990	0.75	9.2	1999
Belgium	0.90	9.1	1990	0.89	8.8	1999
Denmark	0.16	3.1	1990	0.26	4.9	1999
Finland	0.03	0.5	1990	0.09	1.7	1999
France	3.60	6.3	1990	3.26	5.6	1999
Germany	5.34	8.4	1990	7.34	8.9	1999
Ireland	0.08	2.3	1990	0.12	3.1	1999
Italy	0.78	1.4	1990	1.25	2.2	1999
Japan	1.08	0.9	1990	1.56	1.2	1999
Korea	0.05	0.1	1990	0.19	0.4	1999
Luxembourg	0.11	29.4	1990	0.16	36.0	1999
Netherlands	0.69	4.6	1990	0.65	4.1	1999
Norway	0.14	3.4	1990	0.18	4.0	1999
Portugal	0.11	1.1	1990	0.19	1.9	1999
Spain	0.28	0.7	1990	0.80	2.0	1999
Switzerland	1.10	16.3	1990	1.37	19.2	1999
United Kingdom	1.72	3.2	1990	2.21	3.8	1999

Sources: OECD (2002) and various censuses; foreign population data are from population registries or from registries of foreigners except for France (censuses), Portugal, Italy, and Spain (residence permits), and Ireland and the United Kingdom (labor force surveys).

foreign population in Germany in the late 1990s, though inflows from Poland and the Federal Republic of Yugoslavia were larger at the time. Owing to Germany's history of importing largely unskilled guest workers in the 1950s and 1960s, the tertiary educational attainment of its foreign population is 9 percentage points below that of the national population. Neighboring France also has a large foreign population: 3.26 million circa 2000 (or 5.6 percent of the total population). As in Germany, the group's tertiary education attainment lags well behind that of the national population (7.9 percentage points), reflecting large inflows of less skilled individuals from nearby North African countries.

Table 2-9. Shares of Population, Aged 25–64, with Tertiary Education, 1998

Country	Nationals	Foreigners	Difference
Austria	12.5	13.3	−0.8
Belgium	27.6	20.2	7.4
Czech Republic	11.2	23.4	−12.2
Denmark	26.1	27.7	−1.6
Finland	32.0	28.6	3.4
France	21.8	13.9	7.9
Germany	24.2	15.2	9.0
Greece	16.8	19.2	−2.4
Hungary	13.9	28.1	−14.2
Italy	9.5	13.0	−3.5
Luxembourg	16.1	21.7	−5.6
Netherlands	23.9	21.6	2.3
Norway	30.4	36.5	−6.1
Portugal	9.7	14.3	−4.6
Slovak Republic	10.0	15.4	−5.4
Spain	21.0	28.8	−7.8
Switzerland	24.0	23.7	0.3
United Kingdom	27.3	39.3	−12.0

Source: OECD (2002), based on Eurostat data.

In 1998 Morocco accounted for 13.8 percent of the inflows and 16.9 percent of the stock.

In the United Kingdom, the foreign population was estimated at 2.21 million circa 2000, or roughly 3.8 percent of the total population. In contrast to immigrants in Germany and France, this foreign population has relatively high educational attainment, with 39.3 percent possessing a tertiary degree compared with 27.3 percent of the national population. It should be added that such attainment in the foreign population is not unique to the United Kingdom. Eleven of the 18 countries listed in table 2-9 have greater tertiary attainment in their foreign populations than in their national populations. And, as explained in chapter 3, practically all countries have been shifting their immigration policies toward selecting more skilled workers.

Developing-Country Students in OECD Countries

Foreign students at rich-country schools represent a particularly inter-esting component of foreign-born populations from the perspective of

Table 2-10. Stock of Foreign Students in OECD Countries, 2002

Country	Total (thousands)	Total non-OECD (thousands)	Percent non-OECD
Australia	109.4	89.3	81.6
Austria	28.4	9.8	34.4
Belgium	7.3	2.7	36.8
Canada	32.9	19.0	57.9
Czech Republic	4.1	3.0	72.4
Denmark	11	6.4	58.0
Finland	4.3	2.8	64.1
France	148	108.3	73.2
Germany	171.2	74.8	43.7
Hungary	6.7	4.3	64.2
Iceland	0.2	0.0	18.6
Ireland	6.9	1.9	27.7
Italy	23.2	8.2	35.5
Japan	55.8	34.5	61.8
Luxembourg	0.6	0.1	15.7
New Zealand	5.9	4.6	78.5
Norway	5.8	2.6	45.5
Poland	5.4	4.4	82.3
Spain	29	9.9	34.3
Sweden	12.6	4.6	36.9
Switzerland	24.4	6.7	27.3
Turkey	18.7	17.0	91.1
United Kingdom	209.6	84.3	40.2
United States	430.8	262.8	61.0
Total	1,327.20	736.6	55.5

Source: OECD (2002).

skill supplies that are available to developing countries. If students eventually return to ply their skills at home, then poor countries can obviously benefit from the cutting-edge education acquired in rich countries. The trouble is, many students never return, with nonreturn rates especially high for those from poorer countries.

Of the 1.3 million foreign students residing in OECD countries in 1998, some 55.5 percent were from non-OECD countries (table 2-10). The largest number of foreign students, some 430,000, studied in the United States, and 61 percent of these were from non-OECD countries.

Looking at the 10 largest source countries of the U.S. foreign student body for the academic year 1997–98, one finds that Japan barely edged out China as the largest sender of students, although China sent far more graduate students (83 percent of its total; see table 2-11). India also shows up as a large sender of graduate students. Also striking is the concentration of foreign graduate students in science and engineering: as much as 74 percent of Chinese graduate students and 73 percent of Indian graduate students are in science-related disciplines.

But will these students return? Although we do not have access to longitudinal data, some information is available on the *return plans* of foreign doctoral degree recipients from U.S. universities in both 1990 and 1999 (table 2-12). The bad news for developing countries is that large majorities plan to stay in the United States following graduation, though it is possible they are planning to return home at some later stage in life. In 1999 roughly 90 percent of both Chinese and Indian doctoral recipients planned to stay in the United States. The percentage in science and engineering planning to stay was similar for nonscience and nonengineering disciplines. Interestingly, although the overall shares planning to stay were similar in 1990 and 1999, the share expecting to stay in science and engineering was notably higher in the later year. For these graduates, there is little doubt that the booming high-tech economy of the 1990s and the easier availability of temporary work visas for skilled professionals contributed to lower return rates. We now turn to the policy developments that made such choices possible.

Table 2-11. Enrollment of Foreign Graduate Students in United States for Top 10 Locations of Origin, 1997–98, 1993–94, and 1987–88

		Foreign students		Percent foreign graduates across discipline					
Rank	Origin	Total	Graduates (percent)	Social sciences	Physical and life sciences	Math and computer sciences	Engin-eering	Other science and engineering	Non-science and engineering
1997–98									
1	Japan	47,073	19	24	5	4	6	11	51
2	China	46,958	83	5	25	16	26	7	22
3	Korea	42,890	44	10	9	7	18	10	46
4	India	33,818	74	4	9	18	42	4	23
5	Taiwan	30,855	56	7	8	10	20	7	49
6	Canada	22,051	43	14	10	2	7	9	58
7	Thailand	15,090	65	7	5	5	18	8	58
8	Malaysia	14,597	15	8	7	7	24	10	43
9	Indonesia	13,282	26	7	3	4	22	7	57
10	Mexico	9,559	39	13	9	5	20	17	37
	Top 10 total	276,173	50	8	13	11	23	7	38
	Others	205,107	36	n.a.	n.a.	n.a.	n.a.	n.a.	n.a.
	All locations	481,280	44	n.a.	n.a.	n.a.	n.a.	n.a.	n.a.
1993–94									
1	China	44,381	82	6	32	12	24	6	20
2	Japan	43,770	18	17	6	3	8	9	56
3	Taiwan	37,581	66	5	10	11	27	7	39
4	India	34,796	79	5	10	17	44	4	21
5	Korea	31,076	51	13	15	7	18	7	40
6	Canada	22,655	37	14	9	3	6	8	60
7	Malaysia	13,718	15	13	8	8	22	7	42
8	Indonesia	11,744	29	11	7	5	22	10	46
9	Thailand	9,537	59	6	4	6	13	6	65
10	Mexico	8,021	36	13	12	8	17	14	37
	Top 10 total	257,279	52	8	16	11	25	7	34
	Others	192,470	35	n.a.	n.a.	n.a.	n.a.	n.a.	n.a.
	All locations	449,749	45	n.a.	n.a.	n.a.	n.a.	n.a.	n.a.
1987–88									
1	Taiwan	26,660	78	n.a.	n.a.	n.a.	n.a.	n.a.	n.a.
2	China	25,170	81	9	31	13	21	7	19
3	India	21,010	74	7	14	13	38	5	25
4	Korea	20,520	73	16	15	9	21	7	33
5	Malaysia	19,480	21	12	6	13	12	7	50
6	Japan	18,050	24	n.a.	n.a.	n.a.	n.a.	n.a.	n.a.
7	Canada	15,690	38	15	12	3	7	9	55
8	Indonesia	9,010	29	n.a.	n.a.	n.a.	n.a.	n.a.	n.a.
9	Thailand	6,430	56	n.a.	n.a.	n.a.	n.a.	n.a.	n.a.
10	Mexico	6,170	31	15	15	8	15	14	33
	Top 10 total	168,190	56	n.a.	n.a.	n.a.	n.a.	n.a.	n.a.
	Others	187,997	33	n.a.	n.a.	n.a.	n.a.	n.a.	n.a.
	All locations	356,187	44	n.a.	n.a.	n.a.	n.a.	n.a.	n.a.

Source: Institute of International Education, Open Doors: Report on International Educational Exchange (annual series), and Profiles (biennial series), 1987–2000, New York, special tabulations, 2001; Science & Engineering Indicators, 2002.

n.a. = not available.

Table 2-12. Foreign Students Who Received Ph.D.s from U.S. Universities and Plan to Stay in the United States, Top 12 Locations of Origin, 1999 and 1990[a]

	1999				1990			
	Ph.D. recipients		Plan to stay (percent)		Ph.D. recipients		Plan to stay (percent)	
Origin	Total	Science and engineering	Total	Science and engineering	Total	Science and engineering	Total	Science and engineering
China	2,400	2,187	90	91	2,615	1,166	89	59
India	1,077	888	89	90	1,285	709	85	66
South Korea	1,017	738	56	63	1,042	971	46	32
Taiwan	981	732	57	62	1,137	1,012	57	45
Canada	473	283	65	72	419	252	46	48
Germany	266	179	67	65	169	123	50	48
Japan	238	156	50	54	208	147	46	41
Turkey	224	186	54	59	185	106	57	62
United Kingdom	215	141	77	79	172	104	69	70
Brazil	205	156	34	31	129	98	17	17
Mexico	191	158	34	32	130	104	36	33
Greece	117	99	76	78	137	125	49	52
Top 12 total	7,404	5,903	72	76	7,628	4,917	69	49
Other locations	3,889	2,645	61	66	2,806	2,623	49	38
Total all locations	11,293	8,548	68	73	10,434	7,540	64	45

Source: National Science Foundation, Division of Science Resources Statistics (NSF/SRS), Survey of Earned Doctorates, unpublished tabulations, 2001; Science & Engineering Indicators, 2002.

a. Data include foreign doctoral recipients with either permanent or temporary visas. Science includes physics, chemistry, astronomy, and earth, atmospheric, ocean, biological, and agricultural sciences, as well as mathematics and computer sciences.

CHAPTER 3

The International Competition for Talent

To succeed in the new century we need a highly educated and scientifically educated work force. . . . A well-targeted and well-managed Migration Program can help us augment such a labour force. In fact, if I had to sum up one reason for the transformation this government has brought to the Migration Program, it would be this—to help augment the skills, education and knowledge that Australia will need to prosper in the 21st century.

—PHILIP RUDDOCK, AUSTRALIA'S MINISTER FOR IMMIGRATION
AND MULTICULTURAL AND INDIGENOUS AFFAIRS, MAY 2002

While Canada has experienced recent growth in the number of workers entering the country, international competition for educated and skilled workers is now greater than ever before. In response to global labour shortages in certain key economic sectors, the United Kingdom, Japan and Germany, countries not traditionally open to immigration, are beginning to compete for skilled workers. . . . Today Canada finds itself competing in a global marketplace where the demand for skilled immigrants is swiftly increasing.

—CITIZENSHIP AND IMMIGRATION CANADA, 2000

Germany is embedded in a world economy . . . in which the qualifications and knowledge of people are becoming crucial growth factors. In order to ensure it remains competitive, Germany will be more dependent . . . on the international exchange of information and will need to co-operate with people of different origins in order to develop new solutions to problems as well as new ways of thinking and working.

—INDEPENDENT COMMISSION ON MIGRATION TO GERMANY, 2001

Today we will mark up one of most important pieces of legislation that the Senate will consider this year, the "American Competitiveness in the 21st Century Act." . . . We want the high-tech industry to thrive in the U.S. and to continue to serve as the engine for the growth of jobs and opportunities for American workers. If Congress fails to act promptly to alleviate today's high tech labor shortage, today's low jobless rate will be a mere precursor to tomorrow's lost opportunities.

—REPUBLICAN SENATOR ORRIN HATCH, MARCH 9, 2000

The [Highly Skilled Migrant] program represents a further step in developing our immigration system to maximize the benefits to the UK of highly skilled workers who have the qualifications and skills required by UK businesses to compete in the global marketplace. . . . It will allow eminent scientists to base their research projects [in the UK], should encourage the movement of business and financial experts to the City of London and given those at the top of their chosen profession the choice of making the United Kingdom their home.

—LORD ROOKER, U.K. IMMIGRATION MINISTER, DECEMBER 2001

Over the past decade or so, official pronouncements on immigration policy have often been couched in the language of "national competitiveness," especially in knowledge-intensive sectors. The growing concern with competitiveness suggests that governments increasingly see themselves as competing for internationally mobile human capital via their immigration policies. This trend is apparent in the strategies adopted by five "competitors" in the international market for talent: Australia, Canada, Germany, the United Kingdom, and the United States. Two recent reforms also reflect this development: Canada's rationalization of its points system for permanent skilled migration and the temporary U.S. expansion of H-1B visas in response to the tech boom of the late 1990s. Before discussing these policies, we present a simple framework for thinking about how countries compete for talent.

A Market for Talent

Countries compete for the world's workers—engineers, scientists, managers, nurses, and so on—by offering them various mixes of opportunities and imposing selective barriers. As economist George Borjas describes it,

> There . . . exists an immigration market allocating persons wishing to leave their current countries of residence among the few host countries willing to admit them. Potential migrants, like workers

looking for a job, are looking for the best country to live in. Host countries, like firms looking for specific types of workers, set immigration policies so they can attract specific types of migrants. Just as the labor market guides the allocation of workers to firms, the immigration market guides the allocation of persons to countries.[1]

We focus on the demand side of this market—the "deals" that the potential host countries offer. The deals are composed of a mix of incentives in the form of social, economic, and political opportunities and disincentives in the form of immigration barriers. Some would argue, however, that "the phenomenon of international migration is characterized by disincentives rather than incentives."[2] In any case, potential movers will be interested in a long list of socioeconomic and political factors: incomes (adjusted for cost of living), job availability, average tax rates (including income taxes, payroll taxes, expenditure taxes, and property taxes), marginal tax rates, public benefits (such as unemployment benefits), public services, amenities, attitudes toward immigrants (including tolerance of cultural and religious diversity), languages commonly spoken, political and legal rights, strength of relevant diasporic networks, and so on. Most of these factors are only loosely controlled by competing governments, and where they are the direct concern of policy, the choice is dominated by policy objectives other than attracting or repelling immigrants.[3]

As things stand, all rich countries have substantial, though varying, scope to alter the deals they offer by selectively dismantling the barriers—the disincentives—to foreign workers and the domestic firms seeking to employ them. Thus much of what appears to be governments' changing the way they compete for the world's skilled workers is really the selective removal of their own barriers in the international labor market.

Once a would-be migrant meets the immigration authority's selection criteria, the individual receives an offer in the international talent market, which can be called a *migrant value proposition* (MVP). The MVP is the country's offer to the would-be migrant valued in purchasing power parity adjusted to units of the migrant's home currency. The MVP will depend on numerous factors, including the individual's likely purchasing power parity adjusted after-tax earnings, the costs of moving, the quality

1. Borjas (1990).
2. Bhagwati (1991, p. 340).
3. Tax policy is a good example.

of government-provided benefits such as health care and education, the attractiveness of the physical environment, the attitude of domestic residents toward immigrants, and the existence of immigrant networks. Equally important are the conditions under which the individual is admitted. Can the stay be permanent or does it have a time limit? If temporary, are extensions and conversion to permanent status possible? Can one's spouse and children accompany the migrant? Is the spouse allowed to work?

In deciding whether to accept the offer, the potential migrant will establish a *reservation value* (RV)—a value that must be exceeded before the individual will migrate to the country making the offer. This RV depends on the economic and social opportunities in one's home country, *and* on the offers (that is, MVPs) being made by the country's competitors in the immigration market.

Immigration market propositions fall into two main types, determined by whether they offer *permanent* or *temporary* residence.

Policies that permanently admit skilled workers and their families can be subdivided into those that do not include a particular job in the criteria for entry (and instead use a skills-based points system, for example) and those that require certain types of job offers (probably in conjunction with meeting certain standards of qualification). Most points systems are based on the assumption that long-term earnings in the domestic labor market correlate with human capital attributes—education, experience, facility with national languages, and the like—and that points can be assigned to these factors to ensure that only those with sufficiently high likely earnings are accepted.[4] The main alternative is to look at occupations with a short supply of workers. If nurses or software developers are needed, for example, immigrants with qualifications and possibly job offers in these areas will be selectively admitted. A drawback of this approach is that shortages may be temporary; once domestic skill

4. A better measure of the value to natives of an immigrant or group of immigrants is the difference between the social value of the resulting added output less their earnings (after netting out the effects of any additional taxes and government expenditures). Focusing on anticipated earnings can still produce "good selections" if the size of the "immigrant surplus" tends to rise with their earnings. This is more likely to be the case under a progressive fiscal system and one in which knowledge spillovers are greater for workers with more human capital. However, the "immigration surplus" can also be large for less-skilled and thus lower-earning workers. This will be the case, for example, when demand for less-skilled workers is highly inelastic, so that less-skilled immigration significantly drives down the wage (see, for example, Borjas, 1995). In this case, policymakers will have to trade off the relatively large immigration surplus (that is, the aggregate gain to natives) against rising skill differentials (that is, the increased inequality among natives).

supplies catch up with demand, today's selections may not be the workers who would have made the biggest net contributions in the long run.[5] Another key element of an offer of permanent residency is the existence and nature of an option to obtain full citizenship. Although permanent residents typically have many of the rights and obligations of citizens, significant differences exist along such dimensions as voting rights and treatment in the legal system.

Policies that admit workers (and possibly their families) on a temporary basis usually insist on an outstanding job offer. If policymakers are concerned about the impact of temporary migrants on competing domestic workers, they may also ask for a demonstration of no harm to domestic workers or evidence that a suitably qualified domestic substitute is not available. Offers in this category can vary in other important respects. How long is the temporary work visa valid? Is it renewable? If yes, how many times? Are applicants allowed to bring their family? Is a spouse allowed to work? Is it permissible to apply for permanent status while in the country on a temporary visa? What taxes are temporary workers obliged to pay? Which benefits are they entitled to receive?

Permanent Migration Policies in Five Countries

Of the five countries examined here, Australia, Canada, and the United States (countries largely built on immigration) have well-established policies to permanently admit immigrants on the basis of their human capital and job offers. In contrast, Germany and the United Kingdom are relative newcomers to the competition for highly skilled mobile talent with offers of immediate or eventual permanent residency.[6]

As table 3-1 shows, the countries under consideration have experienced a broadly based, if sometimes hesitant, shift to more skill-focused policies. Australia and Canada, the two with established skills-based points systems, increased both the number of skilled immigrants and the

5. Persistent apparent shortages can exist where there is monopsony power in the skill market. We say "apparent shortages" because although employers would like to hire more workers at the going wage, they are unwilling to raise the wage since they would have to pay the higher wage to new and old employees alike. Employers will often lobby to have immigration meet their "excess demand." Such monopsony power is thought to be particularly important in health care skill markets (see Staiger, Spetz, and Phibbs, 1999). One problem with using immigration as a long-term way to relieve the apparent shortages in this market is that it reduces pressure to rationalize the market by introducing more competition between providers or making long-term investments in domestic skills.

6. The contrast should not be drawn too sharply, however, as initially "temporary" entry has morphed into permanent settlement in all of these countries.

Table 3-1. Skilled-Focused Permanent Migration Programs in Selected Countries

	Canada	Australia	Germany	United Kingdom	United States
Program	Independent skilled workers program	Skill migration (multiple programs)[a]	Proposed points-based system[b]	Highly skilled migrant program (introduced on pilot basis in January 2002)	Employment-based preferences (permanent residency)[c]
Number (percent of total)					
1995	81,000 (38)	…	24,100 (29)	…	85,300
2000	118,000 (52)	…	44,730 (56)	…	107,000
Cap	No	No	No	No	Yes (140,000)
Points system	Yes	Yes[d]	Yes	Yes[e]	No
Labor market test	No	No	No	No	Yes (with exceptions)
Selection criteria	Age, language, education, experience, job offer, adaptability	Age, language, education, occupation,[f] experience	(1) Highly skilled professionals with job offers: qualifications and earnings; (2) workers without job offers: points system	Past earnings,[g] education, experience, professional achievement	Job offer (certification from the Department of Labor of no adverse impact on domestic workers required in most cases)[f]
Leading recipient countries in 2000 (percent)	China (23) India (10) Pakistan (8) Korea (4)	United Kingdom (15) South Africa (14) India (10) Indonesia (9)	Not applicable	Not applicable	India (15) China (13) Philippines (10) Canada (7)

a. Included programs (number in 2000–01): employer nominations (7,510); business skills (7,360); distinguished talents (230); skilled independent (22,380); skilled Australian sponsored (7,200); and 1 November onshore (60).

b. The table describes the points system. The actual law passed in 2004 did not include this system. Instead, the existing recruitment ban remains in place with some limited exceptions.

c. There are five preference categories: E1, priority workers (28.6 percent), certification not required; E2, professionals holding advanced degrees (28.6 percent), certification required; E3, professionals holding bachelor's degrees and other workers (28.6 percent), certification required; E4, special immigrants (7.1 percent); and E5, employment creation investors (7.1 percent), who must invest between $0.5 million and $1 million, depending on geographic area, and create at least 10 full-time jobs.

d. A new points system was introduced in July 1999. A new category for skilled independent overseas students was added in July 2001. Applicants with Australian qualifications who apply within six months of completing their studies are exempt from the work experience requirement. No points test applies to the employer nomination stream, though candidates must meet basic requirements.

e. This program is not strictly designed for permanent migration. Initial acceptance is for a period of one year. The applicant can then apply to have the visa extended for a further three years. At the end of the four years, a migrant wishing to remain in the United Kingdom permanently can apply for permanent residence or "settlement." This route to permanent residency is also available to work-permit holders, so the difference between the two programs as a means to permanent residency should not be exaggerated. A key difference, however, is that those entering under the highly skilled migrant program are not tied to a particular employer.

f. Occupation must be on the Skilled Occupations List.

g. Points based on past earnings are country specific, with poorer countries tending to receive more points for a given level of pound sterling earnings. For example, someone from Canada would need to have earned £250,000 to receive the maximum 50 points in this category, whereas someone from India would need to have earned £90,000.

Figure 3-1. Permanent Immigration to Australia by Broad Category, 1990–91 to 2002–03

Number of immigrants

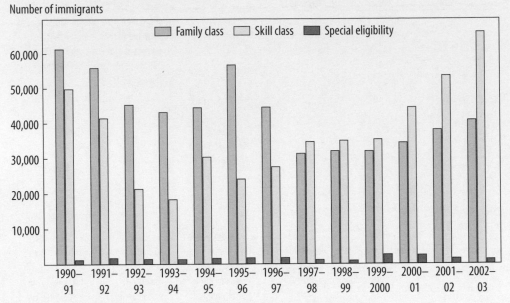

Source: Hugo (2001); Department of Immigration and Multicultural and Indigenous Affairs.

share of skilled immigrants in total permanent immigration in the second half of the 1990s (see figures 3-1 and 3-2). In order to increase the average skill level of the entering pool, the Australian government made major changes to its points system in 1999.[7] The changes included giving points to applicants with an occupation on the Migration Occupations in Demand List (MODL), with further points being granted if the applicant had a job offer in an occupation on this list. Because of concerns about the transferability of foreign human capital, additional points were granted for Australian educational qualifications and experience. And, in a nod to the ever-growing importance of international commerce to the Australian economy, points were to be given for fluency in languages other than English.

Canada's reforms are particularly interesting because, as already mentioned, it is a country built on immigration, with large—if volatile— flows over the last century and a half (figure 3-3). In 1967 Canada pioneered a points-based system for selecting permanent immigrants based on their predicted economic contribution.[8] The system has evolved over

7. Hugo (2001).
8. For an excellent historical overview of Canada's immigration policy, see Green and Green (1999).

Figure 3-2. Gross Immigrant and Refugee Flows to Canada, by Broad Category, 1995–2002

Number of immigrants

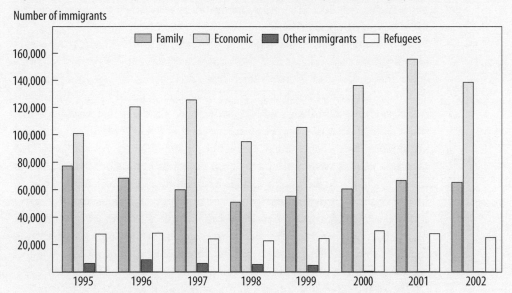

Source: Citizenship and Immigration Canada.

Figure 3-3. Annual Flow and Stock of Temporary Foreign Workers in Canada, 1978–2002

Number of foreign workers

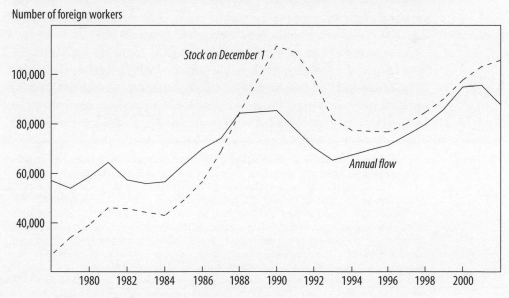

Source: Citizenship and Immigration Canada (2002).

time, initially focusing on meeting cyclical skill shortages and later on augmenting the country's human capital base to improve prospects for long-term economic growth.

The profile of workers admitted to Canada in 2000 via the points-based skill stream reflects a well-educated population: 83 percent of principal applicants (and 59 percent of dependents over the age of 15) have a bachelor's degree or better (table 3-2). The countries of origin are primarily developing countries, with the top three sending countries—China, India, and Pakistan—together accounting for 43 percent of principal applicants. The increased prominence of developing countries in this regard coincides with a fall in the earnings of immigrants compared with those of native workers with similar broad human capital characteristics. In response, the government began putting more emphasis on the selective economic stream compared with the family and refugee streams (see figure 3-2), but, with the deteriorating earning performance also affecting the skill stream, it decided to reform the points system to better select workers with the potential to do well in the Canadian labor market.[9]

The resulting legislation, the Immigration and Refugee Protection Act of June 2002, is undoubtedly the most significant change in Canadian immigration policy since the points system was introduced in the 1960s. Although the new law has changed many aspects of Canada's immigration policy, we focus here on the changes to the points system (table 3-3), which brought a fundamental shift in the focus of the skill stream. Points related to occupation shortages have been eliminated, with the emphasis now on observed attributes that indicate flexible skill sets, suited to an economy with ever-shifting skill demands.

How well has the new policy been designed from the viewpoint of attracting and admitting workers likely to be high earners in the Canadian economy? Empirical work relating earnings to human capital attributes has shown the predictive power of education, experience, and language skills—all of which are emphasized in the new system.[10]

---

9. A related debate and reform effort has focused on removing artificial barriers to immigrants in the labor market, such as nonrecognition of foreign credentials.

10. The vast literature in the tradition of Mincer (1958) provides a useful framework for evaluation. See also McHale (2002), who shows how a simple human capital points system can be designed using a well-specified earnings function for predicting earnings and a chosen earnings cutoff. Points are based on the coefficients in the earnings regression in such a way that immigrants receiving points below a points cutoff have predicted earnings below the chosen earnings cutoff. Thus selections are based on predictions that the applicant's earnings will be sufficiently high. McHale also examines the conditions under which earnings are a good indicator of an immigrant's economic benefit to the native population.

Table 3-2. Profile of Skilled Immigration to Canada in 2000

Profile	Number	Percent
Principal applicants	52,080	44
Dependents	66,415	56
Total	118,495	100
Principal applicants by gender		
Male	39,561	76
Female	12,519	24
Total	52,080	100
Principal applicants by education (15 and older)		
Less than bachelor's degree	9,387	18
Bachelor's degree	29,031	56
Master's degree	11,242	22
Doctorate	2,371	5
Total	52,031	100
Dependents by education (15 and older)		
Less than bachelor's degree	18,137	51
Bachelor's degree	13,887	39
Master's degree	3,406	10
Doctorate	384	1
Total	35,814	100
Principal applicants by source country		
China	12,760	25
India	5,738	11
Pakistan	3,961	8
France	2,356	5
Philippines	1,714	3
Romania	1,465	3
Republic of Korea	1,349	3
United Kingdom	1,307	3
Morocco	1,065	2
Iran	1,049	2

Source: Citizenship and Immigration Canada (2000b).

Table 3-3. New and Old Skilled Worker Points-Based Selection Grids

	Maximum points
New system	
Education	25
Language	24
First	16
Second	8
Experience	21
Age	10
Arranged employment	10
Adaptability	10
Spouse's education	3–5
One year authorized work in Canada	5
Two years postsecondary study in Canada	5
Points received under arranged employment	5
Family relationship in Canada	5
Total	100
Initial pass mark	75
Old system	
Education or training factor (occupation-specific)	18
Education	16
Language	15
First	9
Second	6
Occupation (based on General Occupations List)	10
Age	10
Arranged employment	10
Work experience	8
Relative in Canada	5
Demographic factor	8 (subject to change)
Total	100
Pass mark	70

Source: Citizenship and Immigration Canada.

Empirical evidence also supports giving additional points to principal applicants and spouses with Canadian education and labor market experience, to those with formal job offers, with past acceptance at and graduation from Canadian postsecondary institutions, and even to levels of spousal education.[11]

11. The most obvious reason that the spouse's education matters is that families are admitted and not just individuals. Thus it makes sense to look at the spouse's earning power as well. The theory of positive assortive mating, which predicts that the more educated will tend to match together, suggests the spouse's education can be an additional indicator of the quality of the principal applicant's education.

Some of the design features are harder to understand. For example, providing the full 10 points available for age to anyone between 21 and 49, while deducting two points for every year below or above that range, seems rather more arbitrary than might be expected in a system based on a well-specified earnings function. Given the cost of state pension and health care entitlements for retirees, it is unlikely that individuals in their late 40s yield the same long-term benefits to the economy as those in their early 20s. Other examples of dubious design include the credit for bilingualism—which has the hallmark of politics rather than economics—and the curious requirement of substantial years of full-time study for those targeted as skilled tradespersons, whose skill training is presumably acquired primarily on the job. Although the large credit given for education is consistent with the human capital approach to immigration policy, the manner in which points are credited across varying educational levels appears unlikely to find much basis in a human capital–based earnings regression. The greatest number of points for university-educated applicants is granted to those with a master's or Ph.D. (25), followed by those with two or more bachelor's degrees (22), and then those with two-year university degrees (20). Thus someone with a single four-year bachelor's degree gets the same number of points in the educational category as someone with a two-year degree.

The initial pass mark in the new points system was set at 75 but was subsequently reduced to 67. The initial cutoff did seem high given the substantial numbers entering Canada in the skill stream in the years before the reform and judged by the kind of people who would then be excluded. The number of qualified applicants was sure to drop. For example, a 22-year-old applicant (10 points), with a four-year computer science degree (20 points), one year's experience (15 points), and high proficiency in English but no proficiency in French (16 points) would score only 61 points. Even with a formal job offer or maximum adaptability points based on a Canadian education or experience and a university-educated spouse, this applicant would score only 73 points and be rejected under the initial cutoff score.[12]

Although one can quibble with the design of the new points system, Canada is clearly positioning itself to compete more effectively with selective offers of permanent residency in other countries. But it is facing

12. On the other hand, the fact that the cut would be made by a 45-year-old (10 points) with a two-year degree (20 points), four years of experience (21 points), high proficiency in English and moderate proficiency in French (24 points), and no formal job offer or adaptability points (0 points) hints that the problem lies with the relative point allocations just as much as with the rather stringent cutoff.

increased competition from other countries that are willing to make permanent offers. One drawback of Canada's system is that it takes time, sometimes years, to process backlogs for applicants, especially those from high-volume countries such as China and India. In recent years delays have become even longer because of more intense background security checks following September 11, even though it is widely recognized that approval time and bureaucratic ease carry considerable weight in the competition for the most sought-after workers. A positive element of the new law that should offset the slow processing is that it removes the previous ambiguity concerning the ability to apply for permanent status while working in Canada under a temporary work visa. Status change is now clearly allowed, permitting the most sought-after workers to come on a temporary visa and work while waiting for their permanent residency application to be processed.

Strictly speaking, the United Kingdom's points-based system, the Highly Skilled Migrant Programme introduced on a pilot basis in early 2002, is not for permanent migration, since visas are initially granted for a period of one year but can be extended for an additional three years. After four years the immigrant can apply for permanent residency or "settlement" and is not tied to a particular employer at any time. In a clear signal of competitive intent, the Home Office announced in October 2003 that it was reducing the points cutoff from 75 to 65, granting extra points to those under the age of 28, and providing extra points for partner/spouse qualifications. Another notable feature of the U.K. system is that it allocates points on the basis of past earnings.[13]

Under the shadow of an aging population and massively underfunded social insurance liabilities, Germany intensely debated an immigration reform bill with a points-based system for permanent skilled immigration. An important impetus to the new legislation was a 2001 report by the Independent Commission on Migration to Germany, which opened with the unmistakable exhortation that "Germany needs immigrants." This law has traveled a tough legislative road, however, and the bill that finally passed in 2004 went less far in selective recruitment than first envisioned. Although there are some new skills-focused exceptions to the previous recruitment ban—top-ranking scientists and managers are given the right to permanent residence under certain conditions, for example—the new regime is a shadow of the innovative points system that was initially proposed.

13. Poorer countries, which tend to pay lower wages at given skill levels, receive the available points at lower pound sterling earnings levels than richer countries.

Of the five countries, the United States has probably been the least active in reforming its system of permanent immigration, instead continuing its post-1965 focus on family unification. The Immigration Act of 1990 did increase the cap on visas going to priority workers and professionals with U.S. job offers. This employment preference cap of 140,000 is rarely reached, however, in large part because the application process is a difficult and lengthy one, requiring in most cases a U.S. job offer and Department of Labor certification of no adverse impact on domestic workers.[14] One facilitating feature is that potential immigrants can apply for an employment preference visa while employed in the United States under a temporary work visa such as the H-1B. This is where the United States has been much more active in revising its skill-focused policies.

Temporary Migration Policies in Five Countries

The trend toward opening up entry possibilities to skilled foreigners is also apparent in reforms to the temporary migration policies of all the countries under consideration (table 3-4). All five offer temporary work visas to highly skilled workers with job offers. In the mid-1990s Australia introduced a major new class of temporary (long-stay) visas that are valid for periods of up to four years.[15] Although a job offer is required—a feature of the temporary migration programs in all five countries—Australia does *not* require applicants to demonstrate that domestic workers are not adversely affected. Instead, potential employers must show that the immigrant will provide a "benefit to Australia," which can come through positive employment effects, expanded trade, enhanced links with international markets, improved competitiveness, and the like. This seemingly minor shift in emphasis actually represents a major shift in the official view of immigrants' impact on the economy—they are no longer considered a drag on the economy, driving down wages and taking away jobs, but competitiveness-enhancing assets with the potential to increase productivity.

In Canada, by contrast, employers bringing in workers under its Employment Authorization system must still obtain validation from Human Resources Development Canada (HRDC) to illustrate that

14. There is a provision that a maximum of 7 percent of employment preference visas go to immigrants of any one country, which is a binding constraint for countries such as India and China with a high demand for employment-based green cards.

15. Hugo (2001).

Table 3-4. Skill-Focused Temporary Migration Programs in Selected Countries

	Canada	Australia	Germany	United Kingdom	United States
Program	Employment authorization: temporary residents	Temporary (long stay) business entry	IT specialists temporary relief program ("Green Card")[a]	Work permits	H-1B—Specialty professional workers
Number (2000–01)	86,225[b]	40,493[c]	8,000[d]	82,437[e]	201,079[f]
Job offer required	Yes	Yes	Yes	Yes	Yes
Cap	No	No	Yes (20,000 total)	No	Yes (195,000 per year)[g]
Labor market test	Yes (validation required by HRDC; exception for software developers)	No (but employers must show that the temporary entrant will provide a "benefit to Australia")[h]	Yes (employment agency checks EU worker availability and qualifications/ remuneration)	Yes (waived for "shortage occupations")	No (but employers must "attest" to no adverse affect on U.S. workers)
Tied to employer	Yes	Yes	No[i]	Yes[j]	Yes
Length of visa (max.)	3 years	4 years	3 years	5 years	3 years
Renewable	Yes	Yes	Yes (5-year max.)	Yes (10-year max.)	Yes (6-year max.)
Spousal employment	No[k]	Yes	Yes (after 1 year)	Yes	No
Possibility of permanent settlement	Yes (under new law)	Yes	No (but possible under new law)	Yes (after four years)	Yes[l]

a. Program was introduced in August 2000 to relieve perceived shortages in the IT sector. Germany also operates a much larger work permit system (333,381 in 2000). The aim of the "Green Card" system was to make the recruitment of IT professionals easier through unbureaucratic, rapid, and transparent procedures (McLaughlan and Salt 2002).

b. Number is for 2000. The stock of temporary workers with employment authorizations on December 31, 2000, was 88,962 (Citizenship and Immigration Canada 2000b).

c. Number is for 2000–01 and includes 3,411 independent executives establishing businesses in Australia. In addition, 3,438 visas were issued to medical practitioners and their dependents, and 1,738 visas were issued to people joining educational and research institutions. The estimated stock of long-stay business entrants as of June 30, 2001, was 56,000. The median duration of stay of visa holders as of that date was just under six months.

d. Number is for the period from August 2000 to June 2001.

e. Includes only out-of-country work permit approvals (McLaughlan and Salt 2002).

f. Number is for fiscal 2001 (which begins in October 2000). A further 130,127 petitions were approved for continuing employment (U.S. Immigration and Naturalization Service [INS] 2002).

g. Renewals do not count toward the cap.

h. The benefit can come in various ways: create or maintain employment; expand trade, develop links with international markets, or improve competitiveness. Emphasis is on positive effects rather than the absence of harm.

i. Switching employers is possible without further labor market test. Five-year limit applies to combined employments.

j. Employees switching employers must have new employer apply for a new permit.

k. Spouses can apply for employment authorization on their own merit. Under the Spousal Employment Authorization Program, spouses of workers in engineering, management, technical, and skilled grades can receive an authorization without a labor market test (McLaughlan and Salt 2002).

l. Visa holders can apply for permanent residency while they are in H-1B status. Extensions to H-1B status are possible in one-year increments for those whose visa expires when an application for permanent residency has been pending for more than one year (McLaughlan and Salt 2002).

Figure 3-4. Immigration to Canada, 1860–2002

Number of immigrants

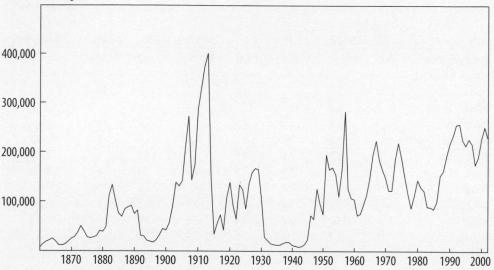

Source: Citizenship and Immigration Canada (2000b).

efforts have been made to find a domestic worker to fill the position and that the temporary worker will not adversely affect domestic workers.[16] The flow and stock declined over the first half of the 1990s, but both moved upward over the second half of the decade as the performance of the Canadian economy improved and shortages in key sectors emerged (figure 3-4).

In Germany, concern about competitiveness in newly emerging information technology (IT) industries was a major reason behind the "Green Card" program for IT specialists introduced in August 2000. Initially, it had some difficulty attracting applicants with the necessary skills, despite a concerted effort to keep bureaucratic hassles and delays to a minimum. In the intense atmosphere of international competition for highly qualified IT specialists in the closing months of the technology boom, these difficulties deterred many mobile Indian specialists in particular, who instead chose to go to the United States on H-1Bs, which are discussed in the next section. These difficulties may also explain the

16. Interestingly, in a move that suggests the government recognizes this cumbersome process can make it hard to compete for the most internationally sought-after workers, the validation requirement was removed on a pilot basis for software developers.

Table 3-5. United Kingdom Work Permits Issued by Country of Origin
Percent

Origin	1995	1996	1997	1998	1999	2000	Change in share (percentage points), 1995–2000
All nationalities	24,161	26,432	31,720	37,528	41,950	64,571	
Country breakdown							
United States	32.6	32.8	30.2	27.1	23.2	19.6	−13.0
India	8.3	10.1	12.7	15.1	13.5	19.0	10.7
Philippines	0.3	0.3	0.3	0.7	5.4	10.5	10.2
Australia and New Zealand	6.5	7.2	8.3	9.2	9.0	8.8	2.3
South Africa	2.7	3.3	4.3	5.8	7.9	6.9	4.2
Japan	10.0	9.8	7.9	7.2	5.9	4.1	−5.9
Canada	3.8	4.2	4.4	4.0	3.6	3.0	−0.8
China	2.7	2.6	2.5	2.4	2.5	2.4	−0.3
Russia	3.0	2.4	2.4	2.3	1.9	1.6	−1.4
Malaysia	1.2	1.4	1.3	2.0	1.8	1.3	0.1
Poland	2.5	1.3	1.4	1.4	1.1	1.1	−1.4
Czech Republic	0.8	0.6	0.6	0.6	0.6	0.7	−0.1

Source: Dobson and others (2001).

pressure on the German government to improve its offer in the skilled immigrant market with skills-related permanent visas.

Another system overhaul of the late 1990s, in the United Kingdom, was marked by a dramatic increase in the number and distribution of work permits. The number jumped from just over 24,000 in 1995 to more than 64,000 in 2000 (table 3-5), and most of the new workers were from developing countries. The share of work permits given to Indians, for instance, increased from 8.3 percent in 1995 to 19.0 percent in 2000, while the share going to workers from the Philippines increased from just 0.3 percent to 10.5 percent. As for immigrant occupations (table 3-6), among holders of work permits from the leading sending countries in 2000, those from India were concentrated in engineering and computing, while those from the Philippines were concentrated in the health professions (notably nursing).

The Case of U.S. H-1Bs

The H-1 visa program in the United States dates from the Immigration and Nationality Act of 1952, its original purpose being to bring workers

Table 3-6. United Kingdom Work Permits and First Permissions Granted by Country and Occupation, 2000
Number

Occupation	United States	India	Philippines	South Africa	Australia	Japan	Canada	China	Russia	Malaysia	Poland
All	12,654	12,292	6,772	4,437	3,979	2,645	1,921	1,541	1054	866	687
Managers and administrators	5,247	1,203	55	589	1,097	1,275	579	211	218	139	143
Professional	1,767	2,947	247	879	916	638	394	285	177	348	104
Engineers and technologists	932	2,616	222	213	200	506	139	147	91	147	63
Health	17	109	17	180	67	1	2	30	0	9	2
Teaching	429	84	1	307	396	91	161	67	53	10	21
Business and finance	154	84	3	91	100	30	34	26	16	119	6
Other	235	54	4	88	153	10	58	15	17	63	12
Associate professional and technical	5,493	7,879	6,442	2,918	1,890	604	911	885	586	329	268
Computer analysts, programmers	1,004	5,973	82	526	486	138	253	108	82	73	54
Health	188	1301	6,327	1,876	535	46	115	179	13	136	42
Business and finance	1,470	257	20	180	360	158	174	135	97	59	41
Artistic and sports	2,020	182	9	174	315	119	275	35	231	8	89
Other	811	166	4	162	194	143	94	428	163	53	42
Other	147	263	28	51	76	128	37	160	73	50	172

Source: Dobson and others (2001).

of "distinguished merit and ability" into the country on a temporary basis to fill positions that were themselves of limited duration.[17] In 1970 Congress relaxed these restrictions, allowing H-1 specialty workers to accept permanent positions, and after 1990 it no longer required applicants to swear they had no intention of "abandoning" their country of origin.

In response to complaints that H-1 workers were filling entry-level positions without a test to determine the harm to domestic workers, the Immigration Act of 1990 created a new class of H-1B visas for workers in occupational specialties. It also introduced new classes for "aliens of prominence": type "O" visas for workers of extraordinary ability in the sciences, education, business, or athletics, and "P" visas for internationally recognized entertainers and athletes. And for the first time it placed a ceiling (65,000) on the number of H-1Bs that could be granted in a fiscal year.[18]

An important feature of the H-1B is that prospective employers must submit a labor condition application to the Department of Labor attesting that wages are in line with those being paid for similar work in the area of skill, that the prospective visa holders will not affect the working conditions of domestic workers, that there has not been a strike or lockout involving the occupational class of the prospective visa holders, and that the employer has provided notice of the application to the existing workforce. Typically, the Department of Labor looks for obvious inaccuracies and incompleteness rather than substantially reviewing the employer's attestations. The process is also fast: barring incompleteness or inaccuracies, applications must be certified within seven days of being submitted.[19]

H-1B visas are granted for a period of three years and can be renewed for an additional three years. A visa holder may change employers provided that a petition from the new employer has been granted. As mentioned earlier, the law allows H-1B holders to have "dual intent," coming initially to work with temporary status but intending to apply for permanent residency. Thus the H-1B visa can be used as a way station for those seeking to immigrate permanently to the United States through the time-consuming process of applying for an employment preference visa.

17. Lowell (2000).
18. Usdansky and Espenshade (2000).
19. Lowell (2000).

Figure 3-5. H-1 Visa Issuances (Initial Employments), 1972–2003

Number of visas

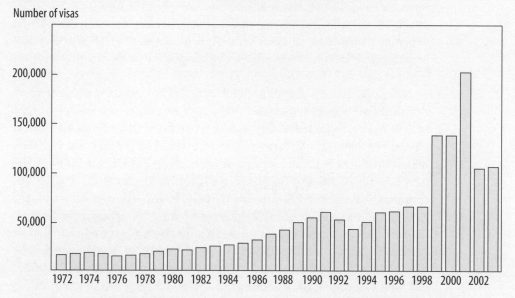

Sources: Lowell (2000); U.S. Immigration and Naturalization Service (2002); Department of Homeland Security (2003).

Although the H-1B cap was initially set high enough so as not to be binding, the number of H-1 visas issued grew rapidly in the late 1980s (figure 3-5), making it reasonable to expect the cap to become binding before too long.[20] Indeed, as the high-technology boom picked up steam in the late 1990s, the demand for H-1Bs grew rapidly, with the result that the cap was reached for the first time in September 1997. Coincidentally, this was the same month that the Commerce Department issued a report predicting a coming shortage of high-tech workers, which, combined with fears of Y2K-related computer system breakdowns, led high-tech industries to lobby intensively for a higher cap.[21] The immigration policy debate became very clearly couched in the language of competitiveness.

The American Competitiveness and Workforce Improvement Act passed in 1998 expanded the available H-1B visas from 65,000 to 115,000 in fiscal 1999 and 2000 and to 107,500 in fiscal 2001. In

---

20. Lowell (2000) explains the dip in the number of H-1 issuances in the early to mid-1990s by the introduction of the new visa categories, notably O and P.

21. Usdansky and Espenshade (2000).

response to domestic labor concerns, the legislation also introduced restrictions on layoffs (both during the three months before the hiring of an H-1B worker and in the three months after) for so-called H-1B dependent firms that had an excessive percentage of H-1B workers and introduced a $500 fee to be used to aid displaced workers and disadvantaged students.[22]

Notwithstanding the expanded cap, H-1Bs were soon in excess demand once more. Renewed lobbying in response to continued high-tech skill shortages led Congress to revisit the legislation again, and it passed the American Competitiveness in the 21st Century Act in 2000, which President Bill Clinton signed reluctantly in October 2000.[23] The new law raised the cap on H-1Bs to 195,000 for fiscal 2001 to 2003, dropping it back to 65,000 in fiscal 2004. It also allowed for an extension of the six-year limit for workers who have an application for permanent residency pending for more the 180 days, permitted visa holders to change employers immediately on the filing of an application by the new employer, and increased the application fee from $500 to $1,000.[24]

Upon examining the operation of the H-1B program in fiscal 2001, the Immigration and Naturalization Service (INS) found that the demand for H-1Bs remained very strong in the months before September 11, even as the high-tech slump gathered momentum. Of the 331,206 petitions approved in fiscal 2001, 201,079 were petitions for initial employment (most of which are subject to the cap), and 130,127 were for continuing employment (which are not subject to the cap). By contrast, a total of 257,640 petitions were approved in fiscal 2000.

In a breakdown of approved petitions by country of origin, age, educational level, and occupation (table 3-7), India emerges as by far the

22. Lowell (2000).

23. At the bill signing, President Clinton stated: "This legislation contains a number of provisions that merit concern. For example, one provision allows an H-1B visa holder to work for an employer who has not yet been approved for participation in the H-1B program. In addition, there are provisions that could have the unintended consequence of allowing an H-1B visa holder who is applying for a permanent visa to remain in H-1B status well beyond the current six-year limit. I am concerned that these provisions could weaken existing protections that ensure that the H-1B program does not undercut the wages and working conditions of U.S. workers, and could also increase the vulnerability of H-1B workers to any unscrupulous employers using the program."

24. This is an important provision for workers from countries facing long waits for permanent residency visas due to country limits on preferential visas. These waits are particularly long for applicants from China and India. Thus this provision is important in allowing many H-1B visa holders to transition to permanent status.

Table 3-7. Characteristics of Approved H-1B Petitions, Fiscal 2001[a]

Characteristic	Number	Percent
Total	331,206	100.0
Country of origin		
Known	330,521	
India	161,561	48.9
China	27,330	8.3
Canada	12,726	3.9
Philippines	10,389	3.1
United Kingdom	9,682	2.9
Other	108,518	32.8
Age		
Known	330,266	
< 20	194	0.0
20–24	38,248	11.6
25–29	138,450	41.9
30–34	85,084	25.8
35–39	39,561	2.0
40–44	16,168	4.9
45–49	7,224	2.2
50–54	3,292	1.0
55–59	1,359	0.4
60–64	483	0.1
> 65	203	0.1
Education		
Known	330,808	
Less than bachelor's	5,608	1.7
Bachelor's	187,735	56.8
Master's	102,996	31.1
Professional degree	9,859	3.0
Doctorate	24,610	7.4
Occupation		
Known	329,866	
Computer-related	191,397	58.0
Other	138,496	42.0

Source: INS (2002).

a. Initial and continuing employment petitions.

largest recipient, receiving almost half of the approvals. India's share increased steadily over the 1990s, from roughly 5 percent to roughly 50 percent, owing to the sharp rise in the demand for computer-related talent.[25] The age distribution shows a strong demand for young, relatively recent graduates, with more than two-thirds of all approvals falling in the narrow 25–34 age group. Not surprisingly, given the skill requirements for the H-1B visa, roughly 98 percent of approvals went to individuals with a bachelor's degree or better, with more than 40 percent falling in the "or better" category. The importance of access to H-1B workers by the high-tech industries (notably information technology) is borne out by the fact that 58 percent of all approvals were in computer-related occupations. Indeed, the largest employers of these workers during the first five months of fiscal 2000 belonged to the U.S. economy's technological elite: Motorola (618), Oracle (455), Cisco (398), Mastech (389), Intel (367), and Microsoft (362).[26]

How is the H-1B program likely to evolve in the future? Following the terrorist attacks of September 11, 2001, and the prolonged technology slump that began in 2000, petition applications and approvals declined in fiscal 2000, while many visa holders fell on hard times and returned home. During the first three quarters of fiscal 2002, the United States approved 60,500 petitions, a number significantly less than the 130,700 approved during the same period of the previous fiscal year. When the expanded cap was not renewed for fiscal 2004, however, the cap allowed was reached by February, which indicates that the demand for visas has nonetheless remained high. Not surprisingly, employers are again pushing for an expanded cap, although prospects are not promising given the fear of terrorism, a relatively weak job market, and grave concern in some quarters about the outsourcing of skilled service sector jobs, especially to India. Indeed, many see the H-1B visa as a factor facilitating the outsourcing of work to India rather than substituting for it. Some employers have been trying to get around the tightened constraint on the availability of H-1Bs by using L-1 visas, which are designed for intracompany transferees. But these visas are also coming under scrutiny from a job-wary Congress. At the same time, there is growing concern about the damage being done to U.S. innovation by policies that restrict industry's access to skilled foreign workers and students.

25. Desai, Kapur, and McHale (2003).
26. INS (2002).

4

Why Is Immigration Policy Becoming More Skill Focused?

In this chapter we explore possible explanations for why rich-country immigration policy has become more skill focused and consider whether it is likely to continue along this path. The central questions of interest are (1) whether and how the economic *costs* and *benefits* of (skilled) immigration have changed, and (2) whether and how the *politics* of (skilled) immigration has changed. They are explored in the context of three widely discussed "big trends" that are likely to have implications for the economics and politics of alternative immigration strategies. The first is *skill-biased technical change*.[1] New technologies in areas such as computing and medicine are making educated workers more valuable, leading governments everywhere to declare that they want more of them. The second is *population aging*. Over the coming decades the share of elderly in the population will rise rapidly owing to increasing life expectancies as well as the aging of the post–World War II baby boom generation, which has the potential to roil labor markets and strain social security systems. The third is the increased international integration of product and capital markets—or simply, *broader global-ization*. While in theory free trade and capital flows can substitute for labor flows, in practice all three forms of integration have tended to occur together.

1. For an excellent survey, see Acemoglu (2002).

It is important to keep in mind, of course, that trends can be interrupted or change direction. Indeed, skill-focused immigration policies have been dampened by terrorist attacks in New York, Bali, Madrid, and elsewhere, and by the deflating of the bubble in the information and communications technology sectors that began in early 2000. It is also possible that rich-country governments will find new policy instruments for appropriating the often-large wage gains from immigration and hence become more willing to accept less-skilled immigrants from poorer countries, for whom wage gaps tend to be especially large, or that rich countries will individually or collectively agree to refrain from competing for highly skilled workers from poorer countries as part of a broader development policy, or that the world will experience a humanitarian crisis that will swamp the available willingness to absorb immigrants.[2] Thus it is not inevitable that competition through selective recruitment of the world's skilled workers will increase. Nevertheless, a plausible case can be made that each of these three trends is changing the economic and political calculus for immigration policy substantially and is having an impact on the restraints on international competition for talent.

Skill-Biased Technical Change

There is mounting evidence that the skill bias of technical change has increased in recent decades.[3] In the United States, for example, the average college wage premium has risen sharply despite large increases in the supply of college-educated workers. A technology-driven increase in the relative value of skilled workers is considered the most likely reason for this development because there has been an increase in the relative use of more skilled workers *across* industries despite their rising relative cost. If the rising education premium were related to increased international trade with poorer countries—the primary competing theory—we would expect to see the rise in the demand for skilled workers coming through a relative expansion of skill-intensive industries rather than a pervasive shift to more skill-intensive production methods within industries.[4] The advancements in information technologies are widely considered the key

2. At present most of this gain is believed to go to the immigrants themselves. There is evidence that the wage gain is large. Jasso, Rosenweigh, and Smith (2002) estimate an average initial income gain for legal immigrants to the United States (in family unification and employment categories) of almost $21,000 (purchasing power parity adjusted).

3. Berman, Bound, and Griliches (1994); Katz (1999); Acemoglu (2002).

4. For further discussion of this argument, see Collins (1998).

skill-using technological development.[5] Although the increase in skill premiums has been most pronounced in the United States, the relative demand for skilled workers has expanded across industrialized countries.[6]

How is this structural change in the labor market likely to affect optimal economic immigration policy? Suppose for a moment that the goal of immigration policy is the narrow economic one of maximizing the average income of domestic residents. In that case, there will be a stronger economic reason for selecting skilled workers over less-skilled workers since the relative value of skilled workers increased. The problem with this argument, however, is that the impact of an immigrant (or group of immigrants) on the average income of natives depends both on the difference between the value of their addition to national output *and* on the wages they are paid—that is, on the *immigration surplus*. Immigrants adding high value do not provide income gains for domestic residents if they take out as much in commensurately high wages as they put into the economy.

To illustrate the immigration effects in the wake of skill-biased technical change, suppose that there are just two factors of production—skilled workers, S, and unskilled workers, U—each with wages determined in competitive labor markets. The economy is closed to international trade, and national output, Y, is given by the (constant returns to scale) constant elasticity of substitution production function,

$$(4\text{-}1) \qquad Y = [(A_s S)^\rho + (A_u U)^\rho]^{\frac{1}{\rho}}.$$

A_s/A_u is a measure of the relative productivity of skilled and unskilled workers, and ρ is less than or equal to one.[7] Initially, we assume that there are no uncompensated externalities, that there is no fiscal system, and that wages are determined in competitive skill markets. Our main interest is to see how changes in A_s/A_u alter the economic case for a skill-focused immigration policy.

This simple model yields a number of noteworthy—and a few surprising—findings about surplus-maximizing immigration policy. First, a

5. See Kruger (1993); Levy and Murnane (1996); Autor, Katz, and Krueger (1998); Bresnahan, Brynjolfsson, and Hitt (1999).

6. Berman, Bound, and Machin (1998). Outside the United States, the rise in the skill premium has been held down by larger increases in the relative supply of skills and by wage-setting institutions that hold down inequalities. See Freeman and Katz (1994); Murphy and others (1998).

7. The elasticity of substitution between skilled and unskilled workers is then $\sigma \equiv 1/(1-\rho)$.

single immigrant (either skilled or unskilled) will not produce an immigration surplus since the immigrant will be paid the value of his or her marginal product in a competitive labor market. Second, there is also no immigration surplus from a balanced immigrant inflow, where "balanced" means that the immigrants have the same kinds of skills as the native population. This is simply a reflection of the well-known fact that under constant returns to scale, a scaling up of the economy has no effect on factor incomes. Third, holding the number of other skill types constant, the size of the immigration surplus rises approximately with the square of the number of immigrants of a particular skill type. The reason is that increases in the number of immigrants of a given skill type lead to increases in the surplus of earlier immigrants of that type as their wage is driven down. Fourth, if the goal is to maximize the immigration surplus from some given number of immigrants, the optimal policy is one that favors the extremes—either all skilled or all unskilled.[8] Most interesting in the present context, skill-biased technical change (as measured by an increase in A_s/A_u) has no effect on which of these extremes yields the larger immigrant surplus. In effect, the higher relative wage received by skilled immigrants offsets the increase in relative productivity, which leads to no overall change in the relative surplus. In this example, the choice between an immigration policy focusing on skilled workers versus one focusing on the unskilled depends only on the relative supplies of skilled and unskilled workers in the domestic population. The superior productivity of skilled workers *does not* create a presumption in favor of skilled immigrants, and so an increase in the relative productivity of skilled workers cannot improve the case for skilled immigrants.

Not surprisingly, it is easy to modify the model so that skill-biased technical change does strengthen the case for a skill-focused immigration policy given a narrow immigrant surplus-maximizing goal. Two obvious ways to do this are to allow for a progressive fiscal system and for uncompensated knowledge spillovers from skilled immigrants to natives. With a progressive fiscal system, high-earning immigrants are likely to be net fiscal contributors, which is an additional source of immigration surplus. In this case, even a single high-skilled immigrant earning the going competitive skill-specific wage will yield a surplus, and skill-biased technical change will raise that surplus to the extent that it raises the skilled wage and net fiscal contribution. Our simple

8. See Borjas (1995).

example also assumes that all the benefits from immigration go to the firms employing the immigrants. In particular, no allowance is made for uncompensated knowledge spillovers from immigrants to domestic workers. To the extent that such spillovers exist, they are probably largest for more skilled knowledge workers, further tilting the advantage to skilled immigrants from a surplus-maximizing perspective.

The foregoing discussion of optimal immigration policy assumes that the government's objective is to maximize the immigration surplus for any given number of immigrants. Of course, the government may also want to minimize wage differentials between skilled and unskilled natives, or at least to prevent wage differentials from rising. Here the case for a skill-focused immigration policy in the presence of skill-biased technical change is more clear-cut. All else equal, such change increases the relative wage of skilled workers, whereas a skill-focused immigration policy reduces the relative wage of skilled workers. Thus a skill-focused immigration policy can be used to reduce wage differentials in the absence of technical change or to counteract rising differentials in the presence of technical change.

It is also interesting to consider how skill-biased technical changes affect the politics of immigration policy. Immigration within a given skill class is more likely to draw political opposition when the wages of that skill class are static or falling. On the other hand, when technology-driven increases in demand lead to sharply rising wages for skilled workers such as programmers, engineers, or scientists, opposition is likely to be muted (though not entirely absent) in response to expansions of skilled visa programs such as the H-1B in the United States or the green card in Germany. By contrast, the rising cost of skilled labor will lead employers to complain that "shortages" are damaging their competitiveness, which may resonate strongly with governments when international competitiveness appears to be at stake. Thus even if the economic case for a skill-focused immigration policy in response to skill-biased technical change is less than overwhelming, the resulting strong wage gains for skilled workers (and the rising costs for the firms employing them) can be important in overcoming political opposition.

Aging Populations

With ongoing improvements in health and longer life spans, industrial-country populations will become substantially older over the next half-century. There will also be a sharp increase in the share of elderly in the population around the end of this decade as the post–World War II baby boomers enter their senior years. When the UN Population Division (UNPD) calculated elderly dependency rates (the population 65 and older divided by the population aged 15–64) for six of the G-7 countries under the assumption of zero net migration (see table 4-1), the rate in the United States was expected to double from roughly 20 percent in 2005 to about 40 percent in 2050. Put differently, the number of (liberally defined) working-age individuals available to support each person of retirement age will fall from 5 at present to roughly 2.5 in 2050, with most of the change occurring by 2030. In Italy, the number of working-age individuals available to support each retiree is already down to roughly 3.3 and will fall to 1.5 by 2050 without migration. Population aging appears to be occurring especially quickly in Japan, where the support ratio is expected to fall to 2.5 as early as 2015.

Such rapid population aging is likely to have significant effects on labor markets and public finances. For one thing, demand and supply in different skill markets are likely to shift substantially. On the demand side, elderly populations will need substantial care services, many of which will have low skill requirements. At the same time, there will be greater demand for high-tech medical services that will be skill intensive in both use and development.[9] On the supply side, it will be hard to acquire increasingly educated domestic workers to fill care positions without sharply raising wages. Although it is hard to predict precise manpower needs and availabilities, a reasonable assumption is that those facing rising health care prices will press to "import" both lower-skilled care workers and highly skilled health care/technology providers.

Many have already contemplated the effect of population aging on industrial-country public finances, and with some sense of alarm. We concentrate here on publicly funded retirement income systems, though aging may have even more significant effects on publicly funded health care. The implications of aging for a pay-as-you-go (PAYGO) retirement income system become quite clear under the following PAYGO identity (or PAYGO constraint), which relates the payroll tax rate required to

---

9. Moreover, as the new medicines and diagnostic technologies rely more on information technologies, there will be an indirect increase in the demand for a broader range of technology professionals.

Table 4-1. Hard Choices: Population Aging and PAYGO Retirement Income Systems without Migration, 2005–50
Percent

a. Projected elderly dependency rates (pop >65 / pop 15–64) with zero post-1995 net migration

Country	2005	2010	2015	2020	2025	2030	2035	2040	2045	2050
United States	0.19	0.20	0.23	0.27	0.32	0.37	0.39	0.39	0.38	0.39
Japan	0.29	0.34	0.40	0.44	0.45	0.46	0.49	0.54	0.57	0.58
Germany	0.28	0.31	0.32	0.36	0.41	0.49	0.57	0.58	0.57	0.57
United Kingdom	0.25	0.26	0.29	0.31	0.34	0.38	0.41	0.42	0.42	0.42
France	0.25	0.25	0.29	0.32	0.36	0.39	0.41	0.43	0.44	0.44
Italy	0.30	0.31	0.34	0.37	0.42	0.49	0.57	0.65	0.67	0.66

b. Implied PAYGO tax rate (assuming constant 1995 benefit generosity rate and zero post-1995 net migration)[a]

Country	1995 benefit generosity rate[b]	2005	2010	2015	2020	2025	2030	2035	2040	2045	2050
United States	0.48	0.09	0.10	0.11	0.13	0.16	0.18	0.19	0.19	0.18	0.19
Japan	0.44	0.13	0.15	0.18	0.19	0.20	0.20	0.21	0.24	0.25	0.26
Germany	0.83	0.24	0.26	0.27	0.30	0.34	0.41	0.47	0.48	0.47	0.47
United Kingdom	0.48	0.12	0.12	0.14	0.15	0.16	0.18	0.20	0.20	0.20	0.20
France	0.84	0.21	0.21	0.24	0.27	0.30	0.32	0.35	0.36	0.37	0.37
Italy	1.05	0.31	0.33	0.36	0.39	0.44	0.51	0.60	0.68	0.70	0.69

c.. Implied benefit generosity rate (assuming constant 1995 tax rate and zero post-1995 net migration)

Country	1995 tax rate	2005	2010	2015	2020	2025	2030	2035	2040	2045	2050
United States	0.09	0.48	0.46	0.40	0.34	0.28	0.25	0.24	0.24	0.24	0.24
Japan	0.09	0.32	0.27	0.23	0.21	0.21	0.20	0.19	0.17	0.16	0.16
Germany	0.19	0.66	0.61	0.58	0.53	0.46	0.38	0.33	0.32	0.33	0.33
United Kingdom	0.12	0.48	0.46	0.41	0.38	0.34	0.31	0.28	0.28	0.28	0.28
France	0.19	0.77	0.76	0.67	0.60	0.54	0.50	0.47	0.45	0.44	0.44
Italy	0.26	0.87	0.82	0.75	0.69	0.62	0.53	0.45	0.40	0.39	0.39

Sources: United Nations Population Division (2000); OECD (2000, 2001); authors' calculations.

a. The PAYGO tax rate, *t*, is the ratio of total (retirement income) taxes to total wages. This is the tax rate required if retirement benefits are funded on a purely pay-as-you-go basis. That is, $t = b \times d$, where d is the elderly dependency rate.

b. The benefit generosity rate, *b*, is the ratio of the average benefit (total benefits/elderly population) to the average wage (total wages/working-age population).

fund benefits on a purely PAYGO basis given the relative generosity of benefits and the elderly dependency rate:

$$\text{PAYGO tax rate}\,(t) = \frac{\text{Total benefits}}{\text{Total wages}} = \frac{\dfrac{\text{Total benefits}}{\text{Elderly population}}}{\dfrac{\text{Total wages}}{\text{Working-age population}}} \times \frac{\text{Elderly population}}{\text{Working-age population}}$$

$$= \text{Benefit generosity rate}\,(b) \times \text{Elderly dependency rate}\,(d).$$

An increase in the elderly dependency rate (d) must be matched by some combination of an increase in the PAYGO tax rate (t) or by a decrease in the benefit generosity rate (b). Note that average benefits to be funded by future taxpayers can be reduced in a number of ways: by raising the normal retirement age, cutting back on inducements for early retirement, adjusting the formula for initial earnings-related benefits, lowering flat-rate benefits, or reducing post-retirement benefit indexation.[10] These benefit-saving methods do not necessarily place the same burden on retirees. Where rules relating to early retirement substantially distort retirement decisions, reforms can be designed to yield benefit cost savings with relatively low burdens on retirees. Nonetheless, to the extent that the benefit generosity rate must bear part of the adjustment to a higher elderly dependency rate, some of the burden will inevitably fall on retirees.

When one examines the implied increases in the PAYGO tax rate holding the benefit generosity rate constant and the reductions in the benefit generosity rate holding the PAYGO tax rate constant (see table 4-1), the implied changes are quite dramatic.[11] For the United States, with no

10. We also treat the prefunding of retirement benefits that were to have been funded on a PAYGO basis as a benefit cut for those doing the prefunding. Individuals are partly funding themselves benefits that were to have been funded by later workers.

11. The benefit generosity rate is the ratio of average benefits (per elderly person) to the average wage (per working-age person). The average benefit in 1995 is calculated as total retirement income benefits excluding survivor benefits as measured in the OECD's comprehensive Social Expenditure Database divided by the population 65 and older. This average benefit measure could be further decomposed into the product of the average benefit per retired person and the ratio of the number of retirees to the population 65 and older. Thus the average benefit measure is affected by both the generosity of benefits for those actually retired and the ease of eligibility for retirement benefits, including the ease of eligibility before age 65. The average wage is the calculated labor share of income multiplied by GDP divided by the working-age population, where an adjustment is made for the output gap in each country in 1995. The PAYGO tax rate is the tax rate required to completely fund benefits on a pay-as-you-go basis in a given year.

change in the ratio of the average benefit payment for those 65 or older to the average earnings of the working-age population, the PAYGO tax rate will rise from 9 percent in 2005 to 18 percent by 2030. On the other hand, if the payroll tax paid by the working-age population to fund the retirement income benefits of those already retired is held constant, the benefit generosity rate will fall from 48 percent in 2005 to 25 percent by 2030. The scale of the implied adjustments is even greater for Italy, with its very generous retirement benefits and even more dramatic population aging. Under a constant benefit rate, the tax rate would rise from 31 percent in 2005 to 69 percent in 2050; under a constant tax rate, the benefit rate would fall from 87 percent to just 39 percent over the same period.

Is there any way to avoid the pain of higher taxes and lower benefits when the domestic population is aging? The PAYGO constraint makes it clear that the only alternative is to stop the demographics from changing. Since rising mortality rates at older ages must obviously be excluded, and the economic and social forces that affect fertility are difficult to change, the only alternative is to "import" younger workers and taxpayers through more relaxed permanent and temporary migration policies.

UNPD projections suggest that *permanent* migration is far from being the sought-after "silver bullet."[12] From assumptions about the age and sex of immigrants, and also immigrant fertility and mortality after arrival, the UNPD has estimated the immigrant inflows required to keep the dependency ratio constant, as shown in table 4-2. If one also assumes that immigrant workers receive the same average wages as native workers, and that immigrant retirees receive the same average benefits as native retirees, these estimated inflows can be viewed as the inflows required to maintain tax and benefit generosity rates at their 1995 levels. Clearly, the numbers are very large in comparison with recent immigration trends. For the United States, the required annual average inflow between 2005 and 2050 is more than 13 million a year (the average legal permanent immigration to the United States in recent years was about 1 million a year)! Such numbers are not politically feasible.

Why are the required numbers of permanent immigrants so large? The simple answer is that today's permanent working immigrants become tomorrow's retirees. Therefore, while immigration may initially increase the taxpayer base, once those immigrants become retirees, they

12. UNPD (2000).

Table 4-2. Migration Required to Keep PAYGO Tax and Benefit Rates Constant at 1995 Levels, 2005–50
Temporary migrant share of total working-age population (θ)

a. Average temporary migrant wage = average nonmigrant wage ($\theta = 0$)

Country	2005	2010	2015	2020	2025	2030	2035	2040	2045	2050
United States	0.00	0.05	0.17	0.30	0.41	0.48	0.50	0.50	0.50	0.51
Japan	0.28	0.38	0.48	0.52	0.53	0.55	0.57	0.61	0.64	0.64
Germany	0.20	0.27	0.30	0.36	0.44	0.54	0.60	0.61	0.60	0.60
United Kingdom	0.01	0.05	0.14	0.21	0.28	0.36	0.41	0.42	0.42	0.42
France	0.08	0.09	0.20	0.29	0.36	0.41	0.44	0.47	0.48	0.48
Italy	0.17	0.22	0.29	0.34	0.41	0.50	0.57	0.62	0.63	0.63

b. Average temporary migrant wage = 150% of average nonmigrant wage ($\theta = 0.5$)

Country	2005	2010	2015	2020	2025	2030	2035	2040	2045	2050
United States	0.00	0.03	0.12	0.22	0.31	0.38	0.40	0.40	0.40	0.41
Japan	0.20	0.29	0.38	0.42	0.43	0.44	0.47	0.51	0.54	0.54
Germany	0.14	0.20	0.22	0.28	0.35	0.44	0.50	0.51	0.50	0.50
United Kingdom	0.00	0.03	0.10	0.15	0.21	0.27	0.32	0.33	0.33	0.33
France	0.05	0.06	0.14	0.21	0.27	0.31	0.35	0.37	0.38	0.38
Italy	0.12	0.16	0.21	0.26	0.32	0.40	0.47	0.52	0.53	0.53

Sources: United Nations Population Division (2000); authors' calculations.

begin increasing the benefit recipient base. Eventually, as the earlier immigrants reach retirement age, even more young immigrants will be required to sustain initial tax and benefit rates.

If permanent immigration is not a silver bullet, what about a policy of selective temporary migration? In the extreme, temporary migrants could be disallowed from staying long enough to gain entitlement to retirement income benefits. In the United States, for example, this would limit total stays to less than 10 years, since this is the amount of work required to qualify for Social Security retirement income benefits. Moreover, by selecting relatively skilled temporary migrants (as is the case with H-1B visas), the policy could raise the average wage in the economy and thus increase the tax take for any given working-age population. To be more concrete, assume the temporary migrant share of the working-age population is given by θ, and the average proportionate wage premium earned by migrants over domestic workers is given by α. It is then easy to show that the PAYGO constraint is given by

$$t = b \times \left(\frac{1 - \theta}{1 + \alpha\theta} \right) \times d,$$

where t is the tax rate levied on all workers, b is the average benefit rate received by domestic workers (average benefit divided by average wage of domestic workers), and d is the dependency rate for the domestic population.[13]

As table 4-2 shows, even in the case of a 50 percent migrant wage premium and no benefit liability, the required migrant shares are very high, averaging more than 37 percent across the six countries in 2030. It seems reasonable to suppose that such high migrant shares would neither be acceptable to the working-age population nor feasible to attract—especially with such a high relative wage. Thus a policy of selective temporary immigration is unlikely to provide the silver bullet either.

Even though migration policies are not a panacea for avoiding tax increases and benefit cuts, it is possible that self-interested younger generations will try to expand the future tax base to forestall the harsh benefit cuts that are likely to occur if tax rates begin to rise too sharply.[14] Given the alternatives of falling benefits or rising taxes, there will be strong incentives to "import" workers to take up at least some of the burden. Such pressures are likely to be especially strong in a number of European countries, where workers know that current benefit rules will

---

13. To understand the basis for the additional term in parentheses, note that the total elderly dependency rate (natives and immigrants) can be written as $(1 - \theta)d$, and the average wage in the economy can be written as $(1 + \alpha\theta)W$, where W is the average wage of natives. The product of the last two terms in the equation can be viewed as an adjusted dependency rate, where the adjustment depends on the share of temporary migrants in the working-age population and the proportionate wage premium that migrants earn over native-born workers.

14. McHale (2003) develops a model of one generation's extraction of benefits from the following generation. The reason that the older generation can extract benefits from the younger generation is that the younger generation has an obligation to make sufficient transfers (tax-funded retirement income or family-funded in-kind benefits) to its elders to allow them to sustain their working-life consumption in retirement. There is a proviso to this obligation, however: the choice of working-life consumption and thus retirement savings must be based on rationally anticipated social security benefits. A key restraint on the benefits that can be extracted is the burden placed on the tax-paying generation by a labor-supply-distorting social security tax. In the model, the working generation can choose an immigration policy (in addition to promising itself social security benefits) that comes into effect with a one-period lag. A selective temporary immigration policy lowers the tax rate on the following generation for any given chosen benefit level. This induces the working generation to credibly promise itself a higher benefit level. With the higher benefit, members of the following generation end up facing an even higher tax burden despite the migration-expanded tax base. The upshot of the model is that the current working generation has an incentive to put in place an immigration policy that will expand the tax base available to pay its benefits. In fact, the only thing that restrains the number of migrants (assuming an infinite willing supply) is a concern on the part of domestic residents that they will increase the political power of a group without a family obligation to sustain their consumption in retirement.

become so expensive that future workers are unlikely to honor them. Although there is undoubtedly more antipathy toward immigrants there than in the more traditional immigration countries (notably Australia, Canada, New Zealand, and the United States), the debate surrounding the new German immigration law shows that the likely scarcity of future taxpayers to share the social security burden is leading politicians to look for ways to selectively augment the working-age population.

Broader Globalization

The next question to consider is to what extent the increasing internationalization of trade, capital flows, and production is pushing rich countries to relax restrictions and indeed compete more intensively for skilled workers. Although broader globalization is knitting together an international labor market, the economist's workhorse model of international trade—the Heckscher-Ohlin (H-O) model—predicts that international trade in goods and services will *substitute* for international migration.[15] Under the standard assumptions of the model, international trade leads to complete factor price equalization. This removes the key incentive to migrate on the supply side: the possibility of earning higher wages abroad. It also means that the standard immigration surplus is zero, since the existence of a surplus depends on the domestic wage being driven down.[16] Of course, the prediction of complete international wage equalization is not borne out by reality. There are vast differences in incomes across countries even after adjusting for the lower prices of nontraded goods in poorer countries.[17] Once allowance is made for productivity differences across countries, however, there is strong evidence of productivity-adjusted factor price equalization.[18] In such a world, there is a willing supply of poor-country residents ready to improve their living standards by moving to a place where they can be more productive and earn higher incomes. But if wages are fixed by productivity-adjusted factor price equalization, the absence of an immigration surplus means that there is no incentive for rich countries to admit them if the goal is to maximize the average income of natives.

Another way to assess the effect of globalization is to assume there are skill-intensive industries in which the government wishes to gain a

15. See, for example, Mundell (1957).
16. See Trefler (1997).
17. Hall and Jones (1999); Parente and Prescott (2000).
18. Trefler (1993).

national competitive advantage but cannot do so with its existing skill supplies. The reasonableness of this assumption is attested by another important prediction of the H-O model: namely, countries will tend to specialize in industries that are intensive in the use of their more abundant factors of production. Thus a country having an abundance of skilled software programmers and microbiologists will tend to specialize in the production and international sale of software and biotechnology products. The special measures that governments are taking to support such industries strongly suggest they believe that national advantage will be served by an internationally competitive domestic presence. One reason often given for this is that knowledge-intensive industries generate localized knowledge spillovers, which means the domestic industry will be too small if left to market forces. According to the HO model, the way to expand these industries without resorting to outright subsidization is to engineer a relative expansion in the factor supplies used intensively in these industries—that is, the skilled workers. The most obvious long-term solution is to educate and train the workers needed for internationally competitive knowledge-intensive industries. But this is a costly and time-consuming exercise, and governments might be enticed to augment the process with skilled immigrants.

Earlier in the chapter we considered spillovers as a reason to support a more skilled immigration policy, on the assumption that knowledge spillovers have become more important given the nature of new technologies. We now consider how openness to international trade induces specialization based on resource availability. It can be argued that as product markets become more internationally integrated, the incentives to "import" skilled workers increase in order to ensure a reasonable presence in the desired knowledge-intensive industries.

The liberalization of international trade in services creates further pressure for the easing of restraints on migration. In many instances, international services cannot be provided without home-country workers operating at the buyer's location. The General Agreement on Trade in Services (GATS) envisions an even more radical liberalization, under which *individuals* can temporarily move to a foreign country to offer their services. This essentially equates "temporary trade migration" with "trade in services." Thus the momentum for greater multilateral trade liberalization may serve to liberalize temporary migration. Although opponents of such a regime might call this wishful thinking, some of the recent high-profile regional trade liberalizations have been accompanied by measures to liberalize migration. The archetypal case is the European

Union, which secures the free movement of goods, capital, *and* people among its members. The eastern expansion of the European Union will allow, probably after a phase-in period, for the free movement of workers from poorer Eastern European countries to their richer Western European neighbors. To take another example, the North American Free Trade Agreement (NAFTA) gives Canadian professionals relatively easy access to the U.S. labor market and vice versa; for Mexican professionals, however, access to the United States is much more limited.

Turning to capital market integration, it is also obvious that capital flows from rich countries to poor countries can substitute for labor flows from poor countries to rich countries. As already noted, poor countries have a reservoir of would-be immigrants of a given skill level because rich countries offer higher productivity and correspondingly higher wages. Productivity varies across countries largely because richer countries have more available capital and use better technology and organization than do the poor countries. Therefore an obvious alternative to bringing poor-country workers to rich-country capital and technology is to bring the capital and technology to the workers. Foreign direct investment—which often brings both capital and technology—can, for example, substitute for immigration. U.S. software multinationals can set up operations in India, rather than petition (and lobby) to have Indian programmers admitted to the United States.

That being said, a freer flow of capital may also create pressure to allow a freer flow of workers. A prime example can be found among internationally footloose corporations that explicitly or implicitly threaten to move their production overseas if the obstacles to immigration are not reduced. Some multinationals also need to move personnel between international locations and may lobby governments to allow this flexibility by issuing special intracompany transfer visas.

A final point meriting a few words concerns the much-disparaged homogenization of cultures. As locations become less culturally distinct and the costs of adapting to new surroundings decline, people are likely to be more willing to move. From the receiving-country side, electorates will become more willing to accept immigrants that they consider "not too different" from themselves. To the extent that this homogenization pervades all socioeconomic groups, it should lead to greater acceptance of immigrants in general. But, realistically, the skilled elites throughout the world are the ones more likely to share common experiences and interests, which may be one more factor shifting immigration policies in a skill-focused direction.

CHAPTER 5

When People Can Leave: The Effect of Prospective Emigration

People do not actually need to leave a country for it to be affected by the existence of outside opportunities for that country's skilled labor. Indeed, the simple *prospect* of leaving one's country can change domestic economic and political outcomes. The prospect of emigration can also affect an individual's decisions to accumulate financial, social, and enterprise capital. Prospective emigration can be examined under three conditions: when an individual is uncertain about his or her chances of emigration but is certain of receiving a higher return on human capital investments should the opportunity to emigrate arise; when emigration is an *option*—one that, under some conditions, might be "bought" with additional education; and when the availability of outside options is uneven across skill levels and can subtly reshape a society, whether in regard to the progressivity of the fiscal system or the incentive to use "voice" to reform domestic institutions.

A Prospect of Emigration

Various models have been constructed to test the "brain drain" theory of skilled emigration, all of which begin with the basic premise that individuals face some probability of getting a foreign visa and will obtain a higher return on their domestically accumulated human capital if they get that visa.[1] The higher expected return induces them to acquire more

1. Mountford (1997); Stark, Helmenstein, and Yegorov (1997); Stark and Chau (1998); Stark and Wang (2001); Beine, Docquier, and Rapoport (2001, 2002).

human capital. Even though emigration does drain off talent, some remain, and these may be greater than would have been present had the prospect to emigrate not arisen. (We develop our own model of this process in the next section.) One model used to estimate the effect of migration on human capital formation leads to the conclusion that "migration prospects exert a positive effect on human capital formation for a cross section of 50 developing countries" and that this holds for different specifications of the human capital equation.[2] According to this model's calculations of the net balance between this "brain gain" and the "brain drain" effect of the actual subsequent migration, mobile human capital makes countries with low levels of human capital and low migration rates for skilled workers net "winners." Even though it turns out that there are more so-called loser countries than winning ones, the winners tend to have larger populations. Indeed, the winners make up 80 percent of the total developing world's population.

One shortcoming of such models is that they assume emigration results from a sort of lottery in which visas are awarded randomly and all individuals have an equal probability of obtaining one. As outlined in chapter 3, rich countries actively screen a large portion of their skilled worker inflows as they attempt to "cream off" the best talent.[3] If workers fully understand the screening process used by a rich country, they can predict with certainty whether they will be granted a work visa.[4] Individuals who qualify and intend to take up the visa may well be induced to acquire additional human capital before leaving. But since they have definite plans to leave, the home country has no chance of gaining from these additional investments. What is more, those individuals whose chances of obtaining a visa are very small will have no added inducement to acquire more human capital.[5]

Besides rich-country screening, three factors may diminish the importance of this prospective channel. First, consider the substitution and

---

2. See Beine and others (2002, p. 37). They use Carrington and Detragiache's (1998) estimates of migration rates.

3. For an excellent discussion of screening and its implications for these models, see Commander, Kangasniemi, and Winters (2002).

4. This will be most likely when the rich country uses objective criteria for selecting immigrants, with little room for subjective judgments. Examples might be entry on the basis of the Canadian or Australian points systems.

5. Rich-country screening may also be biasing the empirical results of Beine and others (2002). The observed correlation between migration rates and human capital formation may be partly due to the effect that the countries more successful at producing human capital are more likely to have workers who pass rich-country immigration screens.

income effects of a higher expected return. An individual might respond to the higher expected return by substituting education for work or leisure at any given level of well-being, in accordance with the model just discussed. If the immediate prospect of emigrating provides a higher expected return for an individual's present skills level, however, the income effect predicts that one would rather enjoy the fruits of one's labor than struggle to acquire more education. This is like the teenagers who have to decide whether or not to work hard to gain admission into a good local university. If they do not emigrate, a university education will be essential to maintaining a good standard of living. However, if they have the opportunity to emigrate to New York or London, where they will earn a decent salary as a construction worker, for example, they might choose to forgo university education. Although they would likely earn more with a degree, the tedium of study might cancel out the expected difference in pay.

Second, skills acquired at home simply might not make the transition abroad. Many cabdrivers in North American cities, for example, seem overqualified for the job. Part of the problem is that foreign credentials are often not recognized in the destination country—even when those very qualifications were the basis for entry under a skills-based screening system. It seems that education and labor market experience acquired abroad are valued significantly less than such human capital acquired domestically.[6] Thus potential immigrants might be better off accumulating human capital after they have immigrated (assuming, of course, that they do not have to acquire that education to overcome the rich-country screening process). Interestingly, it has been found that education acquired after immigration has a very high return.[7] This suggests that even though the value of a foreign education is significantly discounted at first, it complements post-immigration education and thus still might be worth acquiring by those who foresee a high prospect of emigrating.[8]

Third, most of these models assume that just because there is a demand, there will be a corresponding supply. This assumption fails

6. See Friedberg (2000).

7. Friedberg (2000).

8. Findings recently released from Canada's 2001 census show immigrants to be relatively heavy acquirers of education. For example, for those in the 25 to 29 age group, 15.2 percent of immigrants who came during the 1990s were in full-time education and 11.8 percent were in part-time education. The figures for all other residents of Canada were 11.1 and 9.2 percent, respectively.

badly, not only with regard to those countries that people want to leave the most, such as Liberia or Moldova, but also with regard to structural considerations, including unstable university systems and limited faculty, which can severely restrict supply (see chapter 6). Accordingly, even if the prospect of immigration substantially increases the incentive to acquire human capital while still at home, severe weaknesses in the higher education system of poor countries will limit such outcomes.

A Simple Model of Prospective Migration

The key idea underlying this model is that a higher probability of international migration has two opposing effects on the economy's expected stock of human capital when a higher return to human capital is available outside the country. First, an increased probability of migration increases the ex ante return to human capital, thus increasing investments in that capital. Second, for any given level of human capital investment, a higher probability of migration increases the expected human capital loss. For the purposes of the model, we treat the probability of migration as being exogenously determined by the immigration policies of other countries. Thus the model captures the effect of changes in foreign immigration policies on human capital investment and retention.

Each individual is assumed to make a final decision on how much human capital, h, to accumulate at time zero. A unit of human capital yields a dollars in domestic wages per unit of time if the individual works domestically, and a^f dollars if the individual works abroad. The constant instantaneous probability of the individual emigrating at any given point in time (conditional on not having emigrated before) is given by m. We assume that all migrations are permanent. Discounting future expected cash flows by an instantaneous interest rate r, we can write the expected value of an individual's human capital as

$$(5\text{-}1) \qquad V = \frac{1}{1+r} [ah + (1-m)V + mV^f],$$

where V^f is the value of the individual's human capital conditional on having emigrated. Since the individual receives a wage of $a^f h$ in perpetuity post immigration, V^f is simply the value of this perpetuity,

$$(5\text{-}2) \qquad V^f = \frac{a^f h}{r}.$$

Substituting (5-2) into (5-1) allows us to solve for the expected value of the individual's human capital as a function of the level of human capital, the probability of migration, and the interest rate:

$$(5\text{-}3) \qquad V = \frac{1}{r+m}\left(ah + \frac{ma^f h}{r}\right).$$

The marginal value of an additional unit of human capital is given by

$$(5\text{-}4) \qquad \frac{\partial V}{\partial h} = \frac{1}{r+m}\left(a + \frac{ma^f}{r}\right).$$

Turning to the cost of accumulating human capital, C, we assume a simple convex cost function,

$$(5\text{-}5) \qquad C = \frac{1}{2}h^2.$$

Thus the *marginal cost* of acquiring human capital is taken to be a rising function of the level of human capital. One possible rationale for the rising marginal cost is that the opportunity cost in terms of lost wages is greater the more human capital the individual has. With our chosen functional form, the marginal cost is exactly equal to the prior level of human capital:

$$(5\text{-}6) \qquad \frac{\partial C}{\partial h} = h.$$

Equating equations (5-4) and (5-6) allows us to solve for the optimal level of human capital:

$$(5\text{-}7) \qquad h^* = \frac{1}{r+m}\left(a + \frac{ma^f}{r}\right).$$

Not surprisingly, the effect of an increase in the probability of migration on the optimal level of human capital to accumulate depends on the relative return to human capital in domestic and foreign labor markets,

$$(5\text{-}8) \qquad \frac{\partial h^*}{\partial m} = \frac{1}{(r+m)^2}(a^f - a).$$

We assume from this point on that the foreign return is higher than the domestic return (that is, $a^f > a$).

Now consider how the home country is affected by an increase in the probability of migration. For simplicity, we measure this by the worker's domestic wage, ah, and assume that the country gets no benefit once the individual has emigrated. The expected value of an individual who has not yet emigrated, but who faces a constant probability of migration equal to m, is thus given by the perpetuity,

$$(5\text{-}9) \qquad\qquad X = \frac{ab^*}{r + m},$$

where the overall discount rate is now the sum of the interest rate and the (constant) probability of migration. It is now apparent that an increase in the probability of migration affects two factors: (1) the optimal choice of human capital, and (2) the rate at which the future potential human capital flows are discounted:

$$(5\text{-}10) \qquad \frac{\partial X}{\partial m} = \frac{a}{(r + m)^3} \left[(a^f - a) - \left(a + \frac{ma^f}{r} \right) \right].$$

If a^f is sufficiently greater than a, an increase in the probability of migration will actually increase the expected value of the worker to the home country. If m becomes large enough, however, the higher foreign return effect will be outweighed by the higher discount rate effect.[9] It is possible, then, that the optimal (in the narrow sense of X-maximizing) probability of migration, m^*, is non-zero—that is, there is a range where the country actually benefits from a higher probability of losing its workers. Such a case is shown in figure 5-1.[10]

The Option of Emigration

In place of a randomized lottery, rich-country governments are currently developing elaborate screening programs to select the most highly skilled temporary and permanent migrants. In this way, emigration becomes an option rather than a prospect for many highly skilled individuals.

When emigration is an option, there is an increase in domestic human capital accumulation, as demonstrated under the model of emigration as a prospect. As discussed previously, additional education might be necessary to first acquire the option to emigrate. Canada's points system,

9. Note that when m is equal to one the term in brackets is strictly positive given that $af > a$.

10. If this is true, starting from a zero value for m, an increase in m must strictly increase X. It is easy to show using equation (10) that a necessary and sufficient condition for this to be true is that af is at least twice as large as a.

Figure 5-1. Brain Gain with Emigration

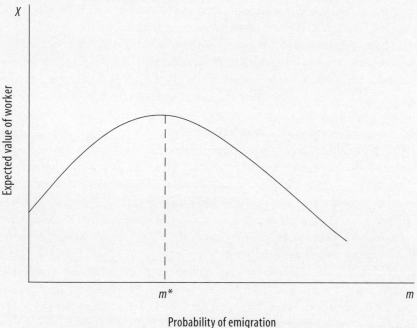

Probability of emigration

for instance, makes it extremely difficult to qualify for entry without a university education.

The existence of the option might also distort the type of education acquired, pushing individuals toward more portable skills rather than toward those narrowly tailored to the home economy. Where a country's existing comparative advantage ties it to low-growth industries, the option to emigrate might actually help the country break out of this growth trap. Suppose that a developing country has a very limited software industry, though it possesses some prospects for developing one. This country might find itself in a catch-22 situation in that its college students might remain wary of studying programming because their future with these skills is presumably uncertain, yet a supply of programmers is exactly what the country needs to get the software industry off the ground. A strong global market for programmers can reduce the risk of acquiring these skills, whether or not a student plans to emigrate. Therefore the option of emigrating can lead students to acquire more forward-looking skills, possibly allowing a country to experiment and thereby better determine where its comparative advantages lie.

Outside Options and Effects on Inequality

It is no secret that international labor mobility can adversely affect the design of an optimal fiscal system (one that maximizes social welfare).[11] The basic problem is clear: once the fiscal system is made too progressive, it will generate an exodus of highly educated and high-earning individuals, who want to avoid becoming large net contributors to the system. When such contributors leave, the country suffers direct fiscal losses (see chapter 6) as well as the losses endured by those remaining behind (TRBs) when the fiscal system is made less progressive in order to keep people from leaving. Some evidence from the past two decades suggests that top marginal tax rates (MTRs) for developing countries dropped from about 56 percent in the mid-1980s to 34 percent in 2001. For industrialized countries, top MTRs dropped to about 40 percent (figure 5-2). Although migration is not the only reason behind these declines, it appears to be limiting the degree to which countries can push the progressivity of the tax regime.

Evidence on the links between the propensity of the skilled to migrate (taken from the *World Competitiveness Handbook*) and income inequality appears in table 5-1 and figure 5-3. The archetypal cases are Brazil and India. The highly skilled in Brazil have a lower propensity to migrate because they can command a much higher income at home than their Indian counterparts. The reason is intuitive: why leave if one can already enjoy a lifestyle that is close to that of the destination country? The share of national income accruing to the top 20 percent of the population in Brazil (64 percent) is substantially greater than that in India (46 percent).

Still, there are other factors that would weigh into one's decision to emigrate. These range from political uncertainty and violence (as in Colombia and Venezuela) and an uncertain future for the country's minority (as for the whites in South Africa) to perhaps a "national culture" (as in the Philippines). Note, too, that the effects of inequality might wane with increasing average income (as in Hungary and Korea). Nonetheless, if one controls for top marginal tax rates and per capita income, there appears to be a fairly strong relationship between inequality and the "brain drain" such that in more unequal societies the elite have less incentive to leave. Furthermore, the results are robust if the

---

11. See the collection of papers in Bhagwati (1982).

Figure 5-2. Top Marginal Tax Rates (MTRs), Developing versus the Top Seventeen OECD Countries, 1985–2001

Average top MTR

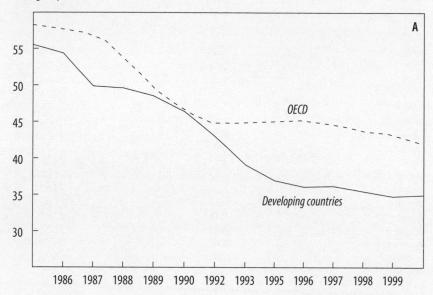

Median top MTR

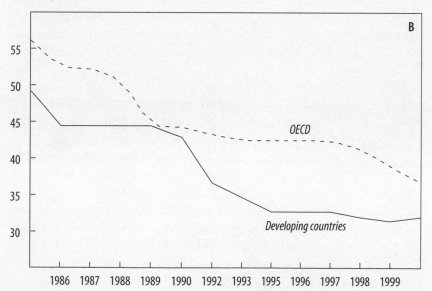

Table 5-1. Inequality and the Propensity of the Highly Skilled to Emigrate

Country	Brain drain (10=high, 0 = low)	Percent income held by top 20 percent
Australia	4.30	41.30
Austria	3.12	33.30
Belgium	4.27	34.50
Brazil	4.07	63.80
Canada	5.88	39.30
Chile	2.68	61.00
China	6.22	46.60
Colombia	8.05	60.90
Czech Republic	3.40	35.90
Denmark	4.59	34.50
Estonia	4.63	41.80
Finland	3.46	35.80
France	4.95	40.20
Germany	3.32	38.50
Greece	4.24	40.30
Hong Kong	4.62	47.00
Hungary	4.48	39.90
Iceland	4.11	37.00
India	6.85	46.10
Indonesia	5.00	44.90
Ireland	2.86	42.90
Israel	3.94	42.50
Italy	5.36	36.30
Japan	3.17	35.70
Korea	5.89	39.90
Malaysia	5.62	53.80
Mexico	4.86	58.20
Netherlands	2.81	40.10
New Zealand	7.17	46.90
Norway	2.84	35.80
Philippines	7.08	52.30
Poland	5.38	40.90
Portugal	4.04	43.40
Russia	5.52	53.70
Singapore	4.42	48.90
Slovak Republic	6.62	31.40
Slovenia	4.11	35.40
South Africa	7.92	64.80
Spain	2.71	40.30
Sweden	5.52	34.50
Switzerland	3.66	40.30
Thailand	3.97	48.40
Turkey	5.54	47.70
United Kingdom	4.22	43.00
United States	1.45	46.40
Venezuela	8.31	53.10

Sources: For propensity to migrate: World Competitiveness Handbook. For inequality: World Development Indicators.

Figure 5-3. Inequality and the Propensity to Migrate

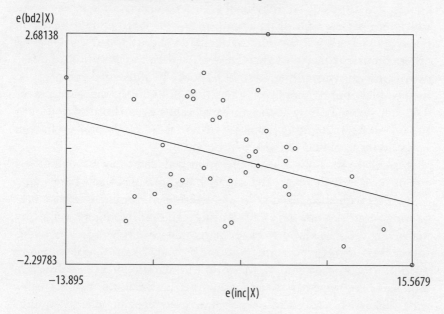

Coefficient = −.06245735, standard error = .02960818, t statistic = −2.11.

share of the top 10 percent is considered instead of the top 20 percent. Low-income countries might well be caught between a rock and a hard place, in that they have to either tolerate much higher levels of income inequality or risk losing their best and brightest.

Outside Options: Other Effects

"Outside options" for a privileged portion of the population may affect a society in a myriad of ways. Three of particular interest here are public spending on education, the unemployment rate, and the incentive to improve domestic policies and institutions.

Public sector funding on education springs from numerous rationales: to overcome pecuniary and nonpecuniary externalities that drive a wedge between the private and social return to education, to counter imperfect capital markets, or to provide a means of generating lifetime redistribution and breaking intergenerational cycles of poverty without too much economic distortion. These arguments become less cogent, of course, if the subsidized individual is likely to leave after receiving an education. For example, if the argument for public funding depends on positive externalities, the external benefits accrue to the residents of other countries if an individual leaves. As with the adoption of a less progressive tax system, the rational response by policymakers might be to spend less public money on education. Of course, the government does not know ex ante who will leave. Thus even those who do not leave, and never had any intention of doing so, might end up having lower access to publicly funded education.

It is easy to see how skilled emigration will lead to larger skill differentials for purely demand- and supply-based reasons. But where wages of workers with specialized skills are determined through domestic bargaining, even the *option* of emigrating can lead to higher wages by improving the specialized workers' bargaining position. Attractive outside options also play an important role in many theories of involuntary unemployment, especially in the form of unemployment benefits.[12] In models where wages are set in bargaining between unions and firms, generous benefits can lead to high unemployment in general equilibrium, for unions push for higher wages as they become less fearful of unemployment. Similar results arise in a shirking-based efficiency wage model, as workers must be paid a higher wage to induce them not to shirk in a world where job loss is not particularly feared. An outside option such as an attractive foreign alternative will affect the working of a domestic labor market by encouraging larger wage demands. The result, however, is that a higher level of domestic unemployment among the workers that choose to remain might be required to bring wage demands into line with what it is feasible for firms to pay. In effect, the options of the potentially mobile group can create higher unemployment for the immobile group through their influence on wage setting.

The prospect of emigration can also have significant political economy consequences. Just after the collapse of the Soviet Union, Cuba faced a severe economic crisis, but the government refused to change any policies. As popular discontent grew in 1994, between 35,000 and 50,000 people fled Cuba in what became known as *la crisis de los balseros,* or the rafters' crisis. The exodus eased the atmosphere somewhat but forced Castro to open up the economy (if only modestly) to

---

12. See, for example, Layard, Nickell, and Jackman (1991).

avert a more ominous crisis. The Cuban government allowed limited forms of domestic private enterprise and foreign investment and also permitted millions of Cubans with relatives in the United States to receive remittances from abroad. The strategy worked. The inflow of new money pulled Cuba's economy back from the brink, even as it undermined the country's socialist system.

Still, when the elites that are best positioned for reform do not see their future (or that of their children) in their country of origin, they are likely to put less effort into making domestic institutions work better. Consider the long-term consequences of rich families sending their children abroad for education, a common phenomenon in developing countries. For decades, Pakistani elites sent their children abroad for their undergraduate education. This was one reason why this sector of the population had little direct stake in reforming the country's higher education system, with deep long-term economic and political consequences for the country.

Outside Options and Other Forms of Capital Accumulation

Obviously, the prospect of emigration can induce financial capital accumulation, as people save the means to fund an expensive move and to set up a new life in another country. Less obvious is the effect on the accumulation of local social capital.[13] On the one hand, people might shy away from developing local social ties when there is a substantial possibility that they will be moving on to a new country. On the other hand, social ties that endure can create valuable opportunities for "brokerage" and for tapping into domestic information that is hard to obtain. The role of such long-distance ties in relation to diaspora is discussed in chapter 7.

The prospect of emigration may also affect the incentive to start new businesses. Given the start-up costs involved, many entrepreneurs might be reluctant to launch a business if they believe the opportunity to emigrate will suddenly arise. Thus the very prospect for emigration that increases the incentives for the acquisition of human capital also reduces the incentives to use that human capital for entrepreneurship.

13. See Agrawal, Cockburn, and McHale (2003).

As this chapter has demonstrated, even the mere possibility of emigration sparks changes in individuals' preferences and behavior toward the accumulation of human, social, and financial capital. However, it is far more difficult to ascertain whether and to what degree this is to the benefit of the home country, the destination country, or both. In chapter 6, we provide some quantitative estimates of the effects on a home country when a portion of the skilled population actually leaves.

Absent Talent:
Out of Sight, Out of Mind?

What does a country lose when a significant fraction of its skilled work-force leaves? For one thing, those remaining behind (TRBs) may be made worse off. The effect on TRBs can be assessed by measuring the direct economic loss due to absent talent. We call this measure the *emigration surplus*—the difference between a comprehensive measure of the value that emigrants would have added in the home economy and the income they would have received. This measure momentarily ignores any benefits from interactions and transactions with the diaspora and from later (capital-augmented) emigrant returns.

This surplus helps guard against the possibility of underestimating or overestimating losses. Those who are sanguine about the extent of such losses tend to view the economy in terms of a "lump of labor," which seems a natural response in an environment of unemployment or under-employment. In the extreme, people of this persuasion assume that there is a fixed amount of work to be done, so that when some workers emi-grate, their jobs are taken over by others, with no loss of total output. Indeed, many think that TRBs gain when emigration occurs, given that they will receive the abandoned jobs. However, recent literature on unem-ployment leads us to believe that a country's unemployment rate is by and large independent of the size of its labor force.[1] To put it a bit differently,

---

1. See, for example, Layard, Nickell, and Jackman (1991).

we assume that supply creates its own demand, where jobs created for skilled workers are similarly destroyed when these workers leave.

As for those who tend to exaggerate the harm done to TRBs, some would go as far as to measure it in terms of the reduction in GDP. Although the overall size of the economy may be relevant in some cases—such as international influence or national defense—it is not a good gauge here because much of the lost GDP was accruing to the emigrants in the first place.[2] Others would measure the harm by the public cost of emigrants' education. However, this cost is sunk at the moment of emigration; its measure is irrelevant to the way in which the TRBs are affected when a significant portion of the labor force leaves.[3] It makes more sense to consider the loss to the economy when a worker with given skills—however acquired—is absent from the economy. The first step is to set a benchmark for the lost surplus due to emigration.

The Benchmark Case

The benchmark case is a simple one: it consists of a closed economy producing a single good (GDP) with skilled workers, and having other factors of production under constant returns-to-scale technology, competitive markets, and no fiscal system (figure 6-1). For any given supply of skilled workers, the area under the marginal value product curve for skilled workers is a measure of the total income of the economy. To see the impact of skilled emigration on the income of TRBs, one can compare their pre- and postemigration income. The shaded area in figure 6-1 shows the size of the aggregate loss to TRBs.[4] A loss stems from the difference between an emigrant's marginal value product (benefit to TRBs) and the wage paid (cost to TRBs). With diminishing returns to skilled workers, skilled emigration pushes up the domestic wage.[5] Since

2. GDP per capita is also a misleading indicator. Skilled emigration will change the composition of the labor force and thus could drive down average incomes without the incomes of TRBs being affected.

3. As noted in chapter 5, a high prospect that an individual will emigrate is likely to make the government more reluctant to fund large education costs. To the extent the TRBs are adversely affected by the government's reduced role in funding education, this is a cost of human capital mobility.

4. Skilled emigration has distributional implications in addition to this loss of aggregate surplus. The skilled workers who remain clearly gain as their wage goes up. If we make the plausible assumption that skilled workers had above-average incomes *before* the emigration, then the emigration will make the distribution of income more unequal.

5. The wage gain will become larger as other factors become less subsitutable for skill. We assume that the supply of domestic skilled labor is perfectly inelastic.

Figure 6-1. Lost Surplus from Emigration

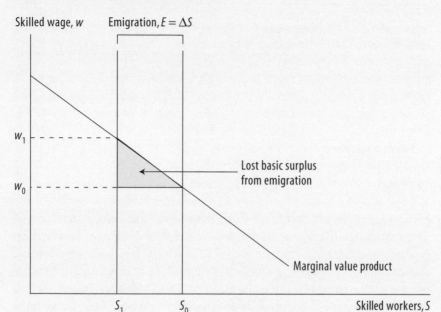

in a competitive labor market skilled workers are paid the value of their marginal product, the loss of a *single* skilled worker will have no effect on the aggregate surplus of TRBs—the lost value of marginal production is exactly equal to the marginal cost of the worker.

It is clear from figure 6-1 that this is not true for the loss of multiple skilled workers. Moreover, the total loss approximately rises with the square of the number of emigrants. The size of the loss can be approximated by using the formula for the area of a triangle. Expressing this loss as a share of total income yields the formula,

$$\frac{Loss}{GDP} = \frac{1}{2} \times \varepsilon \times s \times \left(\frac{Skilled\ Emigration}{Skilled\ Labor\ Force}\right)^2,$$

where ε is the elasticity of the skilled wage with respect to the skilled-labor supply and s is the skilled worker share of GDP.[6] To better understand the source of this loss, note that we are comparing the value lost

6. See Borjas (1995).

Table 6-1. Illustration of Static Losses Borne by TRBs Owing to Skilled Emigration[a]

Emigrant share of skilled labor force	Lost basic surplus, $\varepsilon = 0.5$	Lost fiscal surplus, $t = 0.2$	Lost spillovers, $s = 0.1$	Lost surplus, specialized skills, $\varepsilon = 0.5$
0.1	0.01	0.02	0.01	0.1
0.2	0.02	0.04	0.02	0.2
0.3	0.05	0.06	0.03	0.3
0.4	0.08	0.08	0.04	0.4
0.5	0.13	0.10	0.05	0.5

Source: Authors' calculations.
a. Expressed as a fraction of the preemigration skilled wage bill.

from workers leaving with the wage they were paid before *anyone* left. The real source of the emigration loss is not that the *wage* is pushed up (though it will be in a competitive skill market), but that the *marginal value product* of remaining workers is pushed up as others leave (see figure 6-1).[7] For example, the emigration of a few software engineers will drive the marginal value product of remaining software engineers above the level they were all initially being paid. If more software engineers continue to leave, the loss in value to TRBs will be strictly greater than the amount of money earned by the engineers *before any of them had left*.[8]

As an illustration, table 6-1 shows the lost surplus as a share of the preemigration wage bill for different levels of skilled emigration. It is assumed that a 1 percent reduction in the skilled labor force increases the skilled wage by 0.5 percent. Clearly, the losses are minimal at low levels of emigration, but they become quite substantial as the skilled emigration rate rises. As discussed in chapter 2, a number of smaller

7. An extensive empirical literature describes attempts to measure the effect of immigration on local wages (for surveys, see Borjas, 1994; and Friedberg and Hunt, 1995). These studies fall into three main types: area studies that compare wages across labor markets receiving different numbers of immigrants; natural experiments that look for immigration changes that are independent of developments in local labor markers; and calibration studies that examine how relative factor supplies affect relative wages for different skill groups and then calculate how immigration with a given skill mix affects relative wages. Advocates of the latter method argue that the first two types fail to account for native outflows in response to immigrant inflows; they also tend to find small wage effects (see Card, 1990; and Altonji and Card, 1991). The third type of study tends to find larger wage effects (see Borjas, Freeman, and Katz, 1996).

8. To identify such losses, we consider the skilled emigration in total with the initial wage as our reference point, rather than taking each emigrant individually and previous emigration as given.

Figure 6-2. Net Fiscal Impact of Emigration

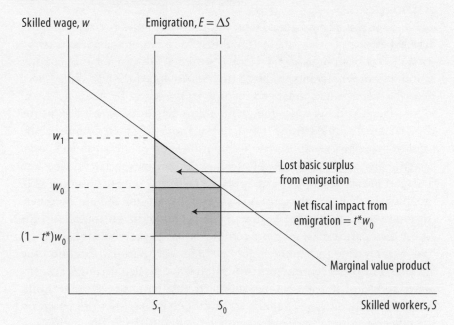

Skilled wage, w

Emigration, $E = \Delta S$

w_1

w_0

Lost basic surplus
from emigration

Net fiscal impact from
emigration $= t^*w_0$

$(1 - t^*)w_0$

Marginal value product

S_1 S_0 Skilled workers, S

countries have lost large fractions of their more educated population, implying relatively large losses even in this benchmark model.

Fiscal Effects

Skilled workers are typically net contributors to a country's fiscal system. Given relatively large incomes and progressive income taxation, skilled workers will usually add more to tax revenue than they do to government expenditures. Thus savings that might accrue when they emigrate—such as lower public health system expenditures—will be swamped by tax losses.

Figure 6-2 adds a very simple fiscal system to the benchmark model by letting skilled workers face a net tax rate of t. The net fiscal loss from a given level of skilled emigration is then easily calculated as the product of the tax rate and the wages of the lost workers. Again, to illustrate the size of the possible loss table 6-1 also shows the fiscal loss as a percentage of the preemigration skilled wage bill at various emigration rates for a net tax rate of 20 percent. The loss is relatively important even at low emigration rates but is surpassed by the lost basic surplus at high emigration rates.

As far as we know, Mihir Desai and his colleagues provide the only detailed attempt to estimate the fiscal loss for a major skilled emigration stream, that from India to the United States.[9] As documented in chapter 2, Indian-born emigrants in the United States appear highly skilled on a relative scale of educational and income attainments. To assess net fiscal losses, Desai and his colleagues estimated what Indians residing in the United States would earn if they lived in India and then combined the resulting counterfactual income distribution with details of India's fiscal system. They estimated the counterfactual incomes in two ways. The first and most straightforward approach was to convert observed U.S. incomes to the purchasing power equivalent in Indian incomes. Although this is likely to overstate the expected Indian incomes in some cases, occupation-based salary comparisons suggest that this is not a bad assumption for many highly skilled occupations. Second, the authors ran observed human capital characteristics through an estimated model of Indian earnings and participation to generate the counterfactual distribution. The human capital characteristics are based on the Current Population Survey, and the Indian earnings/participation model is based on National Sample Survey data. This approach yields considerably lower income estimates, which are likely to be significantly biased because of the huge positive selectivity of Indian emigrants (see chapter 2). Using purchasing power parity for most of their calculations, the authors found fiscal impacts to be quite large, ranging from 0.24 percent to 0.58 percent of India's GDP.[10] Although the Indian-born population residing in the United States represents just a tiny fraction of the total Indian-born population, its skill intensity means that the fiscal impact is substantial.

Spillovers

Another assumption of the benchmark model is that the marginal social value of skilled workers is equal to the marginal private value. There is strong reason to suspect that their knowledge spills over to others in the economy. Such spillovers may be especially important in a developing

9. Desai, Kapur, and McHale (2003).

10. In calculating the expenditure savings from emigration, they err on the side of overestimation by including the per capita savings of all classes of expenditure except interest payments and national defense.

Figure 6-3. Lost Spillovers from Emigration

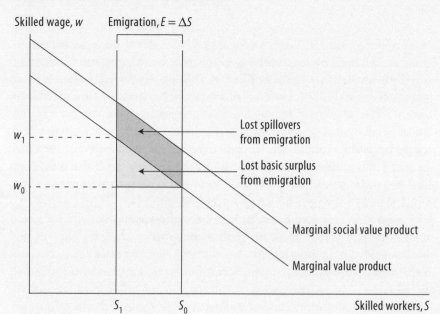

country where knowledge about best technological practices, organization methods, and the like is lacking. Two conditions must be met for spillovers to be relevant to the size of the emigration surplus loss: (1) the spillovers must be disproportionately localized, so that other local workers gain from their proximity to the skilled worker; and (2) once a skilled worker has moved, the tendency for knowledge to flow back to his or her former home through enduring relationships cannot be too strong.

Figure 6-3 crudely captures the implications of such spillovers for the size of the lost surplus by showing a marginal social value product curve that lies above the marginal private value product curve. The vertical gap between the curves measures the size of the spillover stemming from a given worker.[11] Table 6-1 illustrates how the total value of lost spillovers changes with the emigration rate, assuming that the value of spillovers is equal to 10 percent of the workers' private value. In this simple example, the value of lost spillovers rises linearly with the emigration

11. Of course, not all external effects are positive. One possible positive impact of emigration is reduced congestion.

rate, and, as in the fiscal case, loss is experienced even when a single skilled worker leaves.

Such spillovers are anathema to economists because knowledge flows "are invisible; they leave no paper trail by which they can be measured and tracked, and there is nothing to prevent the theorist from assuming anything about them that she likes."[12] It has been found, however, that patent citations can be used to crudely track knowledge flows between inventors.[13] Of course, knowledge flows between inventors even in the absence of citations; and, conversely, citations take place even when knowledge does not directly spill over between the inventors concerned.[14] Thus citations are, at best, a crude proxy. Still, the results of one inventor survey are "consistent with the notion that citations are a noisy signal of the presence of spillovers."[15]

Patent citations also meet the criterion of disproportionate localization in that they tend to occur with disproportionate frequency at the location of the originating inventor.[16] This finding was recently confirmed in a large sample, in which knowledge also appeared to flow disproportionately to inventors' *prior* locations.[17] However, the prior location premium is only about half the size of the current location premium, implying that spillovers are reduced when the inventor leaves.

The value of spillovers, and "learning by copying," depends on the ability (and human capital) of the developing country. A related concept—"demonstration effects"—is also important for developing countries. Although firms there may have poor knowledge about the activities at which they could be internationally competitive, they may be able to quickly copy what is demonstrated to be successful. A model in which the amount of experimentation can be suboptimally low illustrates that the loss of skilled workers and potential entrepreneurs through emigration will compound the lack of experimentation and leave a developing country even more short of successful domestic role models.[18]

12. Krugman (1991, p. 53).
13. Jaffe, Trajtenburg, and Henderson (1993).
14. For example, a patent examiner might demand that a certain citation be made as a means of delineating the scope of a patent.
15. Jaffe and others (1993, p. 400).
16. Jaffe and others (1993).
17. Agrawal, Cockburn, and McHale (2003).
18. For detailed discussion of demonstration effects, see Hausman and Rodrik (2002). In chapter 7, we consider the role that the diaspora can play in changing stereotypes about the country through demonstrations of capabilities.

Specialized Skills

Up to now we have assumed that even skilled workers can be treated as a homogeneous mass, with wages determined in competitive skill markets. However, this assumption could lead us to seriously underestimate the lost surplus stemming from the departure of certain workers with specialized skills, such as a country's few pediatric surgeons. Suppose that a surgeon is adding value equal to $100,000 a year working in a government-run hospital and could earn $40,000 in private practice. If bargaining between the government and the surgeon leads them to split the surplus, the surplus accruing to the employer will be $30,000.[19] If an opportunity arises for a job abroad at a salary of $120,000 (net of moving costs), the surgeon will leave and the surplus will be lost.[20]

There is an obvious similarity here between the loss that results from the absence of specialized skills and Paul Romer's analysis of the loss of surplus that results when trade barriers reduce the range of available imported inputs.[21] In Romer's model, sellers of imported goods have monopoly power on the domestic market but cannot appropriate the entire consumer surplus because they charge a single price to domestic customers. However, it will not be profitable to import the good if the fixed costs of importation are too high, regardless of the consumer surplus. Romer shows that a reduced range of available inputs can severely affect the economy's aggregate output.

Imagine now that the individual is selling engineering services, rather than distributing an imported product. The best salary available abroad can be considered part of the fixed opportunity cost of being in business domestically. If this "cost" rises owing to reduced immigration restrictions in some rich country, then the individual (and the surplus) may be lost.[22] Again, the reduced range of available skills could substantially harm aggregate output. In appendix A, we use Paul Romer's work as a guide in developing a simple model of aggregate output in an economy

19. Alternatively, if restrictions on public sector pay mean that the government can only pay $70,000 to the surgeon, the surplus going the government is again $30,000.

20. Even a foreign offer of $75,000 will be enough to entice the surgeon away if public sector pay scales prevent any move from being made to try to retain the coveted skill.

21. Romer (1993).

22. To get a rough sense of the possible loss, consider the engineer who faces a downward-sloping linear demand curve for his services and can supply extra units of the service at constant marginal cost. In this case, the consumer surplus is exactly half the engineer's total revenue.

with specialized skills. The core of the model is a constant returns-to-scale aggregate production function, in which homogeneous unskilled workers are combined with specialist skilled workers to produce a final output (GDP). Unlike the final goods producers, the specialists are imperfectly substitutable for one another, and they sell their services in monopolistically competitive markets. To calculate the surplus loss to TRBs, we construct an experiment of removing a certain fraction of skilled emigrants from the economy. The result strikingly demonstrates the loss as rising linearly with the emigration rate. Thus, unlike the benchmark model with homogeneous skills, there is a first-order surplus loss. Moreover, for any given emigration rate, the loss is larger the less substitutable the specialists are for one another.

The output loss from the absence of particular specialists is, of course, related to the importance of the role that they play in the economy. Michael Kremer's model of a production process that has multiple tasks—all of which must be completed successfully for there to be final output—suggests the availability of specialized skill can actually be essential.[23] In the extreme, the absence of that skill can stop all production. One activity for which certain highly skilled emigrants may be close to indispensable is building domestic institutions.

Absent Institution Builders

Before World War I, when German science was at its peak, more than half the Nobel prizes in science went to Germany. After Hitler came to power in 1933, Jewish scientists were dismissed en masse from their jobs. Hitler cared little for the damage this would cause German science. "If science cannot do without Jews, then we will have to do without science for a few years," he told physicist Max Planck.[24] As a result, nearly 2,000 Jewish scholars and scientists left Germany for the United States and Britain, having been dismissed or prematurely retired from government service by the Nazi regime because they were not of "Aryan" descent. This movement, though tiny in terms of the number of people it involved, had profound consequences for global science. Within a decade, the locus of global science and technology had moved from Germany to the United States, and English replaced German as the lingua

23. Kremer (1993).
24. Cornwell (2003, p. 34).

franca of science. When an Einstein moves across borders, the loss is not equivalent to that of a single Ph.D. who can be replaced fairly easily. Clearly, people of exceptional talent have a highly nonlinear impact on industrial societies. Perhaps this is also the case for developing countries.

The loss of scarce human capital may be more debilitating than recognized up to now, as recent endogenous growth theories suggest.[25] At least one endogenous growth model shows that the migration of highly skilled workers reduces income levels and long-term economic growth.[26] The brain drain may have an even more inimical effect on the institutions of the countries of origin. Although institutions are considered the sine qua non of development, how successful institutions actually develop is still poorly understood.

One might argue that other factors notwithstanding, successful institutional development generally depends on having a critical mass of individuals with high levels of human capital. They are certainly crucial in the *initial* stages of institutional development, even though the criteria for determining an institution's success rest on whether its fortune is independent of the behavior of particular individuals. To take the United States as an example, it has been argued that an intellectual vanguard of university-trained professionals, economists, and other progressive thinkers was among its most valuable state-building resources during the early twentieth century.[27] These individuals played key roles in developing a more professional and bureaucratic state by providing new ideas about better organization and the exercise of power. Intellectuals also played an important role in advancing various ideas about how to build welfare states in Europe and North America.[28] Similarly, think tanks, research institutes, and university academics (especially economists) have influenced economic policymaking.[29]

To the extent that these ideas are valid, the most adverse consequences of the brain drain may fall on institutional development in the country of origin, which will find it all the more difficult to retain those individuals critical for institution building as the global market increasingly sets their reservation wages. International flows of human capital

25. Lucas (1988); Barro (1991).
26. Haque and Kim (1995).
27. Skowronek (1982).
28. Rueschemeyer and Skocpol (1996).
29. Skowronek (1982); Rueschemeyer and Skocpol (1996); Domhoff (1998).

can have a particularly devastating effect on institutions of higher education, the wellspring of future human capital (see appendix B).

The global demand for Indian information technology (IT) professionals illustrates the consequences of increased human capital flows. As of 2000, India's educational institutions were turning out 178,000 engineers a year, about 92,000 being qualified in IT-related disciplines.[30] In 1998, 34,000 Indian students and 30,000 Indian professionals immigrated to the United States. Including those leaving for other countries, about a fifth of India's annual output of engineers left the country. Although the overall annual output of IT professionals from India exceeds that of the United States, their quality is much weaker, hamstrung by low faculty-to-student ratios (1:45). Moreover, to increase the output, India would need a cadre of well-qualified faculty, but such individuals are currently in very short supply. India's output of master's and Ph.D. students is barely 3 percent of the U.S. output, and more than 60 percent of postgraduate seats in engineering colleges are vacant. The consequent low output of postgraduates has serious implications for the training of future generations, given that India's technical education system already has about 10,000 teaching vacancies.[31]

Indeed, higher education's severe problems in most developing countries are both the result and cause of the brain drain, as illustrated by the post–cold war collapse of Russia's institutions of higher education, once among the strongest establishments in the country. All the same, institutional weakening need not be an inevitable result. For one thing, growth and immigration could increase the pool of students. As noted in chapter 5, emigration to a higher returns-to-skill country might provide an incentive to invest in human capital in the source country rather than deplete it. The level of human capital formation in the source country can therefore be positively correlated with the probability of emigration.[32] Additionally, the technology of education can change, thereby allowing for higher faculty-to-student ratios. Furthermore, a reverse brain drain driven by rising wages and opportunities that are themselves a product of growth—as was the case in Ireland, Taiwan, and South Korea and, to a more limited extent, is happening in China and India—could again augment the supply pool.

30. See www.education.nic.in/htmlweb/itdiscussionpaper1.htm#Introduction.
31. World Bank (2000, annex 1, para. 23).
32. Vidal (1998).

One area of the world that has experienced severe loss of local talent is Africa. Its experience in this regard dates back a few centuries and hence provides a particularly interesting case study.

The Case of Africa: Past and Present

Several hundred years ago, Africa experienced the equivalent of today's brain drain in the loss of young able-bodied men captured by the slave trade.[33] No region of the world suffered this depredation as much as Africa. Although the precise numbers are uncertain, estimates range from 10 million to 28 million forced into slavery, divided almost equally between the Atlantic, North African, and Middle Eastern coasts. Although extensive, the literature on slavery has focused mainly on the effects on either the slaves or on the "new world." Much less is known about the effects on TRBs and Africa itself. As the global community grapples with the political and economic travails of contemporary Africa, it is interesting to speculate about the extent to which they stem from the long-term institutional consequences of forced migration.

Over the course of four centuries, Africa's economic, political, and social institutions have been drastically transformed. To what extent did the slave trade influence this transformation through its impacts on demographics, social structures, and the slave trade within the continent? Although there is general agreement that by the end of the seventeenth century, the European demand for slaves had brought about a profound transformation of African societies, the overall impact of the slave trade on Africa is strongly disputed.

The one clear consequence was that it reduced the supply of labor, making the control of labor the key to power. Power shifted from kings and village headmen, bound to their followers by complicated networks of mutual obligation and exchange, to armed men who gathered around them an often-disproportionate circle of female dependents and slaves. Enslaved men were frequently passed on to new owners and, sometimes, new countries. External conflicts centered primarily on the various struggles to exercise control over a people, and captives became the principal spoils of war. The deep social disruption led to the increased practice of holding slaves within Africa's borders, thereby intensifying

33. Our discussion of the slave trade is based on Rodney (1981); Inikori (1982); Law (1991); Ewald (1992); Iliffe (1995); Spear (1996); and Thornton (1998).

their exploitation and exemplifying what has come to be known as the "transformation thesis." The institutional effects were manifold. Slaves were used by political elites to increase their power, which led to the development of increasingly centralized but also more autocratic states. Household dynamics changed as well. High fertility regimes became institutionalized to ensure large families of potential workers. Women married young and were valued by the number of children they bore. The social status of men was similarly based on the number of wives and children to which they held claim.

While many scholars assert that the slave trade led to dependency and economic inequality, others argue that the scale at which trading occurred was not large enough to have had a major impact on African economic and political conditions, with certain exceptions in some coastal regions. According to this school of thought, slavery was an already widespread and indigenous practice in Africa, and Europeans simply tapped into the existing market.

The Atlantic slave trade transformed African political economies because they were particularly vulnerable to merchant capitalism's network of credit and debt. Africans eagerly accepted European goods on credit, transforming cloth into the ultimate value—rights over people. But the bargain eventually backfired on African debtors. In order to pay, they surrendered the dependent men, women, and children who composed their most valued possession. Thus, according to this theory, many slaves were produced by debt and foreclosure rather than by open and massive violence. Whether or not slavery was an already established institution before Europe became involved in the trade, it caused much demographic damage, especially on a regional and local level. If slaves had not been forced to emigrate, scholars argue, Africans would have numbered almost 100 million instead of 50 million in 1850. Still, because the majority of those exported were men, the number of child-bearing women, and therefore the potential for future population growth, was less drastically reduced. However, the loss of adult males had damaging impacts on sex ratios, dependency rates, and perhaps the sexual division of labor. While one could speculate about the extent to which the absence of this dynamic group affected innovation in Africa, it is clear that the massive social disruptions considerably enfeebled African societies, thus paving the way for an even more disruptive colonial rule and its unhappy aftermath.

In more recent years, international migration from Africa has been more human capital intensive entailing the loss of the middle class, the

Table 6-2. Estimates of the Brain Drain from Africa: Emigration Rates for Tertiary Educated, 2000[a]

Percent	Country of residence
More than 50	Cape Verde, Gambia, Seychelles, Somalia
25–50	Angola, Equatorial Guinea, Eritrea, Ghana, Guinea Bissau, Kenya, Liberia, Madagascar, Mauritius, Mozambique, Nigeria, Sao Tome and Principe, Sierra Leone
5–25	Algeria, Benin, Burundi, Côte d'Ivoire, Cameroon, Chad, Comoros, Republic of the Congo, Democratic Republic of the Congo (formerly Zaire), Djibouti, Ethiopia, Gabon, Guinea, Malawi, Mali, Mauritania, Niger, Morocco, Rwanda, South Africa, Senegal, Sudan, Swaziland, Tanzania, Togo, Tunisia, Uganda, Zambia, Zimbabwe
Less than 5	Botswana, Lesotho, Burkina Faso, Central African Republic, Egypt, Libya, Namibia

Source: Docquier and Marfouk (2004).

a. Percentage of nationals with university education living abroad.

bourgeoisie, which historically has played a critical part in the evolution of Western democracies. The relative scarcity of human capital in that region and the high levels of migration have meant that the loss is particularly problematic. In 1990 about 95,000 African-born individuals residing in the United States had a tertiary education.[34] Since the estimates for OECD countries are much less reliable, we extrapolate from reports indicating that the United States received about half the total OECD migration in 1990. That information, plus the strong historical links and geographical proximity between Africa and Europe and the continued economic and political travails of the continent, leads us to estimate the number of Africans with a tertiary education outside Africa to be about 200,000. According to another estimate, there are about 100,000 highly qualified Africans working in OECD countries, which constitutes nearly a third of its skilled workforce and is about the same as the number of foreign experts working in Africa.[35] In addition, about 23,000 academics migrate out of Africa each year

The loss of human capital in African countries has reached alarming levels (table 6-2). In 2000, 31.4 percent of African immigrants had a tertiary education, whereas the proportion in the continent's population was just 3.6 percent.[36] Along with Central America, countries in Eastern

34. Carrington and Detragiache (1998).
35. IOM (1999).
36. Docquier and Marfouk (2004).

and Western Africa had the highest emigration rates of the highly skilled, as well as the biggest increase between 1990 and 2000.

In 2002 Africa's biggest loss of highly trained professionals to emigration occurred in Ethiopia, followed by Nigeria and Ghana. The migration from Ethiopia has led to a serious shortage of faculty in that country. In 2002 one-third of medical doctors in the country had reportedly left Ethiopia to reside in other countries.[37] By contrast, under the program titled the Return of Qualified African Nationals, which ran from 1995 to December 1999, just 66 Ethiopians returned to their country.

Owing to positive selection, the average quality of emigrants is usually greater than that of the human capital staying behind. This could have several effects on investment and growth. For instance, some researchers report that the entrepreneur's level of education helps explain variances in the growth of African private enterprises.[38] If firms cannot grow because there is a dearth of educated entrepreneurs, the substantial loss of human capital might be one reason why the private sector of African countries has responded poorly to macroeconomic adjustment, and also why foreign direct investment (FDI) has focused on only a limited number of developing countries in recent years, despite a significant increase in flows. Human capital, some argue, is one of the most important determinants of FDI inflows, and its role has been increasing in recent years.[39] Nevertheless, as long as a threshold level of human capital remains in the sending country, international migration may give a reputational signal to investors abroad, thereby increasing the likelihood of investment in that country.

Sector-Specific Effects

Aggregate losses of human capital conceal substantial sector-specific effects. Broad measures of human capital migration shed little light on specific areas of production or even individual countries. In the health care sector, the loss of physicians providing direct services in clinics and hospitals will have a greater short-term negative impact on the health status of residents than the loss of those employed in health research.

37. Michael Eskinder, "Ethiopia the Most Affected by Brain Drain in Africa," *Daily Monitor* (Addis Ababa), November 8, 2002.
38. Ramachandran and Shah (1998).
39. Noorbakhsh, Paloni, and Youssef (2001).

However, the latter loss may be greater over the long term. Similarly, even when specific occupations are taken into consideration, the country in which these losses are occurring is relevant. The loss of Jamaican nurses poses much greater challenges to that country than the loss of the same labor supply in the Philippines, given the latter's strategy of exporting labor. Three sectors in particular seem to have been hit hard: education, research, and health.

In education, some 10 to 15 percent of the estimated 200,000 teachers hired each year in the United States are foreigners, often from the Philippines and India; most are hired to teach math and science subjects in inner-city schools. The teachers arrive with H-1B visas that are good for six years and allow them to convert to immigrant status. Many Filipino teachers wind up in midsize school districts in Southern California, in part because they are "highly qualified" licensed teachers. Pay in the United States usually starts at about $30,000 a year, compared with $5,000 in the Philippines. Most of the teachers arrive in debt, owing a $7,500 fee to a head-hunting firm, later falling further into debt renting apartments and adjusting to the U.S. lifestyle.[40] Given the much lower educational attainments in the source countries, the welfare loss that those countries accumulate from teachers' migration is likely to be greater than the gains to the (richer) receiving country. However, this depends largely on what fraction returns (see chapter 9).

Jamaica, which has a bilateral hospitality worker program with the United States and a Schoolteacher Work Program with the United States and Great Britain, has seen a large outflow of trained employees leave to work temporarily in more developed markets abroad. In principle, this short-term negative impact can be addressed through Jamaica's well-developed infrastructure for training hospitality workers. However, this would require a generally predictable growth in overseas demand. Similarly, under the Schoolteacher Work Program, Jamaican teachers are recruited to meet shortages in inner-city schools in the New York and London areas. Under the direct recruitment drive, without the involvement of the Jamaican government, more than 500 teachers left Jamaican classrooms in 2001 to take up temporary assignments in host countries. The loss of approximately 3 percent of the Jamaican teacher workforce, many of whom were from the more experienced and qualified population, proved to be a large shock to the Jamaican school system. The

40. Joe Mathews, "The New Import: Teachers," *Los Angeles Times*, August 10, 2002.

country does not have a competitive infrastructure for the training of teachers, a process that takes more than four years. The Jamaican government is now seeking to control the outflow of teachers.[41]

In an open economy, one can easily imagine that institutional inflexibilities (such as wages in public sector educational institutions) might cause growing problems for training the next generation of human capital (for an analysis of open economy effects, see appendix C). Thus the exporter of human capital could face a decline in the quality of its human capital over time. Higher education continues to be predominantly concentrated in the public sector, and it is here that the problems and consequences are more worrying, considering the effect on the quality of training of future generations. The bureaucratization of higher education, the prevalence of extreme politicization, and the perpetuation of a system in which quantity vastly trumps quality and inputs alone are monitored will not attract talent, especially if that talent has alternatives to working at home. Where a market is no longer confined within national boundaries, innumerable college teachers in developing countries with the requisite human capital are willing to work in high schools in developed countries, or, in fact, in any other profession, so long as they leave. As developed countries use selective screening tools, a vicious cycle ensues, in which individuals at the upper end of the human capital distribution emigrate and leave behind a pool of poorer quality. This not only prompts others at the higher end to also consider leaving but also discourages anyone who has left in the past from returning home, thereby ensuring that mediocrity becomes entrenched in these institutions.

An important long-term consequence is a further weakening of indigenous research focused on local problems. Researchers require complementary inputs, and this is one reason why the productivity of researchers is much greater in developed countries than in developing ones. Still, the problems they study are much less geared to the problems afflicting the latter. For instance, development economics is, for the most part, a peripheral field in mainstream economics.[42] Unfortunately, the only answer to increase the supply of human capital, more by default than by design, appears to be private sector higher education. This

41. Brown (2003).
42. Bardhan (2001). According to Glenn Ellison, the fraction of development-related papers in the most prestigious journals has declined from 3.8 percent in the 1970s to 1.6 percent in the 1990s. See Ellison, "The Slowdown of the Economics Publishing Process" (econ-www.mit.edu/faculty/gellison/papers.htm, table 19, appx. B [accessed June 2000]).

creates a new set of problems, given that the private sector often concentrates on maximizing profits rather than on attempting to build institutions to serve the public good and enhance public welfare.

Moreover, international recruitment is a growing industry, especially with regard to health care. Companies that were initially established to bring foreign nurses into the United States broadened their business to include teachers, charging them up to $7,500 each as well to arrange a U.S. job. The United Kingdom's National Health Service already recruits nurses from overseas because of local shortages, with an estimated 30,000 working in hospitals across the country.[43] There is an increasing and worldwide demand for nurses that spans the Netherlands, Italy, Norway, the United Kingdom, Canada, Ireland, Japan, Singapore, Guam, the United States, New Zealand, and Australia. The Philippines, the single largest supplier of nurses to the world, is itself facing difficulties in certain specialties, for instance, in hiring emergency room nurses.

During the 1960s in Thailand, more than a third of new medical graduates, who had received a hugely subsidized education, permanently left their homes for the United States. The Thai government implemented a range of policies to deal with the phenomenon, including compulsory public work for a certain period of time, increased supply of doctors, as well as greater opportunities for specialization and higher salaries. In the case of medical professionals, the external brain drain exacerbates the internal brain drain, causing the movement of health care professionals from rural to urban areas. Although Thailand recently had a 300 percent oversupply of private hospital beds, more than 20 rural district hospitals were functioning without a single full-time medical doctor.[44] Meanwhile, the number of foreign medical graduates in the United States rose from 57,000 to 150,000 between 1970 and 1993, with India, Pakistan, and the Philippines accounting for 45 percent of all international medical graduates by 1993. This amounts to about 20 percent of the total stock of doctors in India. Immigration of skilled workers raises the returns to those left behind, and, as in India and Thailand, the migration of physicians has also resulted in a decline of health care workers in rural areas. South Africa is witnessing a somewhat different trend, in that health care professionals have been going to the United Kingdom for only a few months at a time. The situation would be even better if instead of GATS Mode 4 (South African physicians flying to the

43. See http://news.bbc.co.uk/2/hi/health/1513394.stm.
44. Wibulpolparsert (2003).

United Kingdom), the country were to move to GATS Mode 2 (patients coming to South Africa for treatment) through the promotion of health tourism.[45]

The world of sports is perhaps the most visible area in which human talent is globally mobile.[46] Coaches, players, and physiotherapists are all being courted internationally to work in a variety of sports. U.S. basketball leagues (both college and professional), global football (soccer) leagues, and international cricket have all catalyzed the development of an international athletic market. The more competitive a sport and the more money at stake, the more openly countries and teams appear to access the global pool of talent without the fear of nationalist backlash.

In cricket's last World Cup, 10 of the 14 teams had foreign coaches and training staff—something that would have been unheard of even a decade ago. U.S. professional sports—baseball, basketball, and ice hockey—reflect a similar migration of talent. Although international players have been part of the National Basketball Association (NBA) since the late 1940s, the number did not reach double digits until the mid-1980s. The first foreign player was drafted in the first round in 1986. By 2003 the NBA draft "had a bigger foreign influence than ever before," consisting of 73 players from 34 countries, and for the first time a foreign player was the number-one draft pick and had not played college ball. In the 2002 draft, nearly a quarter of total picks (12 of 52) went to foreign athletes; in fact, 5 of the first 16 were foreign (from Africa, Europe, and China).[47] With basketball becoming a global game, the rosters of the NBA have swollen with players from a variety of countries around the world, who are drawn by the sheer talent, competition, and much higher salaries.

The contentious debates regarding the effects of this system on African soccer seem to parallel the opposing views on the effects of human capital flows on the source countries in general. In soccer's last World Cup, Senegal pulled off a dramatic victory when it beat favored

45. GATS distinguishes between four modes of supplying services: Mode 1 is the cross-border supply of services from the territory of one member to another member; Mode 2, consumption abroad, involves a service consumer going to another member's territory to obtain a service; in Mode 3, commercial presence, a service supplier of one member establishes a territorial presence in another member's territory to provide a service; and Mode 4, presence of natural persons, consists of nationals of one member entering the territory of another member to supply a service.

46. Our discussion of the sports drain is based on Armstrong and Guilianotti (2001); Lanfranchi and Taylor (2001); and Foer (2004).

47. See http://cbs.sportsline.com/b/page/pressbox/0,1328,5669795,00.html.

France. Every member of the Senegalese team had played in European leagues—the most competitive (and lucrative) in the world—while abstaining from joining their national team until a new French coach was hired. All 10 nominees for the 2001 African Footballer of the Year played in international leagues outside Africa. And by the mid-1990s, more than 350 African footballers had migrated to first- and second-division European leagues. At the start of the new millennium, this figure had more than doubled (to 770), and an additional 145 Africans were also playing in the lower reaches of European leagues. Many others had joined leagues in Asia. When African countries play each other, their biggest problem is coordinating their star players' national and club commitments, as national teams are often composed entirely of players who have contracts with international leagues during regular season play.

Africa's potential bounty of relatively cheap soccer talent has attracted a large network of agents, who are either talent speculators or venture capitalists dealing in human capital. In the absence of regulatory systems similar to those in Europe, these agents frequently offer positions to boys as young as 15 or 16, with contracts that contain confusing stipulations as to agents' percentages of salaries and transfer fees.

Still, the export of African football talent is not a process solely initiated and driven by European interests, and African players are not consistently duped into signing exploitative contracts. The lure of European football is extremely enticing for African players, and many perceive "making it" in Europe as one of the few opportunities to escape the harsh economic realities of life in many parts of the African continent. And some of the best players continue to give time and money to their national team and their country of origin even after moving overseas.

The dominant European view is that African soccer has benefited from the export of its skilled talent, and that the recent success of African national teams is migration-contingent. Besides helping their bank balances, playing in the world's most competitive leagues has enhanced these players' individual and team skills. Thus African countries can rely on players who have not only improved their own skills but also transferred better playing techniques to their home-based compatriots. Moreover, much as the brain drain might enhance expected returns to education, the possibility of playing in Europe and striking it rich ensures that young African soccer players will try even harder, thereby creating a stronger pool in Africa. The visibility of the most prominent European-based Africans has made a significant contribution to the popularity of soccer within the continent. If anything, according to this viewpoint, the migration of elite talent has had a positive impact on the game in Africa.

Others are more pessimistic, however, complaining that the "expropriation" of Africa's playing resources is actually undermining the development of the game on the continent. The loss of talent lowers the standard of the game in local soccer leagues, so attendance, gate receipts, and media interest all go down. African national teams suffer too, plagued by the difficulties in procuring player releases from European clubs. African critics charge that Europe's "de-skilling" of African football is another manifestation of exploitation comparable to the economic imperialism of the colonial period.

Both the Confederation of African Football and Fédération Internationale de Football Association (FIFA) have tried to remedy the situation. For example, the African Club Champions League was established in 1997 to provide top-level club competition as well as create the administrative structures and economic incentives necessary to encourage players to remain with African clubs. However, such measures are unlikely to prevent European clubs from continuing their recruitment practices. In recent years, a number of the top ones have established training schools and academies in Africa, in some cases even acquiring stakes in clubs. Many within both Africa and FIFA fear that arrangements such as these will soon multiply and become but a front for the systematic draining of the domestic African game.

Conclusion

During the past few decades, developing countries have begun to recognize some of the positive effects of the brain drain. Nonetheless, our analysis of the "absence" effect confirms intuition, which tells us that the displacement of scarce talent ill serves the country from which it stems. Although the literature has focused largely on the adverse economic effects of such displacement, the institutional and political effects are no less important.

Because developing countries have a limited middle class to begin with, when this segment leaves in droves in the aftermath of economic and political crisis, democratic consolidation may well become more difficult. Recalling Barrington Moore's classic dictum, "No bourgeoisie, no democracy," one might easily conclude that their absence has translated into the wider problems associated with nation building. Data from the

World Values Surveys appear to indicate a strong positive relationship between support for democracy, education, and class, though gender and age have little effect. Therefore the fact of positive selection (by education) of migration from virtually all sending countries might weaken support for democracy.[48] If migrants moving to the United States from Mexico have more education than those who stay, that alone could shift societal support for democracy (by lowering the average levels of education of those left behind). Similarly, current patterns of emigration from Argentina seem to be dominated by middle-class professionals who are more educated that those left behind, thus creating possibly negative effects for the support for democracy. Still, income appears to have an equal (or even larger) effect than education in this regard.

To further complicate matters, the migration of lower-income workers generally raises rather than reduces the incomes of that segment of the population, by both reducing the labor supply and increasing financial remittances to their families. If TRBs are less educated but have more income, how does that affect the support for democracy? Furthermore, diasporic networks have the capacity to transmit ideas, making it possible to reshape the attitudes of households with family members in democratic countries (as in the case of Moroccan workers in Spain). Thus, if these mechanisms dominate, the combination of higher incomes and "social remittances" from family members may increase rather than reduce support for democracy.

48. See Feleciano (2003).

CHAPTER 7

Gone but Not Forgotten?
The Role of the Diaspora

When people are absent from their country of birth for an extended period of time, do they have the same impact on their country of origin as other foreigners? In many ways, the members of a country's diaspora—especially first-generation members—have a very different relationship with those remaining behind (TRBs); they also have the collective potential to be an asset and, occasionally, a liability for their country's development. The diaspora affects the domestic economy both *directly*, through its members' disproportionate willingness to interact/transact with TRBs, and *indirectly*, through their role as "reputational intermediaries." The direct effect captures the willingness of diasporas to trade, invest, start businesses, communicate, travel, and remit to their former homes. Aside from providing financial remittances (see chapter 8), skilled and successful emigrants can affect the home economy in a great variety of ways, as demonstrated by the roles played by the Indian and Chinese diasporas in Silicon Valley through their support of domestic high-tech industries.

Indirectly, the members of a diaspora can help connect the home economy to international business networks by leveraging their reputations. Specifically, they can use their superior knowledge of the characteristics of old and new country acquaintances to match economic partners, use long-term relationships with people from both places to facilitate exchange when long-term contracting is difficult, and alter the profiles of home-country individuals through demonstrations of their capabilities.

Of course, even after allowing for differences in size, not all diasporas are equally effective in supporting development. For this reason, it is essential to examine the factors that determine whether a diaspora can be effective, including the selectivity of its member emigrants, their reasons for leaving, the length of time they have been away, their success in their adopted countries, and the conditions and policies in their countries of origin.

Willingness to Interact/Transact

Where a country is reasonably open to international commerce, its population will have a myriad of connections to foreign residents in general, although those residents are likely to maintain disproportionate connections to their country's diaspora. Its members may retain a strong preference for such home-country products as foodstuffs, thereby creating a potential export market.[1] To the extent that they achieve significant income gains as a result of the positive productivity effect of moving abroad, they may also have the capabilities to indulge those preferences (human capital) and possibly the savings to fund home-country investments (financial capital). They will also tend to maintain friendships and acquaintances with people from their former homes, thereby communicating useful market and technological information.

The literature on international trade provides considerable insight into the role of the diaspora. The impact of immigrants on Canada's international trade patterns, for example, has been assessed by adding immigrant stock variables specific to the country of origin to a gravity model of bilateral trade flows.[2] When the model was tested, a 10 percent increase in the immigrant stock led to a 3 percent increase in imports and a 1 percent increase in exports. Another study using a similar gravity-based approach found that immigrant stocks also affect U.S. import patterns, although in this case the number for exports is even larger than for imports, suggesting that the effect on trade patterns may be due more to reduced transaction costs than to immigrant demands for home-country products.[3]

Even casual observation of first-generation diasporas reveals extensive communication with friends and family in their countries of birth—

1. The aisles dedicated to imported goods by country of origin in supermarkets in larger American cities are one visible sign of the importance of such trade.
2. Head and Reis (1998).
3. Gould (1994).

communication that is becoming ever easier to conduct with the falling costs and improving quality of related technologies. Members of the Indian and Chinese diasporas in Silicon Valley, among others, are able to keep in close touch with business acquaintances back home.[4] Data on patents and patent citations also provide evidence of an "enduring social capital" effect whereby relationships developed while inventors are co-located support economically valuable communications even after migration (see chapter 6): in other words, emigrant inventors are "gone but not forgotten."[5]

Although it would seem that the "private" informational advantage of being connected to a network might not be as important in today's information age, this is not the case. One reason is that the informational intensity of goods trade is increasing, in that the share of differentiated products in world trade is climbing. Second, with international migration on the rise, there is a greater supply of diasporic networks. Third, knowledge and technology maintain tacit elements, and their social contexts continue to be critical to how they are transmitted and received. While information is context-invariant, knowledge and understanding are more context-dependent. Personal contacts matter for so-called experience goods. The problem facing economic agents today arises not from a lack of information but from a deluge of it, as people are bombarded with more information than they are equipped to handle. In order to control the flood of knowledge, they have come to rely heavily on social networks in modern economic life.

A substantial network of this type has emerged among the Indian-born population in the United States, which increased by more than half a million over the 1990s.[6] Together with absent Chinese populations, these Indians had a large impact on the economic success of high-tech industries in Silicon Valley. Between 1995 and 1998, Indians were running 9 percent of Silicon Valley start-ups, almost 70 percent of which were in the software sector.[7] Our analysis suggests that a diaspora rich in human capital such as this could be an international business asset. As discussed earlier, the combination of preference, knowledge, and ability to pay may make members of the diaspora willing customers, investors, and purveyors of information. Their knowledge of the needs

4. See Saxenian (2002).

5. Agrawal, Cockburn, and McHale (2003).

6. This section draws heavily from Kapur and McHale (2004).

7. Saxenian (1999). The 70 percent figure is based on all Indian-run start-ups from the period 1990 to 1998.

and capabilities of both U.S.- and India-based firms makes them potentially useful intermediaries in the search and matching process. Because of their ongoing relationships with U.S. and Indian firms (and with other members of the diaspora), they are well situated to use their reputations to support complex transactions when legal contracting is difficult. And their success as technologists, managers, and entrepreneurs in Silicon Valley can change the perceptions of the Indian technology businesses in general.

These groups function as "reputational intermediaries" (see the next section). It is well known that reputational concerns are an obstacle to exporters, especially in services like software. Evidence collected recently suggests that reputation affects the form of contracts established between firms outsourcing customized software and Indian software firms, and that weak reputations are correlated with the tendency to opt for fixed-price contracts over time and materials contracts that are riskier for the buyer.[8] Indian firms have tried to reduce reputational constraints in various ways, notably by entering joint ventures with U.S. firms, acquiring or setting up U.S. firms, getting independent quality certifications, getting listed on the U.S. stock exchanges, and working on-site for the buyer.

According to a survey of Silicon Valley's Asian population in 2002 by AnnaLee Saxenian, members of the Indian diaspora were generally younger than their counterparts from China and Taiwan. While marginally less educated (77 percent had a master's degree or higher compared with 86 and 85 percent, respectively, for China and Taiwan), Indians were more concentrated in executive/managerial occupations than Chinese and Taiwanese (23 and 56 percent, respectively).[9] Of the group interviewed, 38 percent classified themselves as being in the software industry, compared with 26 percent of Chinese-born and 19 percent of Taiwanese-born respondents; 98 percent had a bachelor's degree or better, while 77 percent had a master's or a Ph.D. Interestingly, 68 percent of Indian respondents said that they earned their highest degree in the United States, whereas 81 percent of Chinese and 92 percent of Taiwanese respondents did so.

Of these admittedly elite Indian professionals, 77 percent had one or more friends who returned to India to start a company, 52 percent travel to India on business at least once a year, 27 percent regularly exchange information on jobs or business opportunities with those back home,

8. Banerjee and Duflo (2000).
9. Saxenian (1999).

Table 7-1. Leveraging the Diaspora: Indicators of Emigrant Connectedness in Silicon Valley
Percent

	Country of birth		
	India	China	Taiwan
How many of your friends have returned to their country of birth to start a company?			
More than 10	4	6	17
1–9	73	68	70
None	23	26	13
How often have you traveled to your country of birth for business purposes, on average, in the past three years?			
Never	48	56	36
Once a year	39	31	38
2–4 times a year	9	8	20
More than 5 times a year	4	5	6
Respondents reporting regular exchanges of information with friends, classmates, or business associates in their country of birth			
Jobs or business opportunities in the United States	27	23	16
Jobs or business opportunities in home country	17	12	8
Technology	33	20	19
Have you ever helped businesses in your country of birth by serving as an adviser or arranging a contract?			
Adviser	34	24	15
Contract	46	42	34
Respondents who have invested their own money in start-ups or venture funds in their country of birth			
More than once	10	4	12
Only once	13	6	5
Would you consider returning to live in your country of birth in the future?			
Somewhat likely	20	29	18
Quite likely	25	14	7

Source: Saxenian (2002).

and 33 percent regularly exchange technological information (table 7-1). As for their potential role as reputational intermediaries, 46 percent have been a contact for domestic Indian businesses. On the investment side, 23 percent have invested their own money into Indian start-ups— 10 percent more than once. And, finally, when asked about the possibility of bringing their much-augmented human capital home, 45 percent reported it would be somewhat or quite likely the case. In a more recent and much more comprehensive survey conducted in 2004, members of the Indian-American population were asked, "How likely is it that you will ever move back to India permanently?" and 21 percent responded "very likely"; 20 percent, "somewhat likely"; 40 percent, "somewhat unlikely"; and 26 percent, "very unlikely."[10]

Still, these figures do not coincide with what is known about the activities of the Indian diaspora from other sources. For one thing, the data on investment activity are silent on the magnitude of investments. Foreign direct investment (FDI) from the Indian diaspora is less than 5 percent of its Chinese counterparts, even though the propensity to invest is comparable for the two diasporas in Saxenian's survey. For another, reality belies the conclusion that 45 percent of emigrants would consider returning. While aggregate data on return migration are unavailable, segment-specific data, such as National Science Foundation longitudinal data on Ph.D. students, suggest a number closer to 5 percent.

At the same time, these survey results make it clear that the Silicon Valley–based Indian diaspora has developed a dense network of connections with the Indian economy. At least for this group, skilled emigration is not a one-way brain drain. What is not so clear is whether the loss of such productive/entrepreneurial potential from the Indian economy is counterbalanced by the diaspora's role in breaking down barriers to international business for Indians who remain. One suggestive piece of evidence from the survey itself is that 73 percent of Indians responding to the question, "Which factors would figure most importantly in your decision to start a business in your country of birth?" listed the "availability of skilled workers."[11] This is interesting in the context of the trade-off we discussed earlier between emigration thinning domestic labor markets (and thus reducing the incentive to search for business opportunities) and the role of the diaspora in helping to facilitate and fund such opportunities.

The relative costs and benefits of this migration for the Indian information technology (IT) sector may be inferred in another way, through the revealed preference of Indian IT firms to the increases in the H-1B cap. Given the size and dominance of Indian IT professions in the H-1B quotas, the Indian IT industry might have been expected to oppose the

10. Kapur (2004).
11. Of the Indian-born who had actually set up business relationships in India, 85 percent listed the availability of skilled workers as a key contributing factor to their decision; 73 percent listed the low cost of labor.

increases, in an effort to thwart the brain drain. Instead, it has enthusiastically supported raising of the cap in the wake of changes in the market structure of the global IT industry, itself a lagged effect of the initial brain drain. In fact, 10 of the largest 25 companies hiring foreign nationals with H-1B visas are IT firms based in India or U.S. IT firms run by Indian nationals.

Reputational Intermediaries

International business is greatly complicated by poor information on distant trading partners and the difficulties in contracting across national boundaries. To illustrate how a connected diaspora might facilitate such business, consider the U.S. software firm looking to outsource a once-off software development project, with the following attendant difficulties:[12] poor information on the capabilities of the software firms in various locations, difficulties in communicating requirements to outsourcing partners, and concerns about being "held up" by any overseas party owing to difficulties in writing and enforcing contracts with opportunistic trading partners. Members of the diaspora can serve as what we loosely call "reputational intermediaries" to facilitate international exchange by several means: search and matching, contract fulfillment, and altered profiles.[13]

Search and Matching

If members of the diaspora have an ongoing relationship with the U.S. firm, such as that of an employee to an employer, they might be able to use their own reputation to vouch for a particular overseas firm. The incentive to do so might be monetary, as when employers pay premiums for foreign-country nationals who are well informed about home-country business. But the desire to help home-country businesses is incentive enough in other cases.[14] Suppose employees can build up

12. These are modeled in Grossman and Helpman (2002).

13. As far as we know, the term "reputational intermediary" was first introduced in Kapur (2001).

14. A Fortune magazine article profiling the Indian Silicon Valley businessman and technologist Kanwal Rekhi describes a reputational intermediary of the form we have in mind in action (Warner 2000). Rekhi is the former chief technical officer for Novell and a founding member of the Silicon Valley professional organization the Indus Entrepreneurs (TiE). His value as a reputational intermediary is clear from the number of Indian entrepreneurs who come to him seeking his help. Apparently he himself also takes the value of reputation seriously.

knowledge about suppliers through the normal conduct of their business over time.[15] An employee then faces the choice of going out on his own as a network intermediary (by becoming an entrepreneur) or staying in employment. A network intermediary sells the service of matching buyers with suppliers. Members of the diaspora might be well placed to act as network intermediaries once they have either acquired a richer knowledge of home-country firms or developed a system by which to determine such knowledge.[16]

Contract Fulfillment

Reputational intermediaries also have a part to play in the next stage of this process, when they have the capacity to ensure that each party lives up to its side of the agreement.[17] Once a contract has been signed, the supplying firm may be willing to act opportunistically with its outsourcing partner, but it might be unwilling to risk its reputation with the member of the diaspora vouching for its trustworthiness. Moreover, the ability to "blacklist" an offending home-country businessperson within the diasporic network is always a powerful asset for the vouching party. Similarly, the outsourcing firm, valuing its reputation for engaging in fair business practices within the diasporic network, would be less apt to renege on an agreement forged through an intermediary. In essence, the intermediary leverages his or her long-term relationship with each party to overcome the oft-severe difficulties associated with signing one-shot contracts across weak legal systems.

Altered Profiles

Members of the diaspora can act as reputational intermediaries to the extent that their business behavior affects the "profile" or "brand" of their countrymen. Firms looking for outsourcing partners under uncertainty will rationally engage in statistical discrimination; they will form an expectation of the quality of any given potential trading partner based on observed characteristics *and* their prior beliefs about the distribution

---

15. See the model developed by Rauch and Watson (2002).

16. Reputational intermediaries are likely to matter more where knowledge is tacit. Information is distance invariant, knowledge more contextual. Unlike many manufacturing sectors where ex ante knowledge of quality is more easily discernible through third-party certification (through ISO or ASTM, for example), this is much less the case with services where quality can only be discerned after use.

17. For a fascinating game theoretic model of such intermediary-based contract enforcement, see Dixit (2001).

of characteristics in the population that this firm belongs to. Contacts with members of the diaspora have the power to alter these prior beliefs. For example, when a U.S. firm's interactions with Indian engineers from the elite Indian Institute of Technology (IIT) show them to be excellently trained, this experience can influence an upward revision of prior beliefs about the quality of engineers in India from these and possibly other institutions. This mechanism will be especially important if the industry and firms in question do *not* share the negative attributes of other industries in their country—a fact that the outsourcer may not fully appreciate initially.

Causes of Reputational Barriers

Developing-country firms face reputational barriers to entry in export markets when buyers have limited information about the quality of the firms' products and service reliability. Because buyers in major export markets will have had little prior experience in dealing with these firms, they may be reluctant to do business with them. This places newcomers at a reputational disadvantage in comparison with established firms, effectively creating a reputational barrier to entry. Such barriers arise mainly in two situations: where an individual firm is unfairly "stuck with" an unfavorable reputation because of the poor performance of other firms thought to be similar, and where a firm is at a disadvantage simply because it is a late entrant and little is known about it. The importance of reputational barriers is likely to vary across industries and across segments within industries. Reputational barriers are likely to be greater under the following conditions:

—Quality is more tacit; consequently, passing an ex ante judgment on the product or service is more difficult. Most tradable services fall into this category, software being a good example.

—The risk of extreme adverse outcomes associated with poor quality is high, as in the case of food products and health care. The cost of a cataract operation in India (even including travel costs) is substantially less than the cost in Europe in comparable facilities, but the overall poor reputation of Indian hospitals is unlikely to make this a viable proposition given what is at stake.

—There are large difficulties in designing contractual mechanisms to mitigate information asymmetries.

—Timely, reliable supply is noticeably important.

Diaspora Effectiveness

The mere existence of a diaspora does not guarantee it will have positive effects on domestic industries or firms, however. These effects depend on two broad factors: the characteristics of the diaspora, and the conditions and policies of the home country.

Who Leaves?

The impact of emigration depends foremost on the characteristics of emigrants. A truism of migration studies is that a strong selection bias exists among migrants, meaning that they are not randomly drawn from the general population of a country. The bias may refer to skills, education, occupation, risk averseness and dynamism, ethnic and religious selection, political beliefs, income, or regional and urban/rural selection.

It is widely believed that migrants are a select group, showing, for example, more initiative than their apparent equivalents who choose to stay.[18] However, evidence of positive selection is difficult to pinpoint if characteristics are unobservable. This problem is not insurmountable, however, because the most likely source of positive selection is not voluntary migration decisions but those made by universities, employers, and immigration officials as part of the employment-based temporary and permanent visa system. In the case of the U.S. H-1B visa, employers first decide which individuals to petition for, with immigration officials later deciding which petitions to allow. Employers, aided by the presence of emigrants already in the United States, can observe much more about potential H-1Bs than is discernible in the census or Current Population Survey data. Returning to our earlier example of IIT graduates, an employer can determine firsthand the quality of an institution from which an H-IB applicant has graduated on the basis of the performance of other emigrants with a degree from those institutions. Given the costs of the emigration process, these observable markers of quality will provide a distinct advantage to graduates of the most prestigious schools (see chapter 2).

---

18. Borjas (1987) points out, however, that it is quite possible that immigrants to the United States are negatively selected. Intuitively, the argument is that if income distribution is less compressed in the source country than in the United States—which is the case for many countries in Latin America, for example—it is the high-earner types that will find migration relatively unattractive.

Reasons for Leaving

Economic motives are largely responsible for migration, although political factors are important in certain cases. Where migration is the result of politics, its consequences are likely to be more inimical to the country of origin. Insofar as the economic migrants are members of the erstwhile political elite that is being displaced, their weak links with newer elites are likely to strain commitment to their country of origin. The migration of elites may also open space for new groups. Indeed, the very possibility of exit may make them feel as though they have less stake in the national system, thus diminishing their "voice."[19] On the other hand, the possibility of exit may reduce the intensity of an elite's opposition to the efforts of other social groups to claim a share of the national political space.

Political turmoil spurs international migration and activates diasporic nationalism, which often makes an already bad situation worse. Global trends are weakening the cover of national sovereignty, and diasporic minorities in particular are playing a more activist role in their country of origin, especially where the community faces the threat of violence. "Long-distance" nationalism associated with diasporas has often amplified political tensions and conflict in the country of origin.

Time Abroad

The length of time during which a disaporic community has been abroad is important, for the greater the vintage of a diaspora, the less intimate are its links with its country of origin. Although technological changes that have made it much easier to travel, maintain communication links, and keep abreast of various cultural media are beginning to mitigate this tendency, it does emphasize the need to nurture second-generation links.

Where Did It Go and How Did It Fare?

A diaspora's ability to affect its country of origin varies positively with its own success. This is a function both of the success of the diasporic community within the destination country and of the salience of the destination country itself. The success of the Chinese diaspora in Southeast Asia and the rapid economic growth of the countries there substantially increased their emigrants' capacity to invest in China when

---

19. This term is from Hirschman (1970).

it opened its economy. In contrast, while the Lebanese were successful in West Africa, the downward trajectory of those countries eroded their own financial capacity, thus limiting their impact on Lebanon when the civil war ended there. The Indian diaspora in the United States is having a greater economic and political impact back home than its counterpart in the United Kingdom, and a substantially greater impact than that in the Caribbean, reflecting the U.S.-based diaspora's high initial level of education at the time of emigration and consequent success within the destination country. This is, of course, coupled with the leveraging of that country's global salience as well.

In many cases, disaporas are wealthier than those left behind. A case in point is the U.S.-based population from El Salvador, whose income exceeds the GDP of the home country. Emigrants from Mexico and the Dominican Republic are in much the same situation. Since the wealth is concentrated in fewer hands, collective action is easier. Election financing is now an important channel of diasporic influence. And to the extent that certain diasporic individuals have achieved wealth and prominence, they also attain a "reputational influence." This may occur at either the regional or state level, where a village son makes it somewhat big or a national son, perhaps a Turkish-born entrepreneur, makes it very big in another country, such as Germany.

Does the money make that much difference? Two observations are in order here: on the lines of a tipping point argument, it could make a big difference at the margin; and its negative effects can be much larger than its positive effects. It has been found, for instance, that all other factors being equal, the risk of conflict starting after at least five years of peace is six times greater in nations with the largest diasporas than in those with the smallest. Moreover, "after peace has been restored, the legacy of conflict-induced grievance enables rebel movements to restart conflict by drawing on the support of their diasporas."[20] Others would dispute this claim, however.[21]

Policies and Conditions in the Country of Origin

Even once all these factors are taken into consideration, the policies and conditions in the country of origin continue to mediate the nature of the interplay between the diaspora and its country of origin. Although it played a critical role in China's economic growth after

20. Collier and Hoeffler (2000, p. 5).
21. See, for example, Humphreys (2000, 2003); Humphreys and Garry (2000).

1980, the Chinese diaspora was a silent spectator in the decades before that. As long as China itself was closed and international trade and investment were ideologically suspect, the skills and wealth of overseas Chinese had little effect on the country. Many Central American, African, and Central European countries have large diasporas, but their own economic policies and political instability prevent these diasporas from having much positive effect; on the contrary, they can often have a strong negative effect on their country of origin. The Armenian and Croatian diasporas, for example, played an important role in supporting hard-line political groups in their respective countries, thus exacerbating conflicts with neighbors as well as economic problems at home.

Until recently, the prevailing interests and policies in India paid little attention to international trade. As a result, the country underplayed the advantageous overseas trade networks established by its diaspora, which is why Indian businesses and the government did not court Indians in East Africa and Hong Kong when they were looking for safer pastures. India's policies toward international trade and FDI, as well as an apathy bordering on resentment toward its more materially successful diaspora, reflected the country's fear of the outside world. In the past decade, the transformation of the ideological climate in India and the advances made by the diaspora, especially in the United States, have instilled much greater self-confidence in the domestic and foreign Indian population. The decreasing hostility of the former toward the latter has been an important reason for the growing links and stronger bonds that have transformed relations between India and its diaspora.

A more fruitful line of inquiry may lie in the characteristics of the diaspora and of the policymakers or political elite in the home country. If the ethnic, class, or social differences are large, then the degree of influence is likely to be very different from what it would have been had the diaspora and policymakers belonged to the same groups. To be influential, a diaspora must have sway over those who are influential in the home country. Its power must extend to the social or ideological arena, not just the economic one.

Two broad mechanisms allow a diaspora to influence agents in the country of origin: diasporas are likely to be imitated since they are more economically successful than those remaining at home, and diasporas exhibit more active persuasion stemming from a didactic role in stimulating the international transmission of ideas. If diasporas can induce changes in the preferences of agents in the country of origin, the political economy consequences could be significant. Diasporas are known to transfer financial remittances to the country of origin, but it may well be the less visible, nonquantifiable, and intangible remittances—namely, social remittances or the flow of ideas—that have a greater impact. An interesting example of the long-term impact arising from the home country's imitative tendencies is the unexpected change in fertility rates in Egypt and Morocco.[22] Their emigrants have gone to different geographical areas, primarily the Middle Eastern oil countries and Western Europe, respectively. In general, societies to which Egyptians have emigrated strongly encourage large families (for a variety of reasons). By contrast, Moroccan migrants have gone to host societies in which small families are the norm. In both cases, there was a progressive adaptation to the norms of the host societies. It has been observed that the transfer of "values" has been amplified with the coming of age of the second generation of Moroccan-origin emigrants in Europe.[23] Their fertility decisions were more "European," and the continued close contact with the country of origin affected fertility decisions at home. Thus although in the mid-1970s demographers were predicting a sharp decline in fertility in Egypt and more gradual change in Morocco, two decades later the opposite occurred, despite higher rates of economic growth and levels of education in Egypt. Indeed, international migration can be a powerful vector of norm diffusion, with long-term economic consequences.

Diasporas stimulate the international transmission of ideas at both the elite and nonelite levels of society, whether through a filial connection across nations, a communications revolution, or experience with international finance institutions that returning immigrants carry back home. A panel study of political attitudes in a cross section of Mexico's population prior to the country's 2000 elections shows how emigrants can expose non-elite family members back home to the preferences of a foreign country.[24] The 2,400 respondents were asked for their party affiliation, views on some political issues of the moment, and details about their families. The responses suggest that their preferences are shaped by a closer connection to the United States through immigration. Controlling for monthly household income, the preferences of respondents with relatives in the United States are more "neoliberal" than

---

22. Courbage (1995).
23. Courbage (1995).
24. The Mexico 2000 panel study consists of approximately 7,000 interviews in five separate surveys over the course of the campaign, using a hybrid panel/cross-sectional design. Its first round, conducted from February 19 to 27 (just after the official beginning of the campaign), polled a national cross section of 2,400 adults. We used data mainly from this round. Interviews for the panel component of the project were conducted by the polling staff of *Reforma* newspaper, under the direction of Alejandro Moreno.

Table 7-2. Mexican Attitudes on Economic Policies

Connection to United States	Mean attitude toward electricity privatization and collective bargaining: (1 = neoliberal, 4 = socialist)
None	3.9
Relatives there	3.72
Visited	3.66

those without similar connections (see table 7-2). Of course, it is possible that a reverse causality is at work, in that households having a more neoliberal predisposition to begin with are emigrating. However, the survey question that asked respondents to define themselves politically elicited broadly similar responses across the three groups. Even so, the evidence is strongly suggestive rather than causal.

In a similar vein, consider families that have children or other relatives studying and working in foreign countries. It is not uncommon for policymakers, in particular, to finance an overseas education for their children, especially in the United States, Japan, United Kingdom, France, Canada, and Australia. In this case, the transmission mechanism for the diffusion of policy ideas is policymakers' children who convey their experiences with and adopt the preferences of their temporary homes. A second factor exposing all socioeconomic groups to the flow of new ideas has been the sharply reduced cost of communications devices. This communications revolution has led to the exponential growth of transnational phone calls (see figure 7-1) and e-mails and a sharp increase in international travel.

The cumulative effect of millions of conversations—akin to filling a pond one drop at a time—is likely to be substantial. On the one hand, the resulting information flows convey "deep" (though frequently tacit) knowledge about things to be done and how to do them. On the other hand, it changes expectations of and preferences for what is and is not acceptable, whether in regard to standards of service, the role of the state, or the behavior of politicians.

The influence of diasporas is not unlike that of international financial institutions (IFIs). According to the vast literature on the influence of the IFIs in various developing countries, most of this alleged influence is presumed to derive from the conditionalities that IFIs impose concurrently with a lending program. IFIs can exercise influence in the sense of leverage because of the quid pro quo involved: money. Consider an alternative channel of IFI influence, namely, people who worked in these

Figure 7-1. International Telephone Traffic from the United States to OECD and Developing Countries, 1980–2000

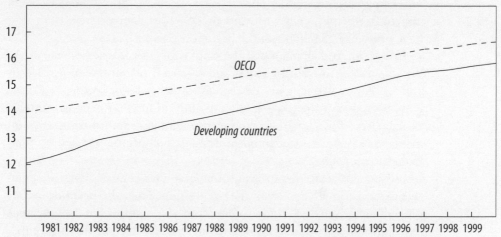

Log of minutes dialed

institutions, returned to their countries, and are employed in central banks, finance ministries, or even in high positions such as that of prime minister (as in Mexico, Turkey, and Peru). In these cases, the IFIs are pushing against an open door—they share an epistemology or "common knowledge." Here, influence takes the form of persuasion. In other words, policymakers in developing countries would act in much the same way an IFI would want them to do but without any overt pressure.

The Importance of Networks

The foregoing discussion suggests that the role of diasporas in contemporary economic life is better understood when markets are seen not just as price-making mechanisms but as social institutions that facilitate exchange in the Coasian sense. Networks embedded in social institutions mimic market structures through signaling and informational exchange among participants, thereby affecting the flow of information in fundamental ways to shape the content of, access to, and credibility of information. Their role in employment and labor markets, as well as in immigration and immigrant entrepreneurship, is well documented. Once in place, networks create self-sustaining migratory flows that gradually break apart from the conditions that generated immigration in the first place. The resulting "chain migration" is an important explanation of why ethnic groups with very small numbers in the overall population concentrate spatially and in occupations and trades. Employers have strong reasons to hire individuals with a credible imprimatur, and existing employees' referrals are important means for achieving such approval. Hiring new employees or contractors from networks that have proven to be reliable in the past reduces search costs.

In addition to helping along the employment process, these networks provide access to informational and financial resources. In the 1970s and 1980s, the wig industry emerged as a niche export sector for Korea. Korean Americans often ran hairdressing salons that became "intelligence posts" for changing fashions, thus passing on information that influenced a quick turnaround in designs to continue popular exports from this industry.

India's experience demonstrates the long-term consequences of cognitive externalities arising from the brain drain. First, the brain drain has played an important role in boosting the confidence of overseas investors in India's potential, despite its innumerable problems. Companies like Yahoo, Hewlett Packard, and General Electric opened operations in India largely because of the confidence engendered by the presence of many Indians working in their U.S. operations. Second, it has helped in the diffusion of knowledge through a variety of mechanisms. Given the technological frontier in the United States, there is a substantial upgrading of skills when Indian technology professionals work in that environment. To the extent that some return while others circulate between the two countries, technological diffusion occurs through imitation, as mimicry is an effective way to reduce search costs. Just as Korea climbed up the technological ladder by importing capital equipment of recent vintage (embodying frontier technologies), diasporic networks embody technologies relating to human, rather than physical, capital. China's and India's success in manufacturing exports and software, respectively, can in part be explained by the strategic role played by the presence of their diasporas in global production networks in these sectors. In both cases, diasporic networks played two key roles: an informational role and a reputational one.

The importance of networks has been amplified by a changing logic of production and industrial organization in global markets. Models of large vertically integrated firms that are dominant in sectors with slow-changing technologies and markets are being supplanted by interorganizational networks of suppliers, production facilities, and collaborative research and development ventures. The new logic of production, which emphasizes flexibility over hierarchy, is a response to rapid technological change and the pressure for shorter product cycles. The resulting decentralized production system consists of dense social networks, flexible labor markets, and collective learning among specialized producers of complex interrelated knowledge, where firms simultaneously compete intensely and collaborate. It possesses a strong spatial dimension manifested in industrial clusters. The importance of spatial concentration is underlined by the IT sector's spatial clustering, despite its own status as the one industry in which production theoretically can be decentralized the most, owing to the minimal movement of intermediate goods.

As already mentioned, diasporic networks act as both reputational intermediaries and credibility-enhancing mechanisms that may be particularly important in economic sectors where knowledge, especially ex ante knowledge of quality, is tacit. For instance, the Indian diaspora's success in Silicon Valley appears to be influencing the way in which the world views India, reflecting the reputational spillover effects of overseas success in a leading sector. It has created a "brand-name," wherein an Indian software programmer sends an ex ante signal of quality within his or her field in the same way that a "made-in-Japan" label sends an ex ante signal of quality among electronic equipment. This, then, helps mitigate the effects of at least one of the reputational barriers discussed earlier in this chapter.

In view of these benefits, perhaps it is time to reevaluate what constitutes comparative advantage in international trade. A country might consider trade strategies that attempt to leverage its diaspora by tapping the potential to increase trade with countries where its emigrants go. In particular, as in India's case, comparative advantage may be greater where reputational barriers for certain goods and services are high, but where the diaspora can augment the country's reputation. Service sectors, in particular—medical, educational, consulting, and tourism—could benefit in this regard. However, as in the case of software services, the diaspora can only augment, not substitute, for domestic capabilities.

The growth of the Internet has provided a new mechanism linking professionals in a diaspora with their counterparts in the country of origin.[25] These networks range in size from a few hundred to a few thousand. The goals are broadly similar: to connect with each other and

25. Examples include the Worldwide Indian Network (India), the Global Korean Network (South Korea), Brain Gain Network (Philippines), and the Reverse Brain Drain Project (Thailand). Jean-Baptiste Meyer and Mercy Brown have identified 41 formal knowledge networks linking 30 countries to their skilled nationals abroad. See Meyer and Brown, "Scientific Diasporas: A New Approach to the Brain Drain" (www.unesco. org/most/ [2003]).

their country of origin, and to promote the exchange of skills and knowledge through joint development projects with government agencies, businesses, and nongovernmental organizations in their countries of origin. The contribution of these networks in comparison with other forms of professional collaboration and knowledge transfer is, however, still unclear.

At the same time, what can be said with some certainty is that the network effects of diasporas are not an unalloyed blessing. Diaspora expertise has also contributed to the success of international criminal groups, which, like other networks, rely on reputation, tacit knowledge, and contract enforcement for their effectiveness. The international migration of criminal talent is a prime reason for the growth of such networks. They merit special attention because the financial flows arising from their activities can be so large as to pose serious threats to national governments, and their impact is often made worse with the use of terrorist acts.

International Migration of Criminal Talent

According to UN estimates, international crime generates $1 trillion to $1.5 trillion a year, with drug trafficking, illegal arms trade, human trafficking and smuggling (especially of women and children for prostitution and servitude), and money laundering constituting the principal activities. While both source and destination countries are hard hit by these activities, the former understandably suffer a much greater impact. The transnational links behind them provide domestic criminal groups in source countries with substantial financial resources, at times enough to bestow on them significant political power, even to destabilize weak states. The profits from drugs, often funneled through diasporic networks, have played an important role in Haiti's narco-coup in 2004, the ongoing violence in Colombia, and the warlordism in Afghanistan. These activities not only bring in billions of dollars of revenue to source countries each year but also increase their economic dependence on drug trafficking, prostitution, and other forms of illegal activity. Virtually all international criminal networks—whether Albanian, Italian, Colombian, or Chinese—rely on their respective diaspora as a base for their activity.

Diasporas have been a boon to international crime for a number of reasons. As with any business, international criminal activity requires enforcement mechanisms and trust, which diasporic networks can easily internalize. Increased migration—much of which stems from states with weak economies and political instability—has created a large demand for both financial support and larger global networks. In many cases, such networks become particularly prominent where immigrant groups are not fully integrated into their host societies, as one policy group has observed. Forced repatriation of felons (for example, from the United States to Central America) has given these networks additional strength.

Much like any international industry, many criminal networks rely on expatriated populations to help facilitate their activities abroad. The most well-known example in the last century is the Italian Mafia, which built its structure on a large migratory population, especially to the New World. The Chinese triads have an even longer history and continue to thrive today with strong connections to Chinese populations around the world, particularly in the Netherlands, the United Kingdom, Germany, and the United States. In recent years, traditional triad groups from Hong Kong and Taiwan have been hooked up with mainland Chinese criminal gangs, whose activities extend beyond the usual extortion, gambling, people smuggling, and drug trafficking to more sophisticated crimes such as credit card fraud, computer chip theft, and violations of intellectual property rights. Nigerian criminal gangs (about 500 are thought to be operating in at least 80 countries) are known to take advantage of large West African populations worldwide to operate global networks of drug trafficking and sophisticated, lucrative fraud schemes. According to recent estimates of U.S. customs officials, Nigerian criminal syndicates have established themselves as the world's most active traffickers of Asian heroin, with 25–30 percent of the heroin seized at U.S. international airports found on couriers employed by Nigerian trafficking groups.

The end of the cold war and the conflict in the Balkans prompted an exodus from that part of the world that served, in turn, as the impetus for the establishment of some of today's thriving criminal networks. Ethnic Albanian groups, whether originating from Albania or Kosovo, have been the most prominent and are particularly active in trafficking drugs, arms, cigarettes, illegal aliens, and women for prostitution. They reportedly dominate the market for heroin in Norway, Sweden, southern Germany, and Switzerland. By 1999, Albanian groups controlled most of Italy's prostitution and had displaced the Russian Mafia as the controlling power of central London's lucrative prostitution racket.

Arguably the most educated among the various international crime groups, the Russian Mafia blossomed under the Soviet regime by supplying hard-to-find products to government officials and by greasing the wheels of a command economy. In the 1990s, the organization profited from the chaotic economic situation, rapidly garnering economic and political influence. This power, combined with the personal ties that many top crime leaders developed during the 1970s and 1980s while serving time in prison, still helps them to coordinate illegal activities today. The group relies heavily on the overseas Russian population, particularly in Eastern and Central Europe, for support and resources.

The following list summarizes the activities of the major crime networks:

—*Italian:* Wide variety of activities including gambling, extortion, drug smuggling, arms dealing, alien smuggling, and environmental crimes, particularly illegal hazardous waste dumping. Extensive presence via expatriate Italian populations throughout Europe, Central and South America, the Caribbean, the United States and Canada. Italian diaspora crime groups in the United States include the Cosa Nostra.

—*Russian:* Particularly active in oil and gas trading sectors, financial markets, and sale of arms overseas. Presence in more than 60 countries. Russian Mafia commonly establishes illegal operations in overseas resorts frequented by Russian speakers. Most influential in Eastern and Central Europe.

—*Ethnic Albanian:* Active in trafficking drugs, arms, cigarettes, illegal aliens, and women for prostitution. Albanian gangs now dominate the market for heroin in Norway, Sweden, southern Germany, and Switzerland, and dominate prostitution in Italy and London. Small-scale operations in northeastern United States. Whether originating from Albania or Kosovo, ethnic Albanian groups are typically from tight-knit clans. Since the end of the cold war, Albanian groups have expanded beyond their borders to become the most significant of smaller criminal groups.

—*Chinese:* Mainland Chinese criminal gangs expanded beyond traditional triad activities of extortion, gambling, and illegal alien and drug trafficking into more sophisticated areas such as credit card fraud, computer chip theft, and IPR violations. Strong connections in Chinese enclaves around the world, particularly in the Netherlands, the United Kingdom, and Germany.

—*Nigerian:* Particularly active in drug trafficking and sophisticated fraud schemes. Nigerian criminal syndicates are the world's most active traffickers of Asian heroin and are increasingly trafficking South American cocaine. Nigerian criminal groups take advantage of large West African populations worldwide. Recent estimates suggest 500 Nigerian criminal cells are operating in at least 80 countries. The United States and Britain are key targets.

—*Latin American:* In the past decade, have expanded beyond drug production and trafficking into money laundering and production of counterfeit goods. Nevertheless, major Latin American criminal organizations are not involved in the smuggling of illegal aliens into the United States. Trafficking networks have been established across the Western Hemisphere.

An even greater challenge facing the international community lies in the combined support for terrorism and civil wars emanating from these criminal networks. Although the fear of terrorism has in some cases become full-blown paranoia, it is seriously disrupting the transnational flows of human capital, with the costs to U.S. businesses alone beyond $30 billion since 2002.[26]

Conclusion

This chapter has provided a wide-ranging review of the role modern diasporas play in integrating developing countries with the global economy—mostly, though not exclusively, for the good. The main drivers of globalization are technological breakthroughs in transport and communications combined with the dismantling of politically imposed barriers on international trade and investment. But social relationships still matter a great deal in facilitating economic exchange, imparting a continuing local bias to business despite these revolutions in technology and policy. The emergence of diasporas helps overcome some of the remaining "social barriers" that lock poor countries out of international commerce. It remains an open question as to whether these linkages outweigh the more direct absence-related losses discussed in chapter 6. The next two chapters continue our exploration of the complex effects of skilled emigration by looking at two additional ways in which a diaspora can alter the fortunes of those remaining behind: their willingness to send money home and the possibility that they themselves might eventually come home.

26. "Do Visa Delays Hurt U.S. Business?" (www.nftc.org/default/visasurveyresults% 20final.pdf [June 2, 2004]).

CHAPTER 8

Financial Remittances and Development

Remittances are financial flows arising from the cross-border movement of a country's nationals. In their narrowest sense, they refer to "unrequited transfers," meaning primarily money that migrants send to family and friends without attaching any claims to it (in contrast to other financial flows such as debt or equity). In our opinion, the definition should also include two categories that are recorded separately in a country's balance of payments statistics: "migrant transfers," which arise from the migration (change of residence for at least a year) of individuals from one economy to another and are equal to the net worth of the migrants; and "compensation of employees," which are funds sent back by temporary workers (who work abroad for less than a year).[1]

This broader definition is not without problems. In practice, it is difficult to distinguish between persons whose earnings are classified as compensation of employees and migrants who have become residents of economies by virtue of being expected to live there for a year or more. Since compensation of employees includes contributions paid by employers, on behalf of employees, to social security schemes or to private insurance or pension funds, it overstates the resources transferred to the country of origin. On the other hand, these amounts exclude unrecorded and in-kind transfers, which are likely to be substantial.

1. The World Bank (*Global Development Finance*, 2003, statistical appendix to chap. 7) appears to have recently adopted this practice as well.

Table 8-1. Remittance Flows, 1970–2001: Percentage of Cells for Which No Data Are Available[a]

Year	1970–79	1980–89	1990–99	2000–01
Inflows	77	53	39	34
Outflows	77	52	43	45

Source: Global Development Finance (2003).

a. A cell is a country-year data point.

They also exclude funds sent through the capital account by overseas residents (for example, via special savings accounts), which are then withdrawn in local currency.[2]

Despite the volume and importance of remittances, data regarding this phenomenon are of poor quality and limited availability, the principal source being the International Monetary Fund's information on balance of payments. IMF figures come from member countries but contain many gaps in the area of remittances. Even for countries with a population of a million or more, a good deal of this information is either missing or unreported (table 8-1).

Given that a considerable volume of remittances passes through unofficial channels, while those transferred through official channels incur high transaction costs, one might reasonably expect more outflows (from the sending countries) to be reported than inflows. The figures actually show the opposite. Countries like Cuba, Liberia, Haiti, and Vietnam show zero remittance inflows, while Hong Kong, Singapore, and Canada also show zero or very small outflows, despite large immigrant populations in all cases. Many countries have sudden surges, which are inexplicable under most plausible scenarios. And there are large variations in remittances across countries per foreign worker (see figure 8-1). High remittances from Belgium/Luxembourg and Switzerland are a puzzle and could simply reflect the fact that all three are banking centers, so remittance outflows may simply be masking money laundering. Alternatively, low tax rates may be luring multinational companies to set up offices in these financial centers.

The great uncertainty surrounding remittances is reflected in the varying numbers recorded by the sources: according to the Inter-American

2. In the balance of payments, such transactions show up as contra entries—a reduction in the capital account and an increase in the current account. For instance remittances to India increase by more than $2 billion if this is taken into account. This is also a feature of the so-called Dresdner scheme in Turkey.

Figure 8-1. Variation in Remittances per Foreign Worker

Percent

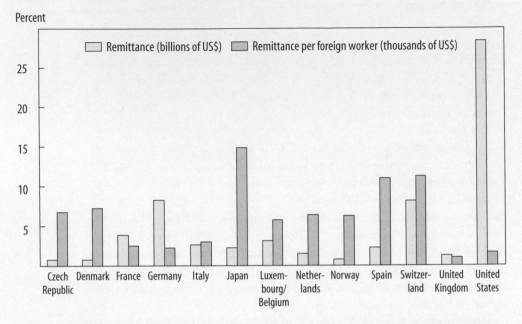

Source: For remittance data, see Global Development Finance (2003, p. 160, figure 7.5). For stock of foreign and foreign-born labor, see OECD (2002) and *Trends in International Migration: SOPEMI* (Paris: OECD, 2002, table A.2.3). All figures are for 2000, except for Spain, Belgium, and the Netherlands.

Development Bank's Multilateral Investment Fund, for instance, remittances to Latin America reached $40 billion in 2004 whereas the World Bank put the figure at $36.9 billion. By contrast, data on international financial flows are more abundant and of better quality, because data-gathering techniques have improved tremendously over the decades. The concepts there have been systematically refined, the data are timely, and the coverage of countries and issues has become broader and deeper. The World Bank's Global Development Finance (formerly World Debt Tables), the IMF's International Financial Statistics, the Bank for International Settlements, and the Organization for Economic Cooperation and Development (OECD) are the standard sources of data on international financial flows. Their attention to detail is not too difficult to understand. The institutional channels through which financial capital flows from north to south have a strong interest in maintaining good data. Creditors are fewer in number and have the capability as well as the power to ensure that data mandates are adhered to. Moreover, poor data on international financial flows have been implicated in numerous financial crises, be it the Latin American debt crisis or the various financial crises of the 1990s. Since these crises have repercussions for source countries, mainly the industrialized countries, each systemic crisis has resulted in an improvement in data quality. It is far harder to track down the numerous individual sources of remittances, while the recipient countries—developing countries—lack the capability and perhaps even the incentive to compile better data.

Financial Remittances: Size, Sources, and Destinations

Official interest in remittances is on the rise, however, owing to a number of their features.

First, remittances have become a significant source of external financing for developing countries, emerging as their second largest source of net financial flows over the past decade (see figure 8-2a).[3] By contrast, *net official flows* (aid plus debt) over this period have stagnated, if not declined. The total volume of remittances to developing countries in 2004 was $125.8 billion, nearly four times net official development assistance in that year ($32.9 billion) and *net private flows* (foreign direct investment [FDI] plus debt flows) of nearly $247.7 billion (table 8-2). But if instead one examines the figures for *net transfers* (figure 8-2b)—which is the bottom line after deducting all payments including profit repatriation, interest payments, and remittance outflows (since most developing countries have some outflows as well)—then the significance of remittances for developing countries is much more apparent.

Remittance flows were 11 times net official transfers and 1.6 times net private transfers in 2004 (table 8-2). While this reflects in part the large stock resulting from flows of private and official finance in previous years, it is precisely the "unrequited" nature of remittances that makes this big difference—all other sources have a corresponding claim on the receiving country, which can be substantial in view of the stock of FDI and debt. The welfare and growth effects from these sources are in all likelihood quite different. However, if one is interested in the financial bottom line, remittances were clearly the most important source of net foreign exchange flows to developing countries in that year. For reasons discussed in the next section, the growing importance

3. We are grateful to Dilip Rath of the World Bank for the data used in this section and discussions related to the same. See also Rath (2003).

Figure 8-2. Financial Flows to Developing Countries, 1990–2004

a. Net flows

Billions of U.S. dollars

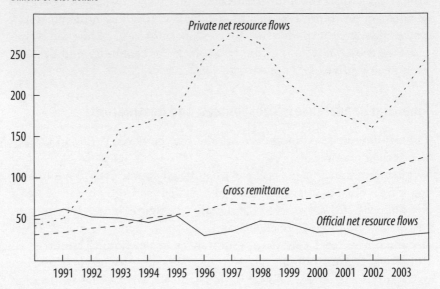

b. Net transfers

Billions of U.S. dollars

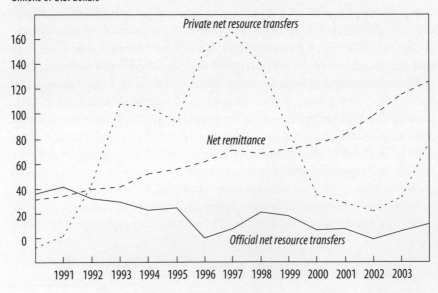

Table 8-2. Net Flows and Transfers of External Finance for Developing Countries, 2004
Billions of dollars

Region	Private	Official	Remittances	Total (net)	Remittances (net %)
Flows					
East Asia & Pacific	62	−4.5	17.6	75.1	23
Europe & Central Asia	67.1	4.4	10.4	81.9	13
Latin America & Carribean	41	2.3	29.6	72.9	41
Middle East & North Africa	4.8	1.6	13	19.4	67
South Asia	11.1	2.2	18.2	31.5	58
Sub-Saharan Africa	13.2	22.9	4.1	40.2	10
Transfers					
East Asia & Pacific	20.2	−9.8	17.6	28	63
Europe & Central Asia	22.1	−0.7	10.4	31.8	33
Latin America & Caribbean	−11.7	−4.3	29.6	45.4	65
Middle East & North Africa	−0.9	−1.6	13	10.5	123
South Asia	1.9	0.3	18.2	20.4	89
Sub-Saharan Africa	1.7	21.4	4.1	27.2	15

Source: Global Development Finance (2005).

a. Private flows include equity (FDI and portfolio flows), and both long- and short-term debt flows. Private transfers include equity (FDI and portfolio flows), and both long- and short-term debt flows.

b. Official flows include lending from multilateral banks, the IMF, and bilateral loans and grants. Official transfers include lending from multilateral banks, the IMF, and bilateral loans and grants.

of remittances compared with other sources of external finance is likely to continue. Aid levels declined in the 1990s, and a more than modest upturn is unlikely. Furthermore, private capital flows are unlikely to reach the euphoric levels that preceded the Asian crisis any time soon.

The 10 largest sources and recipients of remittances in the last decade include both developed and developing countries (table 8-3). Not surprisingly, the United States is the largest source, and 4 countries of the Middle East (Saudi Arabia, Israel, Kuwait, and Oman) are among the largest. Three G-7 members—Japan, the United Kingdom, and Canada—do not make this list, which is especially surprising when the small countries Belgium/Luxembourg and Switzerland do.[4]

The general impression is that remittances flow mainly to poor countries. That is only partly true. Of the 10 largest recipients of remittances

4. Belgium's data are not reported separately but are usually combined with Luxembourg's.

Table 8-3. Largest Sources and Recipients of Remittances, Annual Average, 1992–2001

Source country	Billions of dollars	Recipient country	Billions of dollars
United States	20.7	India	7.7
Saudi Arabia	15.4	France	6.9
Germany	8.8	Mexico	5.7
Switzerland	8.1	Philippines	5.0
France	4.9	Germany	4.1
Italy	2.2	Portugal	3.8
Israel	2.1	Egypt	3.8
Belgium/ Luxembourg	1.8	Turkey	3.7
Kuwait	1.4	Spain	3.0
Oman	1.4	Greece	2.7

Source: International Monetary Fund, balance of payments statistics.

between 1992 and 2001, 7 were members of the OECD, and 2 of the top 5 recipients were G-5 countries (France and Germany). Of the $173 billion in total remittances in 2003, about two-thirds (or $116 billion) accrued to developing countries. The share of developing countries has ranged from less than half in the late 1980s to about three-fourths in recent years. The largest 10 recipients have been quite stable since the early 1990s (except that Morocco has replaced Greece in recent years). Although private in nature, remittance flows are less concentrated than private flows. Thus whereas the top 10 recipients of FDI accounted for 70 percent of FDI flows to developing countries in 2001, the top 10 recipients of remittances accounted for 59 percent of those flows.

Second, the bulk of international remittances does not accrue to the poorest countries. Nearly half of all remittances received by developing countries flows to lower-middle-income countries, while the other half flows about equally to upper-middle-income and low-income countries (figure 8-3). Remittances are benefiting some regions more than others, particularly Latin America (primarily the Andean countries, Central America, and Mexico), South Asia, the Middle East (where, however, they have been growing very slowly compared with other regions) and Maghreb, and some countries in East Asia (especially the Philippines and Indonesia). The fact that sub-Saharan Africa receives the least amount of reported remittances (unlike other regions with little growth) is a sobering indication that this source of finance is unlikely to contribute significantly to ameliorating the external financing problems of the region.

Figure 8-3. Remittance Inflows

Billions of U.S. dollars

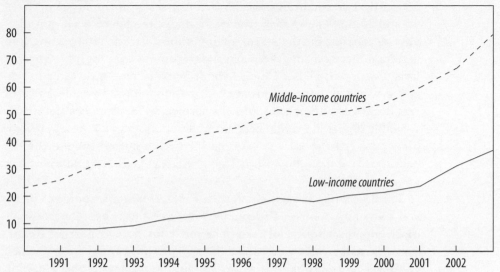

Source: Citizenship and Immigration Canada (2002).

The limited remittance inflows to Africa reconfirm that geography does matter. There are indeed large migrations from African countries, but the civil strife in that region sends migrants across borders to other impoverished African countries rather than to rich countries. Geographical contiguousness to rich countries is clearly important, especially for illegal migration. This puts Mexico, Central America, and the Maghreb at an advantage, although nationals of other Latin American countries may have access to European labor markets because of the prior history of migration from the latter to the former. With the likelihood of greater curbs on net migration to the Middle East, its formerly large remittances to South Asia will decline unless compensated by migration to other regions.

The two countries with the largest global migrations, China and India, report substantial differences in remittances. Surprisingly, China receives comparatively little in the way of remittances—the figure was about $1.4 billion a year between 1992 and 2003, or about one-seventh of India's receipts, which amounted to $9.34 billion a year over the same period. These large differences probably have less to do with the characteristics, size, or vintage of their large migrant populations and more with incentives (especially tax policies) and economic opportunities in the two countries. In contrast to the remittances figures, diaspora FDI in the two countries indicates that overseas Chinese invest between 10 and 20 times more than overseas Indians (the figures vary considerably depending on the status of investments from Hong Kong and assumptions regarding the magnitude of round tripping). However, a large fraction of FDI in China—about one-quarter—is invested in real estate.[5] Since this type of investment is common to the deployment of remittances as well, it reinforces the suspicion that there is a not inconsiderable statistical overlap between remittances and FDI, which, if combined, makes financial inflows from the two countries' emigrants more comparable—with inflows into China being between two and four times those into India.

Third, remittances have emerged as the *least unstable* source of financial flows for countries afflicted by "shocks" and constitute the single most important source of insurance for many poor countries. Remittance flows are much more stable than private capital flows, which exhibit strong herdlike behavior, amplifying the boom-bust cycles in many emerging markets (figure 8-2). Consequently, remittances can be viewed as a self-insurance mechanism for developing countries in that overseas migrants help diversify the home country's sources of external finance. This role is strengthened by the low risk correlation between the country of residence and the country of origin and is especially important for poor countries since (much like poor people) they find it difficult to secure insurance otherwise. It is therefore not surprising that remittances have taken on this role for residents of countries afflicted by economic and political crisis (such as Lebanon during its civil war or Haiti), those hit by natural disasters (such as Central America in the aftermath of Hurricane Mitch), those pressured by international sanctions (such as Cuba), or those in which state authority has crumbled (such as Somalia and other "failed" states). Ecuador was certainly on the list of countries in crisis in the late 1990s, when it experienced its worst economic crisis of the century. The resulting political chaos, social upheaval, and economic collapse led to the largest out-migration in the country's history (particularly to Spain). In just two years, more than a quarter million Ecuadorians left the country. Remittances jumped from $648 million in 1997 to more than $1.4 billion in 2001 (10 percent of GDP), emerging as the second largest source of foreign exchange after

5. Tseng and Zebregs (2002).

petroleum exports.[6] Cuba, too, suffered a sharp economic downturn in the aftermath of the collapse of the Soviet Union in the early 1990s, leaving it without any geopolitical benefactor to prop up its inefficient statist economy. Not only did overseas assistance dry up but the output and prices of its principal export (sugar) collapsed in global markets just as the United States was trying to tighten its embargo on the island. Until then the country had curbed overseas remittances from its rich diaspora, which was (in large part) deeply hostile to the regime. For the first time, the Cuban government took steps to attract remittances, offering a slew of incentives to residents receiving dollars. By 1995 remittances were approximately $530 million (up from just $50 million in 1990). At a time when foreign aid and FDI combined came to only about $100 million and exports just $1.1 billion, and an acute foreign exchange crisis threatened to take the country the route of North Korea, remittances provided a crucial lifeline.[7]

Fourth, for the many small countries—especially island economies, be it in the Caribbean or the Pacific—remittances, along with foreign aid and tourism, have become the only viable sources of income. As much as two-thirds of families on a small island like Cape Verde receive money from abroad. For many of them, remittances offer the only source of income, which is not surprising with a population of only 435,000 in 2000 and twice as many abroad.[8] Such high levels of migration and remittances might well indicate that these countries are simply unviable economic entities, but given political realities they will continue to exist—surviving to a considerable extent on the labors of their overseas population.

Fifth, as with the euphoria over private capital flows in the mid-1990s, the attractiveness of remittances is in part a reaction to previous failed development mantras. Development thinking has been as prone to fads and fashions as private capital flows are alleged to be. Remittances strike the right cognitive chords. They fit in with a communitarian "third-way" approach and exemplify the principle of self-help. People from poor countries need only migrate and send back money to help not only their families but also their countries. Immigrants, rather than governments, then become the biggest provider of "foreign aid." The general feeling is that this "private" foreign aid is much more likely to go to

6. Jokisch and Pribilsky (2002).
7. Eckstein (2003).
8. IMF and IDA, Poverty Reduction Strategy Paper, Cape Verde (www.imf.org/external/np/jsa/2002/cpv/eng/032102,pdf [March 2002]).

people who really need it. On the sending side, it does not require a costly government bureaucracy, and on the receiving side, far less of it is likely to be siphoned off into the pockets of corrupt government officials. It appears to be good for equity and for poverty and yet imposes few budgetary costs. What could be better—if these hopes are valid?

Why Have Remittances Grown?

The most obvious factor behind the recent upswing in remittances is the steady growth of the underlying cause, namely migration, especially to rich countries. Although legal flows of migrants have been uneven, illegal migration and the stock of emigrants have increased steadily. The United Nations estimates that roughly 175 million people were living outside their country of birth or citizenship in 2000, up from 120 million in 1990.[9] An analysis of the 2000 U.S. census reveals that of the foreign population in the United States in that year, nearly half (47 percent) entered the country in just the previous decade. In another notable change, the foreign population of 17 European economies tracked by the OECD rose from 15.8 million in 1990 to 21.7 million in 1998—which amounts to an increase of 37.2 percent.[10] In the oil-exporting Gulf States, foreign workers continue to represent more than 50 percent of their labor force; in Saudi Arabia, they account for 70 percent of the labor force, now 10 million strong.[11]

The frequency and intensity of economic and financial crises in many developing countries over the past two decades has increased the need for social safety nets, amplifying the demand for remittances. Of course, some of the reported increase in remittances is in all likelihood a statistical artifact since the quality of data has improved, and changes in economic policies of many developing countries, especially with regard to foreign exchange controls, have sharply reduced the black market premium for foreign exchange. As a result, part of the increase in officially recorded remittances reflects a shift from informal to formal channels. Nonetheless, remittances continue to go through informal channels in some countries, either because of foreign exchange controls (as in Myanmar and Zimbabwe) or because state machinery is lacking (as in Afghanistan).

9. UNPD (2002); Martin and Widgren (2002).
10. OECD (2001).
11. Martin and Widgren (2002).

There is, however, another less obvious factor driving the growth in remittances—a burgeoning infrastructure that has helped ease the movement of money across borders. For a long time, the remittance business was dominated by money-transfer companies like Western Union, which in 2002 alone processed almost $700 billion in transfers and payments worldwide through 68 million customer-to-customer transactions (and another 173 million customer-to-business transactions). In 1994 it had 24,000 agents worldwide, but two-thirds were in North America. By mid-2003 this figure had increased nearly sevenfold (to 165,000), and 70 percent of these agents were outside the United States.

The exorbitant costs of remittances (about 10 to 12 percent of the estimated $25 billion transferred from the United States) and the implied large profits have brought forth new entrants. The most striking change has been in the strategies of major commercial banks, which had been slow to recognize that the remittance business was a potential source of significant new opportunities. Portuguese banks, realizing this in the early 1980s, established branches in areas with concentrations of emigrants (such as France), offered free transfer services, and arranged to have local agents deliver the funds back home. By the late 1990s deposits from emigrants represented about 20 percent of the total deposits in Portugal. In the Americas, the collapse of the Mexican banking system in the aftermath of the "tequila" crisis of the mid-1990s opened up the Mexican banking sector to foreign direct investment. As major Spanish and U.S. banks began buying Mexican banks, remittances gradually moved to the center of their strategies. They began to buy complementary U.S. assets as well as form alliances with other banks to leverage the remittance business.[12] It soon became evident that users of their remittance service could be drawn into becoming full banking customers—spearheading a large expansion of retail banking to two severely underserved groups on both sides of the border. The banks

12. Thus Spain's Banco Bilbao Vizcaya Argentaria bought Bancomer and then emerged as a dominant player in the electronic transfer business. Its volume grew from 657,000 transactions in 1999 to 12.65 million in 2004, thanks largely to the alliance it started in 2000 with another U.S. bank (Wells Fargo), links with a number of money transfer services in the New York area, and with the U.S. Postal Service. Following Citibank's purchase of Banamex in 2001, it introduced a single account that can be operated on either side of the border, using branches of either Citibank or Banamex. In 2002 Bank of America, the biggest U.S. retail bank, took a stake in Santander Serfin, the third largest Mexican bank, which was controlled by Spain's Santander Central Hispano. The remittance business also drove HSBC's decision to buy Grupo Financiero Bital, a large Mexican retail bank along with Household International, a consumer credit lender with branches across the United States, as a base for the remittance business.

have also been surprised by the relative wealth of Mexican customers. The transfer business is already paying dividends. Bank of America has found that 33 percent of its U.S.-Mexican remittance customers have opened a current account. Citigroup is using its transfer business to attract new customers and some to other products—for example, by lowering fees on transfers between Citigroup accounts in the United States and Mexico. Banks are now extending the products and technologies developed in the Mexico-U.S. remittance business to other Hispanic remittance markets both in the United States and in Spain, as well as the Spanish North Africa remittance market.

Informal Value Transfer Systems

Remittances flowing through informal (and sometimes underground) channels, outside the purview of government supervision and regulation, go back centuries, particularly in Asia. Examples include *hawala* and *hundi* in South Asia, *fei ch'ien* in China, *Phoe kuan* in Thailand, *Hui* in Vietnam, and *casa de cambio* in South America. Informal Value Transfer Systems (IVTSs) flourish in countries with economic controls, political instability, and low levels of financial development. Using rudimentary low-cost technologies, they rely more on trust than violence, riding on the social capital of ethnic groups. These systems transfer "at a minimum, tens of billions of dollars" globally, offering speed, easy access, low costs, and anonymity.[13] Basically, the sender gives money to an IVTS agent (usually in an ethnic neighborhood) who calls or faxes instructions to his counterpart in the region where the money is to be sent. The counterpart makes the payment within a few hours. Settlements are made either with a transfer in the opposite direction or periodic wire transfers or through over(under)invoicing of cross-border trade.

These services transfer funds derived from both legitimate and illegitimate activities, ranging from funds deployed by intelligence agencies to those related to corruption, tax evasion, drugs, and terrorism. However, there is more hype than evidence on the scale of the latter.[14] Attempts by Western governments to regulate IVTS activities have arisen in the context of measures to deter money laundering and most recently terrorist financing.

13. David Aufhauser, General Counsel, Department of the U.S. Treasury, *Hearings before the Senate Judiciary Committee*, 108 Cong. 1 sess. (GPO, June 26, 2003).
14. Passas (1999).

Effects of Financial Remittances

Remittances have complex effects, which are a function of the characteristics of migrants and the households they leave behind, their motivations, and the overall economic environment. Remittances are a form of household transfers motivated by, among other things, altruism as an implicit intrafamily contractual arrangement or as an implicit family loan. The importance of motives appears to vary with the institutional setting.[15]

Remittances finance consumption, land and housing purchases, and philanthropy, and, as already mentioned, they are an important source of social insurance in lower-income countries. They also provide liquidity for small enterprises (in the absence of well-functioning credit markets) as well as capital investments—in equipment, land, wells, irrigation works, and education—with long-term implications for economic development.

At this point, it is important to dispel one myth surrounding remittances, namely, that they compensate for the brain drain, substituting one scarce factor (financial resources) for another (human capital) that is critical for development. The two are not substitutes, even though emigrants are usually positively selected. The real detrimental effects of the brain drain for developing countries arise from the migration of the upper end of human capital distribution, comprising engineers, scientists, physicians, professors, and so on. This scarce human capital is usually drawn from the upper decile of the income distribution rather than the middle. Although there are exceptions (for example, temporary skilled migrants like the H1-B information technology workers in the United States), for the most part these households are in less need of remittances, unless the country of origin undergoes a major crisis. Indeed, if the brain drain is a response to political repression or economic and political instability rather than simply better economic opportunities abroad, human capital flight and financial capital flight complement each other. Instead of one form of capital outflow being "compensated" by another type of capital inflow, the migration simply precipitates the outflow of financial capital as well. Countries such as Afghanistan, Colombia, Ghana, Haiti, or Venezuela, as well as Cuba in the late 1950s and early 1960s, which have witnessed violent regime changes and civil wars, are examples of this phenomenon. This is not to

15. Foster and Rosenzweig (2001).

say that the brain drain of professionals might not have other benefits for the country of origin, such as business and commercial networks or investment flows and diasporic philanthropy as discussed in chapter 7, but those effects are distinct from financial remittances.

Remittances as Social Insurance

To reiterate, remittances play an important insurance role—and this has a significant impact on both poverty and equity. For people in failed states, remittances are critical for personal consumption. In Haiti, remittances have amounted to between a sixth and a fifth of GDP. In Somalia, following the collapse of a formal government in the early 1990s, remittances from the Somali diaspora based in the Gulf states, several European countries, the United States, and Canada were the sole source of survival for many Somali families, particularly during the harsh years of the 1990s. By the end of the decade, remittances had risen to about 25 and 40 percent of GDP, and some regions, such as southern Somalia, began investing these resources in construction and commerce.[16]

Remittances tend to increase in the aftermath of shocks, whether macroeconomic or natural disasters. The many recent economic and financial crises have resulted in two simultaneous shocks that affect remittances: either a positive income shock to the remitter because of devaluation or a negative income shock to the remittee because of an economic downturn. Both predict an increase in remittances (in domestic currency terms). To study this effect, we looked at countries that had suffered an economic shock (defined as a 2 percent decline in GDP in year t) and examined remittances in relation to private consumption in the years preceding and following the crisis. If the insurance hypothesis holds, we would expect the share of remittances in private consumption to increase. Because it was difficult to obtain consistent annual data on remittances for the countries suffering a shock, we examined this issue in both an unbalanced panel (figure 8-4a) and in a balanced panel (figure 8-4b). In the latter case, annual data were available for a set of countries for three years preceding and following a shock. In both cases, remittances increase sharply if a country suffers a macroeconomic shock.

This suggests that with globalization, factor markets can play a crucial role in alleviating poverty. Households tend to be much more specialized

---

16. Idil Salah, Som-Can Institute for Research and Development, and Bernard Taylor, Partnership Africa Canada, "Somalia: Peace and Development" (www.web.net/pac/pacnet-l/msg00008.html [September 12, 1999]).

Figure 8-4. Unweighted Average of Remittances as Share of Private Consumption[a]

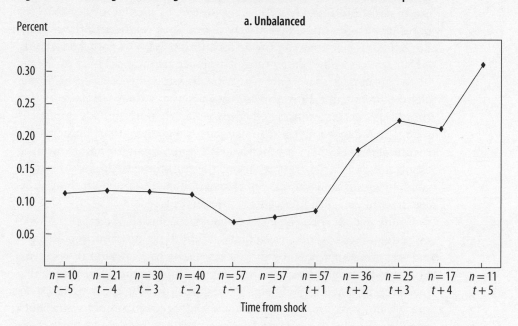

Percent

a. Unbalanced

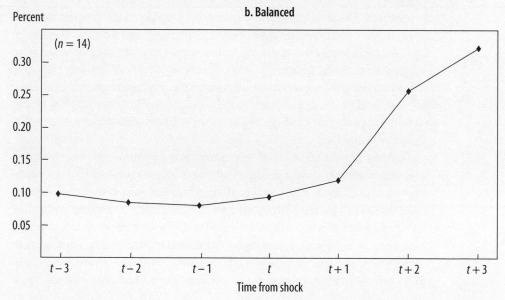

Percent

b. Balanced

a. Includes Barbados (1988–94), Colombia (1981–97), Comoros (1985–91), Ghana (1983–89), Guinea-Bissau (1988–94), India (1980–86), Jamaica (1992–98), Mauritania (1989–95), Mexico (1991–97), Morocco (1989–95), Panama (1984–90), Trinidad and Tobago (1989–95), Tunisia (1989–95), and Turkey (1990–96).

in income (or factor earnings such as land, labor, or capital) than they are in consumption. Hence it is the source of income rather than the pattern of expenditure that affects the poor in relation to the average household.[17] Remittances provide social protection to poor households, which reduces vulnerability to shocks. Since remittances have an immediate impact on transient poverty, which is known to be a serious obstacle to human capital investment, they also have long-term effects that should not be underestimated. Because an income shock's impact on school attendance is consistently larger for daughters than sons, ensuing remittances could have a beneficial effect on human capital investment, especially girls.[18] For this to occur, the remittances should of course accrue to poor households, but that will depend on whether migrants are drawn from such households in the first place.

Equity may also be enhanced by the particular characteristics of who migrates—the so-called selection effects. The distributional consequences are complicated by the uneven access to migration flows across households, ethnic groups, communities, and regions. Households that receive remittances rapidly attain standards of living greater than those that do not have family members working abroad. Should some shock trigger a devaluation and economic downturn, households with more diversified portfolios—both in financial assets and human capital assets—will weather the storm better than those with domestic portfolios. After a devaluation, the income stream from an overseas portfolio increases in terms of the domestic currency, thereby increasing their income compared with that of lower-income groups. If remittances flow to poorer households concentrated in a particular region, this might reduce inequality within the region even while increasing it among different regions.

Following the Asian crisis, for example, Philippine households with overseas migrants did substantially better than those that had no members abroad. This is to be expected since migration is a form of coinsurance and gives families diversified portfolios. Indeed, among Philippine families above a certain income threshold, those with members abroad appear to use remittances to invest in human capital, which would then make it easier to migrate abroad, while those below this threshold use it to meet subsistence consumption.[19] This is particularly the case during a

17. Winters (2000); Reimer (2002).
18. Sawada (2003).
19. Yang (2003).

Figure 8-5. Population 25 or Older with Tertiary Education

Percent

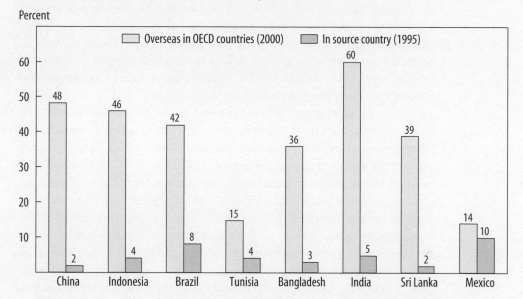

Source: Doquier and Marfouk (2004); Thomas, Wang, and Fan (2000); International Bank for Reconstruction and Development (2000).

crisis when households face substantial financial and economic stress and resultant pressure on consumption.

Migrants are rarely drawn randomly from the population pool but instead are selected from specific communities—be it regional, ethnic, or religious—as well as educational and income levels. Selection therefore plays a large role in migration, remittances, and poverty and equity outcomes in the country of origin. The average level of education of immigrants is greater than that in the country of origin—often substantially so (figure 8-5). In Latin America, only about one-fifth of those remaining behind have completed high school or college, whereas a little more than half of the Latino immigrants in the United States have a secondary education or better. Well-educated Latin Americans are at least two and a half times more likely to be in the United States rather than the home country. According to one analysis of Mexican migration to the United States, Mexican immigrants, while much less educated than U.S. natives, are on average more educated than residents of Mexico.[20] If Mexican

20. Chiquiar and Hanson (2002).

immigrants in the United States were paid prevailing wages for those skills in Mexico, they would tend to occupy the middle and upper parts of Mexico's wage distribution structure. In contrast to earlier work that posits a negative selection hypothesis, these findings suggest that in terms of observable skills there is intermediate or positive selection of immigrants from Mexico.[21] The results also suggest that migration abroad may raise wage inequality in Mexico.

The fact that migrants are not being drawn from the poorest households in their country of origin means that even though remittances are poor-friendly they may have only a limited direct effect on the poorest groups. Instead, structural poverty is likely to experience substantial indirect effects, in the demand for labor-intensive services (such as construction work when remittances are used for home building) and perhaps even in redirecting government social expenditures from areas benefiting from remittances to those that are not. Of course, these results may not be the same where immigrants are illegal, since they are much more likely to come from poorer households. Large-scale illegal immigration tends to occur in areas of geographical proximity—for example, from Mexico and Central America to the United States, from Myanmar to Thailand, from Bangladesh to India, or from the Maghreb countries to Europe. In the case of the many poor people who do make it across borders, there is strong anecdotal evidence that they incur substantial debt from the upfront cost of making the often-illegal journey across borders. Many of them become indentured laborers working to pay off the loan (often to criminal syndicates) and have little left to remit. On balance, however, the beneficial impact on poverty and inequality is maximized for the sending country when migrants have fewer skills. It is not just that the ensuing remittances are directed at poorer households, but that the supply of unskilled labor in the source country is reduced, thereby increasing unskilled wages of those left behind.

Although little evidence is available to assess the direct impact of remittances on economic development and growth, officials often lament that the bulk of remittances is spent on consumption. Nonetheless, insofar as remittances finance the consumption of domestically produced goods and services such as housing, there appear to be wide multiplier effects. Moreover, additional consumption increases indirect tax receipts.[22] There is also some suggestion that the propensity to save

21. On negative selection, see Borjas (1987).
22. Desai, Kapur, and McHale (2003).

is higher among remittance-receiving households than among others.[23] If so, then remittances that help augment national savings could be leveraged for broader economic development.

To take another example, it has long been recognized that capital and liquidity constraints greatly affect small enterprise development, especially in poorer communities with imperfect capital markets, such as those in urban Mexico. Thus it is not surprising that remittances from migration by the owner or family members working in the United States have helped in supplying capital for investment in microenterprises throughout urban Mexico. In the 10 states with the highest rate of migration from Mexico to the United States, almost a third of the capital invested in microenterprises was associated with remittances.[24] Insofar as remittances are driving retail banking strategies of foreign investment in Mexican banks, remittances could also have the inadvertent but potentially far-reaching effect of transforming Mexico's banking system. Fewer than one in five Mexicans have a bank account and many rural areas of central Mexico, which send the most migrant laborers to the United States, lack any bank branch. Weak formal credit markets have been particularly inimical to Mexico's small and medium enterprises. If retail banking does radically change these practices, the long-term economic benefits of remittances to the country might be greatest here.

Interestingly, some immigrant communities have sought to pool remittances for public use back home. To this end, Hispanic immigrants across the United States have organized themselves into hometown associations (HTAs) that finance public works projects and small businesses in the towns from which they have migrated. The Mexican government has taken the initiative to leverage their remittances by creating a "three-for-program" in which all HTA remittances used to improve infrastructure or establish businesses are matched dollar for dollar by the Mexican federal, state, and local authorities.[25] This threefold leveraging has had some notable successes at the local level, but the cumulative impact remains limited.

Often communities do not have the resources to maintain what has been built through these contributions. Hype notwithstanding, HTAs have not so far been used significantly to fund direct income-generating projects. Furthermore, it is unclear if these initiatives are creating jobs so

23. Orozco (2003a).
24. Woodruff and Zenteno (2001).
25. Alarcon (2002).

that Mexicans do not have to emigrate or are instead simply subsidizing future migration through improved training. Perhaps the biggest benefit is that the HTAs have become a magnet for local collective action in both the sending and the receiving country. For migrants, these associations help maintain ties to their hometown, which in turn may help sustain private remittances.

So What's the Problem?

In assessing the impact of remittances, micro-level studies (principally by anthropologists) tend to be less sanguine than more macro-level studies (usually by economists). The former tend to see a dual effect: greater wealth but fewer economic opportunities for those left behind—a Pyrrhic victory, as it were. Remittances, they point out, have helped physically transform so-called migra-villages in Latin America, but many of the new handsome houses are empty because their owners live in the United States. Likewise, remittances have helped build better schools, but enrollment has been declining. Though simply a consequence of migration initially, remittances in these regions have now become its principal driver. The very money that has increased the material wealth of these villages appears to be gradually undermining their long-term future. What is good for individual migrants and households may not be as beneficial for the communities. Whether economic development is more about the former or the latter is something that can be reasonably debated.

Remittances can have ambiguous effects even at the household level, as can be seen in the case of homecare workers such as Jamaican nannies in New York or Filipino nannies in Hong Kong. Many of these women are mothers who have left their own children behind to take care of children in wealthier households. The household in the home country enjoys higher consumption because of remittances, but the children of these homecare workers grow up without their mother. The migration decision of the mother could be considered a "revealed preference" of an improvement in household welfare. Why would she leave otherwise? However, independent analysis is not available to confirm that this is indeed the case.

Communities heavily dependent on remittances often develop a culture of dependency. In a variety of contexts it has been observed that household members simply stop working and wait from month to month for the overseas remittance. Such negative incentive effects—a form of moral hazard—in turn cause the reservation wage to increase.

Young men prefer to remain unemployed and wait for the possibility that they themselves will migrate, rather than take up jobs at the local market-clearing wage. That remittances increase consumption much faster than production raises issues of long-term sustainability, for they will inevitably decline as migrants settle in new communities and their links with home communities gradually erode. Of course, this is a moot point if most people leave the community in any case.

Similar negative incentive effects can act at the national level. If remittances are substantial and a large share is spent on nontradables—housing and land are particularly favored—the country is likely to suffer Dutch disease effects. The real exchange rate is then likely to appreciate, rendering exports less competitive. The country's principal export—labor—could become the cheap factor, rather than labor-intensive products. At an aggregate level, remittances constitute a form of rents. Exporting products requires painstaking effort to build the institutions and infrastructure that help develop the necessary productive capacity. Exporting people, on the other hand, occurs in most cases by default rather than by design. Nonetheless, if the latter also results in large foreign exchange receipts, the pressure to undertake reforms needed for export-led growth is considerably attenuated. For instance, countries can maintain larger fiscal deficits in the context of international migration and remittances. In the absence of remittances, high fiscal deficits would imply higher current account imbalances and hence greater reliance on foreign savings (assuming the deficit is not monetized—which is less likely given that central banks are more independent today), with a subsequent increase in capital account inflows.[26] However, if remittances are high, current account deficits would be lower, thereby reducing the likelihood that high fiscal deficits will precipitate a balance of payments crisis—the most common trigger for economic reforms in developing countries. Thus countries with high remittance levels can sustain higher fiscal deficits—while at the same time keeping international financial institutions like the International Monetary Fund and the World Bank at bay.[27] With the increasing politicization of these institutions, potential borrowers no longer seek co-insurance through

26. Moreover, the general trend of greater trade openness and increasing domestic liberalization means that excess demand has much less effect on inflation.

27. For instance, India has maintained exceedingly high fiscal deficits (about 10 percent of GDP) even in the presence of modest inflation (about 5 percent). In part this is because its current account—buoyed by remittances exceeding $12 billion (2.5 percent of GDP)—is positive. For a more detailed discussion, see Kapur and Patel (2003).

these institutions as much as self-insurance, in the form of higher foreign exchange reserves and international migration and remittances.

Political Effects

Money buys influence. Therefore it should not be surprising that in countries where remittances are important, the political effects are not inconsequential. In the Dominican Republic (where remittances are 10 percent of GDP), presidential candidates campaign in the United States. From Mexico to India, the lucre of remittances has led politicians to switch positions toward their diaspora from benign neglect to active courtship. Regimes in socialist economies such as Cuba and North Korea have used remittances to augment scarce hard currency resources to strengthen themselves in the short term. Cuba draws remittances from its U.S.-based diaspora, while North Koreans earn remittances mostly from pachinko parlors run by Koreans living in Japan. But insofar as these remittances sow the seeds of economic transformation, they can also quietly erode the political system. In Cuba, access to remittances has increased inequality in a political system that draws its legitimacy from its commitment to equity.[28] Furthermore, remittances have a strong racial bias there, since the diaspora is predominantly white while the island is mostly black. The latter gained under Castro and were therefore less likely to emigrate, but as a result they have less access to the emerging cross-border informal dollarized economy. Access to remittances is also heavily urban and regional; Havana, with 20 percent of the island's population, receives approximately 60 percent of remittances. Therefore rural-urban inequality is also likely to widen.

Second, remittances can be viewed as a political weapon of the weak. International migration and remittances have forced states to accommodate new realities rather than simply react to state policies. In lieu of political voice, migration becomes an exit strategy, and remittances either fuel further exit or empower political voice by making available resources to new groups. In several Latin American countries, even as economists debated the relative merits of dollarization, the influx of "migradollars" was in several cases rendering the debate moot.

Nor is the political impact confined to source countries. In receiving countries, remittances have been quietly reshaping immigration policies. Recently, the Mexican government negotiated with banks and wire transfer agencies in the United States to make it easier and cheaper for

28. Eckstein (2003).

immigrants to send money home. The Mexican government began to distribute "matrícula" consular identification cards and persuaded U.S. banks to accept them as identification cards for the purpose of opening bank accounts, irrespective of the legality of the applicant's immigration status.[29] Major U.S. banks, attracted by the high fees and volumes, began to accept these cards. The remittance market was also a good complement to U.S. banks' strategy of expanding operations in Latin America by buying local banks in the region. After all, if a bank could get a customer to step inside and make a deposit (in the United States) or a withdrawal (in, say, Mexico), it might interest him or her in other financial products. In turn, by simply offering to do business with any illegal foreign resident who got a consular identification card, U.S. banks have quietly reshaped their country's migration policy toward illegal immigrants from Latin America or Mexico. As Mexican consulates began to be flooded with applications for identity cards, local governments and law enforcement agencies in the United States began accepting these cards to allow migrants to get other forms of identification such as driver's licenses, making the lives of illegal migrants less onerous.

Since international remittances are a form of cross-border financial flows, it should not be surprising that they also have international political effects. In many countries they are so important and the flows so large that they affect bilateral relationships and foreign policy. While at the local level remittances have an impact on politics, at the macro level causality runs the other way—it is politics that has an impact on remittances. This is particularly the case when migrants are concentrated in countries or regions that become unstable. Source and destination migration dyads (table 8-4) increase the harm resulting from covariant shocks. Indeed, controlling remittance outflows can become a coercive instrument on the part of a migrant destination country. To cite one example, remittances from migrants in the Ivory Coast accounted for a quarter of the GDP of Burkina Faso, and a civil war in the former rapidly reverberated to the latter.

The oil shocks and the Gulf crisis in the Middle East have not only affected oil-producing countries but have had a regional contagion effect through their demand for labor. A similar phenomenon was

29. The cards are digitally coded and check an applicant's information against computerized census and voter rolls in Mexico. The accounts will allow immigrants to send ATM cards to relatives back home, so rather than spending $25 to send $200 at a typical money transfer counter, immigrants can give their families access to funds in the United States for about $3 per transaction.

Table 8-4. Some Prominent Source–Destination Migration Dyads

Source country	Destination country
Afghanistan	Pakistan
Albania	Greece
Algeria	France
Argentina	Italy
Armenia	Russia
Bangladesh	Saudi Arabia
Brazil	Japan
Burkina Faso	Côte d'Ivoire
China	South Korea
Colombia	Venezuela
Dominican Republic	United States
Ecuador	Spain
Ghana	Nigeria (1970s), United Kingdom
Guatemala	Mexico
Haiti	Dominican Republic
India	Gulf countries, United States
Indonesia	Malaysia
Mexico	United States
Mozambique	South Africa
Myanmar	Thailand
Nepal	India
Pakistan	Saudi Arabia
Peru	Chile
Philippines	Hong Kong
Surinam	Netherlands
Turkey	Germany

observed in Southeast Asia during the Asian crisis when the expulsion of Indonesian labor from Malaysia and Thailand exacerbated the crisis in the former, increased tensions between the countries, and weakened the Association of Southeast Asian Nations. Following the 1991 Gulf War, the Gulf countries punished workers from Jordan and Yemen and especially Palestinians for supporting Saddam Hussein and expelled them from their countries. In all these cases, remittances from family members earning money in the Gulf states were crucial. The heavy price paid then and the continued dependence on remittances from the Gulf was one reason that some countries were opposed to the second Gulf War in Iraq, fearing its disruptive economic effects.

Control of remittances as a form of economic warfare has been most evident in the Israeli-Palestinian conflict. In September 2000, Israel began revoking the work permits of Palestinians because of security concerns. At that time, some 100,000 Palestinian workers from the West Bank and Gaza Strip crossed into Israel every day. By January 2002, only 25,000 Palestinian workers and 8,000 merchants had permits to enter, and the number has continued to drop. In their place, Israel began to import foreign workers (an estimated 230,000, largely from China, Thailand, Africa, and the Philippines) to work in agriculture and construction. As a result, remittance outflows from Israel tripled from less than $1 billion in the early 1990s to nearly $3 billion in 2001. The economic effects on the West Bank and Gaza have been devastating. Gross national income per capita fell by 11.7 percent in 2001 and a further 18.7 percent in 2002, while poverty levels jumped from 21 percent in 1999 to 46 percent in 2002. The drop in remittances had even larger indirect effects since the loss of income dampened the demand for Palestinian goods, and imports from Israel declined sharply—which in turn adversely affected Israel's economy as well.[30]

Like much else in today's world, remittances changed in the aftermath of September 11. This proved a blessing for Pakistan, a "frontline" state caught in the vortex. In 2000 remittances to Pakistan totaled about $1 billion (about a third of their peak in 1982–83), but after September 11 many Pakistanis with savings in offshore accounts repatriated their funds, fearful of being caught in U.S.-led investigations into terrorist financing. Under pressure from the United States, the Pakistani central bank tightened controls on the web of moneychangers (locally known as *hundi* operators) and introduced a law restoring immunity against disclosure of the sources of income for holders of foreign currency accounts. As a result, the difference between the official and market rates narrowed (to less than 1 percent), and by 2003 remittances in Pakistan rose to nearly $4 billion.

In contrast, the effects were much more disruptive for Somalia, a country with no recognized government and without a functioning state apparatus. After the international community largely washed its hands of the country following the disastrous peacekeeping foray in 1994, remittances became the inhabitants' lifeline. With no recognized private

30. See http://lnweb18.worldbank.org/mna/mena.nsf/Attachments/Ecomomic+and+Social+Impact.

banking system, the remittance trade was dominated by a single firm (Al Barakaat).[31] In 2001 the United States shut down Al Barakaat's overseas money remittance channel, labeling it "the quartermasters of terror." With remittances representing between a quarter and 40 percent of total GNP, closure of the channel was devastating. The humanitarian impact of having money frozen in transit was considerable. Remittances provided many times what the aid agencies could offer to rebuild the deeply impoverished country. Although evidence of Al Barakaat's backing for terrorism was weak, the effects of the ban on the country's well-being were significant.[32]

Policy Options

The Somali case brings up two important points. First, there is little doubt that remittances have helped to fund terrorism, civil wars, and liberation struggles, the nomenclature depending on the beholder. There is no shortage of examples: the beneficiaries range from the revolutionary council of the Free Aceh Movement (or Gam) in Sweden and the Liberation Tigers of Tamil Eelan in Canada to the Kashmiri cause in the United Kingdom. In Somalia itself a large portion of the remittances went to supply arms to the rural guerrillas who toppled the government in January 1991. For the peoples of collapsed or failed states in Congo, Somalia, and Afghanistan, as well as for nationalities without states (Palestinians, Kurds, and pre-independence Eritrea and East Timor), overseas remittances are the oxygen essential not just for family survival and household consumption but also to finance the militant causes and support leaderships that may use the struggle in turn to maintain their own hold. In other cases, such as Armenia and Croatia, remittances underwrote long-distance nationalism, boosting hard-line regimes and complicating efforts to resolve regional conflicts.

Second, the Somali case illustrates the need for a greater international effort to create an acceptable international money transfer system in the growing number of countries where the state has collapsed, the paucity of international aid is acute, and nationals are trying to do more for themselves. The biggest challenge facing the international community is

---

31. Al Barakaat operated in 40 countries, was Somalia's largest private sector employer, handled about $140 million a year from the diaspora, and offered phone and Internet services.

32. By early 2003 only four criminal prosecutions had been filed, and none involved charges of aiding terrorists.

how to improve the well-being of people living in such states. Currently, it is relying principally on a "big stick" approach—proscriptions and sanctions against countries and financial intermediaries. Along these lines, the United States recently considered sanctions to cut off remittances to North Korea, and together with the Paris-based Financial Action Task Force, is pressuring countries to start monitoring "door-to-door" remittances, fearing that this unregulated flow of money could be used for terrorist activities. New legislation is forcing money transmitters to install expensive new compliance technologies. It is certainly the case, as the United Nations Development Program (UNDP) found in Somalia, that current money transfer systems in that country do not meet acceptable international standards and lack the means to identify suspicious transactions and money-laundering schemes. But international efforts will be more meaningful if they are directed at building a financial architecture rather than just deploying the blunt instrument of sanctions. An alternative policy action of this type has been initiated by the UNDP, which is working with foreign governments and Somalia's remaining money transfer and remittance companies to comply with standard financial rules and regulations and help firms institute standard bookkeeping, auditing, and reporting.

The international community can best serve the channels through which remittances are transmitted by helping construct a financial architecture that reduces the transaction costs of intermediation and increases its transparency. Recently, the World Council of Credit Unions launched the International Remittance Network to facilitate remittance transfers from the United States. It does not charge recipients a fee and offers better exchange rates, but as yet its services are confined to its members. The Inter-American Development Bank is helping create a common electronic platform in the region between sending and receiving countries and within receiving countries.[33] But there is considerably greater scope in this regard. In particular, the international community should fund a more substantial effort to underwrite the development and maintenance of a common electronic platform (including clearinghouse and payment systems) that would facilitate remittance transfers. If the facility were maintained under the aegis of a multilateral organization (the UNDP, for instance), it could ensure both greater transparency and lower transactional costs. Indeed, by allowing registered IVTS operators as well as INTERPOL access to such a platform at low

---

33. Buencamino and Gorbunov (2002).

costs, many of the advantages of informal banking would be coupled with the transparency of such a facility. It should be remembered that public subsidies for such an endeavor would in all likelihood be much lower than the costs of policing and monitoring as well as the transactional costs currently being incurred.

Another step to help lubricate international remittance transfers would be to work on transforming the role of post offices, the single biggest global distributional channel. The U.S. Postal Service began a program called Dinero Seguro (safe money) for sending remittances, but with charges at nearly 10 percent of the face amount, it has had little success. Postal "giro" payment systems are widely used in Europe and Japan. Linking the postal giro systems worldwide would facilitate international postal transfers, paralleling the agreement for the exchange of mail among member countries of the Universal Postal Union.

What can receiving country governments do to enhance the development impact of remittances? For one thing, they should try to get a better idea of the magnitudes and sources of these flows. In contrast to the massive effort they have devoted to monitoring and managing foreign aid flows, governments have paid little attention to these flows. Remittance data should become part of the IMF's Special Data Dissemination Standards to ensure the consistency and timeliness of remittance data, which would help improve the data on remittance flows but also allow for some cross-checks, similar to those currently done in trade flows. Remittance-receiving countries need to create a spatial map of their overseas communities, showing not just the country but specific geographical location. This would allow financial intermediaries to better target these communities.

To increase the long-term productive impact of remittances, governments need to promote greater competition and entice formal financial intermediaries, especially banks, to expand operations in areas with higher levels of emigration. Although it is true that *hawala*-like informal transfer systems are extremely efficient in that they provide much-needed services at low cost, *the net amount of capital they bring in is virtually zero.* The reason is that *hawala* can only function if inflows are equal to outflows, which means that the transactions are balanced through capital flight. Thus while remittance-receiving households benefit from the operation of such systems, the net financial and foreign exchange gains to the country are significantly less than if the flows came through formal channels. Moreover, if the propensity to save is higher among remittance-receiving households than in others, formal systems are likely to raise national savings rates. This would suggest that the presence of an extensive network of financial intermediaries in these areas could help leverage remittances for broader economic development. Countries with large remittance flows through informal channels could consider subsidizing the intermediation costs through formal channels as well as offer other incentives, such as less costly financial products like life insurance or access to mortgages.[34] Remittances could also be used to securitize future receivables to augment foreign credit ratings.[35] In addition, governments also need to more actively monitor and regulate labor market intermediaries, who often fleece potential migrants. Intermediaries lubricate flows—but they can also divert a substantial stream of income to themselves. Finally, governments should be aware that attempts to encourage or require remittances to be invested are unlikely to have significant economic benefits. The best way for recipient countries to ensure that a greater proportion of remittances are utilized for productive investments (rather than simply consumption) is to have a supportive economic environment for investment per se. Countries such as India and Turkey have tried to increase remittances by offering various preferential schemes under the capital account, such as tax-free status, but this inevitably leads to round tripping. Instead, governments should direct their efforts to the financial sector.

Conclusion

Are remittances a new development paradigm or another destabilizing force of globalization? They are certainly one of the most visible—and beneficial—aspects of the role of international migration in reshaping the countries of origin. In a variety of settings, remittances are quietly transforming societies and regions and are the most manifest example of self-help undertaken by poor households in the global arena. In particular, they are augmenting private consumption and alleviating transient poverty in receiving countries. However, their effects on structural poverty and long-term economic development are still poorly understood, which is surprising given their importance. By contrast, a substantial body of literature has grown up around the other principal sources of development finance: foreign aid, flows from the Bretton Woods institutions, and foreign direct investment and private debt flows.

34. This is being attempted in Mexico with the assistance of Fannie Mae and JP Morgan.
35. Ketkar and Ratha (2001).

Unlike foreign aid, remittance flows do not put any burden on tax-payers in rich countries. Nonetheless, they occur only to the extent that emigrants from poor countries can work in richer countries. Since countries that are more open to immigration are also the principal sources of remittances, which constitute substantial sources of external finance to poorer countries, should they not be viewed as a country's contribution to poor countries?[36] From this point of view, the U.S. contribution substantially increases (and in proportionate terms that of Saudi Arabia even more), while that of more immigrant-resistant countries, such as Japan, falls. The critical difference between foreign aid and remittances is that the former consists of transfers from public entities in the donor country to public agencies in receiving countries. Even when it is directed to agents in civil society such as NGOs, foreign aid goes to organized entities. Remittances, of course, simply go directly to households and in that sense their immediate poverty alleviation impact—through increased consumption—can be greater than that of traditional foreign aid, depending on the income characteristics of the receiving household. The transaction costs are lower, and there is less leakage to rent-seeking bureaucracies and consultants.

However, the long-term impact may be more questionable, especially if few productive assets are being created. Thus it would appear that remittances are a better instrument for alleviating transient poverty arising in response to shocks, whether at the household or national level, rather than structural poverty. There is as yet no evidence that remittances can catalyze broad economic transformation, the kind that is essential to alleviate structural poverty in the long term.

36. A new research initiative currently undertaken by the Center for Global Development and *Foreign Policy* magazine on the impact of an array of rich-country policies on poor countries does take this into account.

9

Better than Before?
The Role of Returning Emigrants

Thus far our discussion of emigration and its implications has assumed that it is a permanent decision. In reality, many emigrants eventually return to their country of birth, raising the possibility that the "time spent away" can be turned to the advantage of the home country. The question of interest here is how time spent abroad allows emigrants to accumulate human, entrepreneurial, financial, and social capital beyond what they would have accumulated if they had never left. With such accumulation, any negative effects from their absence on those remaining behind (TRBs) must be balanced against the enhanced impacts upon return. It is also important to consider why emigrants might return, what is known about the numbers and types that are returning, and the effects that they can have on their home countries upon resettlement.

Why Return?

A crude but useful distinction to make in examining returns is between those stemming from "mistakes" and those from "plans." We interpret mistakes broadly. The most obvious mistake occurs when someone emigrates on the expectation that the income gain will outweigh the costs of emigrating, including the money equivalent of the utility loss from being away from family and friends. If the anticipated income gain does not materialize, or being away proves more of a hardship than expected, the emigrant may later reverse the decision to live abroad. The mistake

Figure 9-1. New Irish Graduates Overseas, 1982–97

Percent

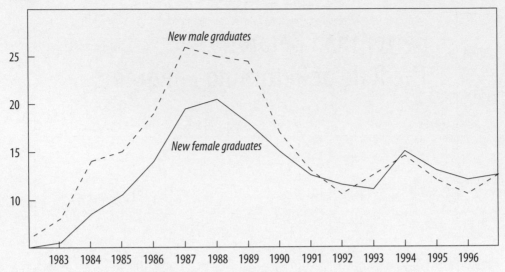

Source: Adapted from Lydon (1999); original data from Higher Education Authority, First Destinations Survey.

might not be due to an obvious miscalculation on the part of the emigrant, however, but to unforeseeable changes in circumstances at home or abroad. By way of example, consider the huge turnaround in the Irish economy in the 1990s, which lured many emigrants to return—a large number of whom left thinking they had bleak economic futures in Ireland in the 1980s, when Irish economic performance was anemic at best.

Between 1982 and 1989 employment fell by 5 percent, causing unemployment to hover in the midteens.[1] Throughout this period, tertiary education enrollments continued to expand strongly, growing by 64 percent over the course of the decade.[2] This followed the rapid growth of the 1950s (56 percent), 1960s (129 percent), and 1970s (92 percent). The dire labor market and the precedent of emigration in hard economic times were bound to lead a number of new graduates to move abroad.

Government surveys on Irish graduate emigration from 1982 to 1997 show that male graduate emigration rose from around 6 to 25 percent over this period (figure 9-1).[3] Female graduate emigration

1. OECD (2000).
2. Clancy (2001).
3. See Lydon (1999).

Figure 9-2. Estimated Annual Net Migration to Ireland

Estimated net migration (annual average)   Estimated net migration per thousand of population (annual average)

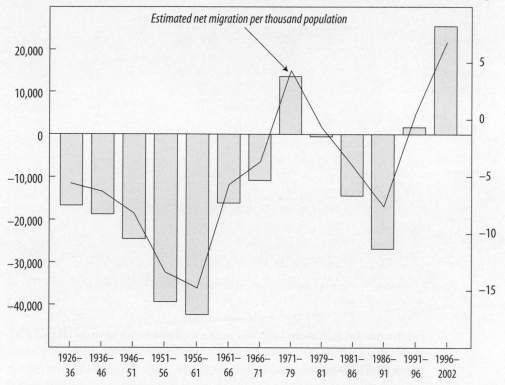

Estimated net migration per thousand population

Source: Central Statistics Office, *Census 2002, Preliminary Report* (Dublin: Stationery Office, 2002).

exhibited a similar trend, peaking at around 20 percent. The Irish economy was clearly losing a substantial fraction of the human capital it was producing.

These numbers changed with the economic turnaround of the 1990s. Employment almost doubled (47 percent) between 1989 and 1999.[4] At that point, graduate emigration fell sharply (figure 9-1), especially for male graduates. Moreover, as the boom gathered pace, graduates who had left during the 1980s began to return home.

This upturn came at the end of a long period of migration that started at Irish independence in the 1920s (figure 9-2). Conditions grew particularly bleak in the 1950s, prompting many young people with limited

4. OECD (2000).

Table 9-1. Residents of Ireland on Census Night 2002 Who Lived outside the State for One Year or More
Number of residents

Year residence taken up in Ireland	Country of previous residence				
	Total	U.K.	Other EU	U.S.	Other
Before 1951	7,520	5,980	191	604	745
1951–60	16,048	12,973	369	1,153	1,553
1961–70	50,615	39,492	1,330	4,573	5,220
1971–80	86,967	66,752	3,375	5,825	10,745
1981–90	89,258	56,263	6,844	9,899	15,892
1991–95	98,379	62,171	8,952	10,489	16,767
1996–2002	252,383	121,226	27,991	24,431	78,735
Not stated	43,544	9,961	2,700	1,708	29,175
Total	644,444	375,178	51,752	58,682	158,832

Source: Central Statistics Office, *Census 2002, Principal Demographic Results* (Dublin Stationery Office, 2003).

educations to leave for the United Kingdom. As the economy picked up in the 1960s and 1970s, the outflows subsided, and a significant net inflow was recorded during the 1970s. However, macroeconomic mismanagement, industrial restructuring away from indigenous labor-intensive manufacturing, and poor global economic conditions combined to produce net emigration again in the 1980s. Although many observers are divided on the factors responsible for the changes of the late 1980s, few would disagree that Ireland experienced a growth miracle through the 1990s.[5]

Table 9-1 shows the number of people aged one year and older (usually resident in Ireland and present on census night in 2002) who had spent at least one year outside the country. This measure captures both immigrants and the returning Irish population. In total, 644,444, or 16.5 percent of the entire population, were classified as such. Of those who stated the year they took up residence in Ireland, 42 percent reported doing so between 1996 and 2002.[6] Assuming that relatively

5. The most plausible explanation is that Ireland had been on a path of long-term fast growth for some time, underpinned by its initial backwardness and thus the opportunity for catch-up growth, increased investments in education starting in the 1950s, and its openness to trade and foreign investment. The 1980s debacle was the result of poor macroeconomic conditions—partly brought on by earlier fiscal profligacy—and the unfolding of the creative destruction of older labor-intensive manufacturing industries in the context of rigid and excessive real wages in low-productivity firms.

6. Of the total, 36 percent were between the ages of 25 and 39 on census night.

Figure 9-3. Migration Flows to Ireland: Returning Irish Emigrants and Non-Irish Nationals, 1995–2001

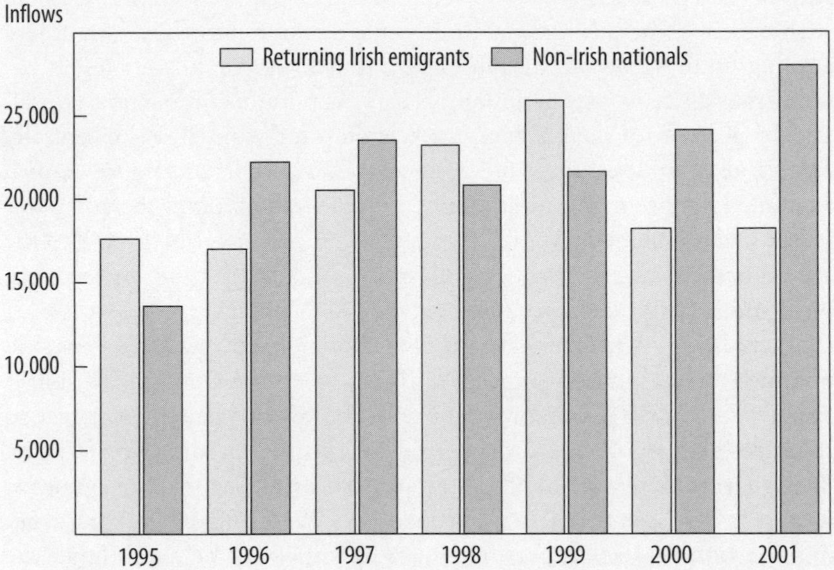

Inflows

Source: Central Statistics Office, *Population and Migration Estimates* (Dublin: Stationery Office, 2001).

few U.S. citizens moved to Ireland during this period, it is reasonable to suppose that most of the 24,431 individuals who reported the United States as their previous residence were returning Irish emigrants.

Between 1995 and 2001 the number of returnees peaked at more than 26,000 (in 1999), before falling to just over 18,000 in 2000 and 2001 (figure 9-3). Labor force survey data from the mid-1990s confirm that the returning Irish were highly educated:[7] 58 percent of those born in Ireland but not resident there in the previous 12 months had a third-level degree, whereas only 29 percent of the nonreturnees in the labor force had reached the same level. For the 30–39 age group, 50 percent of returnees had a third-level education, compared with 26 percent of the nonreturnee population. Thus returning emigrants provided a significant boost to human capital resources at a time that skill shortages were becoming more apparent.

To determine how the time spent abroad affects the productivity of returnees, Alan Barrett and Philip O'Connell estimated an earnings

7. Barrett and O'Connell (2001).

equation for the 1992 cohort of graduates.[8] Using earnings data from 1998, they found that returnees earned a 5 percent premium over those who never left. The premium differed sharply between men and women, with male returnees earning a 10 percent premium and female returnees earning no premium at all. For emigrants who seemed to have left for labor market reasons, the premium was even higher: 8 percent overall and 15 percent for men. Again, the premium for women was essentially zero (with a point estimate of –1 percent). When Barrett and O'Connell examined the premium for separate industries, they found the computer sector had the highest overall premium, at 16 percent. In contrast to the all-industry results, women actually had a higher premium in the computer industry (21 percent) than men did (11 percent).[9]

There is also evidence that returning skilled emigrants have kept skill premiums from increasing much at a time when the demand for skill is rising strongly.[10] This is consistent with the overall beneficial effect of returnees because the increased surplus to existing factors of production due to returning emigrants depends, in part, on their effect on domestic wages. It has been calculated that between 1996 and 1999, with a net immigration of 16,000 persons a year (assumed to be all skilled), the supply of skilled labor increased by 3.2 percent and skilled wages declined by 4.7 percent.[11] A standard social surplus calculation based on these estimates yields a total gain to the preexisting population of less that one-tenth of 1 percent of the skilled wage bill.[12] This calculation, however, ignores any fiscal benefits from bringing in individuals likely to make positive net fiscal contributions, any benefits from increased scale

8. Barrett and O'Connell (2001).

9. Barrett and O'Connell considered different explanations for why returnees have higher earnings than those who stay. In addition to the human capital accumulation story, they also considered the possibility that emigration is a signal of quality (positive or negative) and that it is the more able individuals (with ability unobserved by the econometrician) who choose to emigrate. Although cautious in their conclusions, they consider their results more supportive of the explanation based on human capital than on the signaling of self-selection.

10. Barrett and O'Connell (2001).

11. Barrett and others (2000).

12. Applying the standard social surplus calculation (ignoring fiscal effects and externalities) yields a small surplus gain, equal to 0.07 percent of the skilled wage bill. We can calculate the surplus gain as a share of the initial skilled wage bill as $1/2 \times \varepsilon \times (N/S)^2$, where ε is the elasticity of the skilled wage with respect to the skilled labor supply, N is the net immigration of skilled workers, and S is the initial supply of skilled workers (see Borjas 1995). The elasticity of the wage with respect to the supply of skilled labor is given by the ratio of the percentage change in the wage divided by the percentage increase in skilled labor, approximately 1.5.

or spillovers from the expanded skilled labor supply, the benefits of providing unique skills to the Irish economy, or the investment induced by larger (and cheaper) supplies of skills.[13]

Thus it appears that over the latter half of the 1990s returning Irish with augmented skills fueled the Irish economy in general, and the high-tech sector, in particular. With current evidence, it is hard to determine exactly how much the Irish economy has benefited from the resulting improvement in skill availability and cost. The Irish high-tech industry's active recruitment of citizens living abroad indicates that it had much to gain by their return home. Consider, for example, the establishment of Opportunity Ireland in 1998 by Enterprise Ireland, the agency responsible for indigenous industry development. The purpose of this new service was to highlight opportunities for expatriates in the software and electronics industries. That Opportunity Ireland has been disbanded, however, may be a sign that the pendulum is swinging once again.

As in other mistake-driven returns, emigrants in the Irish case initially expected the departure to be permanent. By contrast, some emigrants plan an eventual return, in many cases for retirement. Christian Dustman has developed a life-cycle planning model in which emigrants actually plan for a return during their *working life* and thus have the potential to generate substantial surpluses for TRBs.[14] What sort of factors would lead someone to go abroad with a firm intention of returning? Most obviously, people leave temporarily to accumulate capital—human, entrepreneurial, financial, and social. Someone hoping to set up a software business at home, for instance, might first go abroad to get an advanced degree and gain experience in a particular field, with a view to developing business ideas and confidence, accumulating start-up capital, and establishing connections and reputations. But there are other reasons for planned returns. Complementarities between consumption and home location often provide a strong incentive to return—a preference for the type of lifestyle and prestige that money can bring at home, for example. Another factor drawing people home might be the lower price of nontraded goods, which can mean that wealth

13. On the other hand, it also ignores negative spillovers from rising road congestion and increased pollution. Furthermore, it ignores any distributional effects that stem from rising housing and land prices.

14. Dustman (1996, 2001). In the later model, Dustman shows that migration durations may actually be negatively related to the wage differential. Micro data for Germany are used to provide evidence consistent with the hypothesis on the negative wage differential effect.

accumulated from high incomes in rich countries can have much greater purchasing power when brought back to poor countries.[15] In addition, people are likely to value different things at different stages in their lives, such as having foreign experiences when young but later wanting to expose their children to home-country traditions and values.

Who Returns?

Return migration is by no means infrequent. Although there is little longitudinal evidence on immigrant cohorts, figures that are available suggest that large numbers of emigrants eventually return to their home countries. A study of immigrants who moved to Sweden in 1970 found that more than half had returned to their home countries after 20 years.[16] Looking instead at long-term inflows and outflows, the U.S. Bureau for Citizenship and Immigration (formerly the Immigration and Naturalization Service) reports that between 1900 and 1990 approximately 38 million immigrants were admitted to the United States and approximately 12 million foreign-born persons emigrated, suggesting a return rate of roughly 30 percent. The bureau also reports an increase in the return rate over time.

Some estimates also exist for the rates of immigrants who came to the United States between 1970 and 1974 and between 1975 and 1980 and had left by 1980.[17] The figures were arrived at by comparing the number of legal immigrants admitted during the two periods with census estimates of both the foreign-born population present in the United States in 1980 and the breakdown of who had entered during those periods. Adjustments were made for the illegal population and legal nonpermanent residents. Considering the difficulty of making such adjustments, one must approach the results with considerable caution, although they do capture the undoubtedly great variation in the incidence of return across regions and countries, as well as the relatively high return rates after even a short period away. For the 1970 to 1974 cohort, the overall return rate was 21.5 percent. Broken down by region, return rates were 23.8 percent for Europe, 11.5 percent for Asia, 39.3 percent for Africa,

15. Thus while real incomes may fall dramatically upon return, even after correcting for a lower cost of living, overall purchasing power may be substantially higher when the purchasing power of wealth is accounted for.

16. Klinthall (2003).

17. Borjas and Bratsberg (1996).

26.0 percent for North America, 25.1 percent for South America, and 43.4 percent for Oceania.

Empirical interest in the issue of who returns appears to have focused more on how well immigrants assimilate in destination countries than on the likely contributions of returnees once they return. To see how returnee "selectivity" affects assimilation estimates, suppose that it is the least skilled that return. In this case, the average "quality" (as measured by earnings, for example) of a given immigrant cohort will tend to rise over time, giving a distorted impression of assimilation.

The limited literature on assimilation suggests that returnees are *negatively selected*. According to recent estimates for Denmark, Norway, and Sweden, the least successful emigrants, as measured by earnings and labor market attachment, tend to return.[18] A cross-country sample that provides evidence of a more subtle selectivity effect indicates that returns tend to augment the direction of the initial selectivity of the immigrant pool from a given country.[19] Suppose that immigrants from Mexico are by and large low skilled. The returnees from any given cohort will tend to be the more skilled, further lowering the skill level of a given immigrant cohort over time. On the other hand, if a country loses many of its highly skilled (India is a good example), the findings suggest that it is the less skilled from this group that are most likely to return. This implies that the most talented are likely to make their contributions—if any—to the economy of the country of origin as members of the diaspora rather than on their return.

Domestic residents who have gone abroad for high-level study are a very important class of potential returnees. In this case, the express purpose of the emigration is to acquire additional human capital. But how many foreign students eventually return? Looking at the number of doctoral recipients from U.S. universities by country of origin for 1990 and for 1999 and at the percentage of the emigrant population that has "firm plans to stay" in the United States (see table 2-11), one can use the percentage without such plans as a crude measure of the return rate.[20] Of this group, 64 percent had firm plans to stay in 1990, and the figure rose to 68 percent in 1999. In the science and engineering fields,

18. See Husted and others (2000), Longva (2001), and Edin and others (2001), respectively. A second common finding is that the probability of return decreases with time spent in the destination country.

19. Borjas and Bratsberg (1996).

20. Of course, some students without firm plans to stay will end up choosing to stay, and some of those with firm plans to stay will eventually return.

the percentage planning to stay jumped from 45 to 73 percent. For doctoral students from China and India, the percentage in science and engineering without firm plans to stay in 1999 was only around 10 percent. This is consistent with a survey of the Silicon Valley diaspora (see chapter 7) in which many of the highly educated individuals interviewed had received their highest degree in the United States.[21] It is likely that the high-tech boom in the late 1990s had something to do with this group's increased reluctance to return.[22] However, anecdotal evidence suggests that the bursting of the technology bubble and the sharp growth of offshoring has generated an increase in return rates, especially to China and India. This is to be expected, however, for, as in the case of South Korea and Taiwan in earlier years, once technology sectors take off in source-country economies, return migration of the highly skilled increases.

Nonetheless, the aforementioned studies on the negative selection effects of return migration seem to miss several critical elements in the selectivity attributes of return migrants. Although few among the highly skilled return, those who do are likely to have a utility function that places greater weight on the public good rather than private returns. Indeed, if only the latter mattered, there would be little reason to return. Furthermore, such individuals are likely to have a greater commitment to institution building, which is a nontradable public good with returns that cannot be appropriated privately. If this is true, the benefits for the country of origin may be quite substantial.

What Effects?

The impact of the highly skilled on development is just beginning to capture the attention of economists.[23] Studies to date range from econometric analysis of labor force samples to detailed interview-based research.[24] In a work on the entrepreneurial behavior of returnees to Egypt, the authors conclude:

21. Saxenian (2002).

22. Note that the return rates are somewhat high for Brazil and Mexico. Both of these countries have fairly high inequality, so that the highly skilled fare quite well in domestic labor markets. The high return rate is consistent with Borjas and Bratsberg's (1996) argument that emigration from high-inequality countries will be biased toward the low skilled and return emigration will be biased toward the high skilled.

23. Sociologists have long studied the effect of returns on receiving communities.

24. For an econometric analysis, see McCormick and Wahba (2003) and Barrett and O'Connell (2001). Ammassari's (2003) work was based on interviews.

The evidence provides a clear indication of how overseas migration to higher wage economies, for even comparatively short spells, can enable future new entrepreneurs to accumulate financial capital on a scale not otherwise possible, and to accumulate useful new skills. We find a higher rate of "entrepreneurship" amongst return migrants than in the same sample prior to international migration; relatively high education levels and longer durations overseas amongst new entrepreneurs. . . . In an econometric model of entrepreneurial activity we find evidence supporting the hypotheses that overseas savings, [and] the duration of the stay overseas, both have positive effects on becoming an entrepreneur. The economic contribution of return migrants in this sample supports the view that overseas work experience in a high wage country can play a useful role in the development process.[25]

As mentioned earlier, returning Irish emigrants have been found to be more skilled than the permanent labor force, and, after controlling for observable human capital characteristics, returning male emigrants earn a premium over their nonemigrant counterparts, though no such premium is found for female returnees.[26] Thus, at least for the men, it seems that time spent abroad does increase nonobservable human capital. Still, a positive selection explanation—the most skilled were the most likely to leave in the first place—cannot be ruled out.

Interviews exploring migration and development in West Africa reveal that while older cohorts of emigrants were more concerned with nation-building tasks, more recent cohorts are likely to create an impact through entrepreneurship.[27] In certain instances, returnees were instrumental in introducing new work practices and technologies and in stimulating investment. On the negative side, access to capital and regulatory constraints on private sector enterprise restricted the entrepreneurial efforts of returnees, as did the conflicting perspectives of the returnees and TRBs.

At one end of the returnee spectrum, exiles and diasporas have played an important part in the experiences of some of the renowned political figures of the last century who returned to transform their countries: Lenin, Gandhi, Nehru, Nkrumah, Ho Chi Minh, Kenyatta, the Young Turks, Cho En Lai. In the last few years, in Kampuchea, East

25. McCormick and Wahba (2003, p. 5).
26. Barrett and O'Connell (2001).
27. Ammassari (2003).

Timor, Afghanistan (Karzai), Palestine (Arafat and Abu Mazen), Lebanon (Hariri), and perhaps Iraq, returning elites are playing an important, if not necessarily positive, role in their societies. On an even broader scale in Jamaica—with a diaspora about as large as the island's population—there has been a recent upturn in return migration, driven by an improvement in the country's fortunes and "a perception that returning exiles can assume higher levels of responsibility at home, and at a much younger age, than they could in Britain or America."[28] And this is not only in business but also in politics, where political parties are giving returnees prominent positions because weary voters see this group as an improvement on the "often sterile, partisan pettiness" of entrenched politicians.

Similarly, many residents in industrialized countries view members of a diaspora, especially those of the professional classes, as the experts on their countries of origin. Insofar as some professional emigrants have political ambitions of their own, their interpretation of their country of origin can be designed to ingratiate themselves with the country of residence rather than as an objective analysis. Even if that is not the case, many of them have been out of touch with their countries of origin and are locked in an imagined past.

In some cases, even brief periods of exposure can have long-term influence, as illustrated by cultural exchanges, which were important channels of influence and persuasion in Soviet-American relations during the final decades of communism. Some 50,000 skilled Soviet citizens—scholars and students, scientists and engineers, writers and journalists, government and party officials, musicians, dancers, and athletes (and embedded KGB personnel)—visited the United States between 1958 and 1988 under various exchange programs, which brought an even larger number of Americans to the Soviet Union. These programs helped raise the Iron Curtain by paving the way for changes that led to Gorbachev's *glasnost* and *perestroika*, and to the end of the cold war.[29]

Millions of lower-skilled migrants, many of whom left because of economic distress or political chaos, occupy the other end of the spectrum. They either take up jobs that make little use of their human capital (as in the case of Ecuadorian graduates acting as home-care workers in Spain) or low-skilled ones that lead to a dead end (such as retail jobs in the Middle East). Although these jobs pay much better than comparable ones

28. "Bright Jamaicans Are Going Home, Which Is Good News for Their Country," *Economist,* October 11, 2003, p. 62.
29. Yale (2003).

in the country of origin, they do little to augment human capital and networks. The many domestic-care jobs that are performed by immigrants from South Asia in the Gulf or from Central America in the United States offer few opportunities for learning. However, the social effects may be more important, in that return migrations can be a powerful force for social change. Japanese women who went abroad in the 1980s and 1990s as the wives of executives involved in foreign direct investment, for example, "saw how women were treated in the West today; and many went back as silent, sometimes active revolutionaries."[30]

In some areas, such as agriculture and construction, human capital may be augmented largely through learning by doing. Many immigrants work in these sectors, frequently in seasonal jobs, which entail substantial circulation. Examples include Romanian farm labor in France, North Africans in Spain, or Mexicans in California. One might think that such movement could lead to the diffusion of agricultural technologies from the host to the source country. There is little systematic evidence that this is happening, however. Insofar as agricultural labor is migrating across ecological zones, the technologies may simply be inappropriate to the home county's soils and climates. It is also possible that there are no systematic programs to provide the complementary inputs (credit, roads, and the like) that could harness the technological skills acquired by large numbers of returning agricultural laborers.

In the case of construction, overseas Korean and Bangladeshi construction workers provide an instructive contrast. When Korea was hard hit by oil price hikes in 1973–74, it sought to earn foreign exchange to pay for the more expensive oil by sending workers to the Middle East. Domestic firms bid on construction projects in the Middle East and took Korean workers with them.[31] The project management skills learned by Korean construction firms and the new skills acquired by workers were then applied to the large construction projects in the Korean heavy and chemical industry drive of the 1970s and 1980s. By contrast, the high numbers of Bangladeshi workers currently employed in construction in Singapore are showing little sign of stimulating technological change in that sector back home despite their exposure to superior technologies.

---

30. Jagdish Bhagwati, "The Same the Whole World Over," *Times Literary Supplement,* November 8, 2002, p. 12.

31. There were 395 Koreans in the Middle East in 1974 and 162,000 in 1981, by which time about a seventh of Korean construction workers were employed in the Middle East. For a 48-hour week, they earned monthly wages of $750, and in 1981 they remitted $1.4 billion to Korea.

The return of augmented human capital is not an unequivocal blessing for the receiving country, especially if it brings someone with a criminal record to the country of citizenship. These criminals are much more experienced in the use of firearms than those at home and have substantially greater human capital in criminal technology. As a result, violent crime in many Central American countries soared following the return of these criminals.[32] Under a March 2002 agreement, Cambodia agreed to take back about 1,400 Cambodians convicted of crimes in the United States over the next decade (about 10 a month). Most of the returnees left as small children in 1979 and 1980 and have no memory of Cambodia. These criminals, many of whom were convicted of crimes in Southern California gang wars, are more proficient with sophisticated technology, and the return of such human capital to a country still recovering from three ruinous decades could prove to be disastrous.

Conclusion

Several trends can be inferred from the limited data on the return rates and characteristics of emigrants. First, return is not uncommon, though how many actually return to their countries of origin is unclear. Second, returnees from rich countries appear to have been "negatively selected" from the emigrant pool. Third, notwithstanding this negative selection, highly skilled returnees to poorer countries can play an important role in development, particularly as entrepreneurs with internationally acquired skills, ideas, savings, and contacts. Returnees have indeed played diverse economic and political roles in their country's development. The differences stem from variances in the emigrating population, the experiences in destination countries, the returning population, and home-country policies that can make use of their skills.

32. See Taylor and Aleinikoff (1998). The chapters by Christopher Mitchell and by Rafael Fernandez de Castro and Carlos Rosales in Dominguez (1998) also touch on the deportations of criminals, though their main focus is Latin American countries influencing the U.S. government on immigration policy.

10

Policy Options

Skilled individuals will continue to flow from poor to rich countries as long as massive gaps in living standards persist and the latter see advantage in buttressing their talent and taxpayer ranks. As we hope the preceding chapters have made clear, the stakes are large for both migrants and receiving countries, but especially for those remaining behind (TRBs) in sending countries. All countries, receiving and sending alike, could improve the overall balance of effects on poor countries. Given the global nature of the problem, effective policy solutions to improve the overall balance of effects on countries losing their skilled workforce will lie in a concerted effort by rich receiving and poor sending countries and the help of international organizations.

At the risk of oversimplification, we offer a four-legged typology of policy responses open to both receiving and sending countries: it centers on control, compensation, creation, and connection (see table 10-1). *Control* policies relate to efforts to directly stem skilled inflows or outflows. *Compensation* policies relate to efforts to share the often-considerable spoils of emigration with those remaining behind in poor countries. *Creation* policies focus on the implications for the human capital policies of both rich and poor countries. And *connection* policies are concerned with strengthening economically valuable diasporic interactions and increasing the possibility of capital-enhanced return.

Two caveats are in order here, however. First, as mentioned earlier, data on human capital flows are woefully inadequate when compared

Table 10-1. Policy Matrix

Policies	Instruments		
	Rich countries	Poor countries	International organizations
Control	Shift balance toward unskilled immigration Curb skill-poaching programs unless compensation schemes are in place	Curb illegal migration Improve economic and political stability	Promote economic development
Creation	Avoid shortages in areas such as health and education due to poor human capital planning Transparent mechanisms for recognition of foreign credentials	Higher education reforms Liberalize skilled immigration	Increase support for higher education
Compensation	Share social security taxes Tie development aid to skilled emigration Firms pay headhunter fees to source country	Exit tax Tax foreign income	Improve migration-related data
Connection	Encourage circulatory migration Strengthen temporary migration programs	Develop systems of IRAs for migrants Dual citizenship	Develop network infrastructure

with data on all other transnational flows in goods, services, and capital. We reiterate this point because policies cannot accord with reality unless they are backed by strong data.

Second, the importance of policies will vary significantly across countries of different population sizes. The very small countries—with populations of less than a couple of million people—simply lack the capabilities necessary to be able to retain talent in many sectors. Just as small towns in rich countries find it extremely difficult to prevent their bright young people from leaving, so too do the small states that lack a critical population mass. This means, then, that public policy priorities are best directed to *facilitate* the movement of talent from these countries to proximate larger countries and regional integration of labor markets that can help build a critical mass of human capital. At the other end of the spectrum are the giants like China and India that, on the one hand, provide the greatest numbers of skilled migrants on the global scene but, on the other hand, have such enormous bases at home that they will manage not only to cope with this loss but also to benefit from the resulting networks.

The most significant challenge for public policy lies with the many medium-sized countries of the world.[1] While their populations are large enough to sustain self-replicating human capital, their current human capital capabilities are "thin." Out-migration can further deplete this already weak pool and trigger a downward spiral as TRBs also try to move out. If weak institutions are the central cause of state failure and human capital is critical to institutional strength, the global externalities of skilled out-migration may be quite worrisome. Indeed, it is the specter of the latter that should make rich countries pay greater attention to this issue. When a Humpty Dumpty falls and cracks, just who is going to put it together again?

The crux of our argument is that developing countries can do a great deal themselves. Something they should not do, of course, is bemoan the loss of highly educated individuals even while constructing obstacles to prevent these individuals from engaging with the population at home. As for rich countries, they need to integrate policies that affect the level and nature of immigration into their broader development efforts. It makes little sense to provide funding for AIDS drugs for a poor African country and simultaneously recruit scarce doctors and nurses from that same country. On the other hand, it is hard to argue against policies that increase the "asset value" of the diaspora through enhanced connections. As the preceding chapters have shown, there is much to be gained from the establishment of global diasporic networks and the eventual return of skilled emigrants from abroad. The most controversial of policy options are those designed to compensate poor countries that are losing scarce talent so as to better share the considerable "spoils" resulting from international migration.

Policies of Rich (Receiving) Countries

Propelled by concerns for national competitiveness, rich countries are increasingly targeting mobile skilled workers through selective dismantling of immigration barriers. In principle, and to varying extents in substance, these countries have also pledged support for poor-country development. This presents them with something of a quandary, however.

---

1. We owe this observation to Alan Winters.

Although emigration can be beneficial to the source country, the absence of talented individuals—individuals who provide specialized skills, build institutions, or even simply make large fiscal contributions—is often inimical to development. How, then, should rich countries respond?

Control: Stop Targeting Scarce Talent

Should rich countries simply stop targeting poor-country talent? Even if one is sure that skilled emigration hurts the remaining population, the large income gains that often accrue to the emigrants themselves is something to consider. At the same time, pressuring rich-country governments to curb skilled immigration seems to be a questionable way to try to raise living standards of those born in developing countries.

Actually, there are better ways for the destination countries to help the source countries than by raising existing barriers.[2] But there may be times when some restraint is needed. The most obvious case is the targeting of scarce doctors, nurses, and teachers from very poor countries in the midst of health and education crises. In other words, rich countries should be sensitive to the development implications of their recruitment of scarce personnel from particularly vulnerable countries. It is one thing when this is an individual decision. It is quite another when governments promote schemes that target particularly scarce skills. As discussed in chapter 6, the loss of people with such skills—say, pediatricians or professors interested in building up world-class research and teaching departments—directly hurts those remaining behind. Yet many rich countries give special preference—and sometimes actively recruit—professionals that are in short supply domestically even though they may be in even shorter supply in the source countries. This is not to say that emigration options should be removed from doctors and teachers just because they might be particularly valuable at home. However, a policy based on development sensitivity might avoid explicit targeting or "poaching" of these types of workers.

The U.K. National Health Service (NHS) has long drawn on clinicians from overseas but lately has changed its approach somewhat, in response to requests from the government of South Africa that both the United Kingdom and Canada stop recruiting its health professionals.

---

2. There are inevitable conflicts in any set of principles that could guide migration. A basic principle is that immigration and emigration barriers are constraints on a basic freedom—the freedom to live and work where one wishes. Barriers seem especially pernicious when people want to leave a country because they no longer wish to live in it.

Instead of persuading South African medical personnel to relocate, the NHS has been using them for short-term assignments to tackle a backlog of operations.[3] Such policies allow health professionals to augment their incomes, build their skills in top-class facilities, fill particular gaps in rich-country health systems, but still keep specialized talent available to poor countries. However, while pressures have forced the public sector to shift its stance, the recruitment of health care personnel appears to have simply shifted to the private sector.

Compensation: Share the Spoils

Beyond the substantial income gains that often come from poor-to rich-country migration, skilled migrants are likely to enjoy a surplus gain in the destination country when the social value added by them exceeds their post-tax earnings.[4] These gains suggest that it should be possible to at least partly compensate the source country for the loss of scarce talent.

DIRECT COMPENSATION. Where the loss to the poor country is highly apparent, the rich country could pay direct compensation. To take an extreme example, suppose that a public hospital in a rich country has recruited a doctor from a poor African country or that a private hospital recruits a nurse. In this case, the government or private agency could be asked to pay a fee similar to that charged by "headhunters" in rich countries, equivalent to a few months' pay. Although the monetary compensation could be paid directly to governments, it would probably have a greater payoff if transferred directly to the institutions losing their staff—universities, hospitals, and the like.

TAX SHARING. At a time of fiscal deficits and large unfunded liabilities in social security systems, it may seem fanciful to suggest that rich countries share tax revenues with poor countries. Indeed, as noted in chapter 4, fiscal problems will undoubtedly be a driving force behind skill-focused immigration reforms. But if the development agendas of rich countries are to be something more than empty rhetoric, the potential damage done by skill-focused recruitment must be recognized. Perhaps it is not

3. Under the Netcare program, surgeons from South Africa travel to the United Kingdom to conduct operations ranging from cataract removal to hip and knee replacement. The South African team is integrated into the existing hospital service and subject to the same supervision as local medical staff. The doctors even plan to fly back for the six-week checkups and 12-month follow-up appointments. See "Overseas Medics Tackle Ops Backlog" (http://news.bbc.co.uk/2/hi/uk_news/england/2778059.stm).

4. Any additional public expenditure on the migrant is here treated as a negative tax.

wishful thinking to hope that a share of revenues raised from emigrants would be remitted to source-country governments, possibly in recognition of the human capital investments funded by that government.

Of course, the relevance of such tax sharing depends on whether poor-country emigrants are sizable contributors to rich-country tax systems. In the United States, estimates of tax payments based on the Current Population Survey reveal that the foreign-born—both foreign-born U.S. citizens and (more interestingly) foreign-born non-U.S. citizens—are major contributors to tax revenues. In the year 2000, foreign-born citizens and noncitizens paid an estimated $17.6 and $18.7 billion in Social Security (or Federal Insurance Contributions Act) contributions, respectively. These payments amounted to roughly 5.5 percent and 6.0 percent of total Social Security taxes. Income tax payments by the foreign-born are even higher—$43.4 billion for citizens and $31.8 billion for noncitizens—though the share in total payments is lower than for the payroll taxes, at 4.4 percent and 3.2 percent, respectively. Looking at developing countries alone, the contributions are still large:[5] $28.4 billion in Social Security taxes ($13.9 billion by citizens and $14.5 billion by noncitizens) and $52.3 billion in income taxes ($31.9 billion by citizens and $20.4 billion by noncitizens).

The most obvious scope for tax sharing lies in the Social Security taxes paid by temporary migrants, but this possibility is currently hampered by the absence of "totalization" agreements between developing and industrialized countries. Thus while H1-B visas are valid for a maximum of 6 years in the United States, eligibility for Social Security benefits requires contributions over 40 quarters, which means a minimum of 10 years (immigrants who stay that long are very unlikely to return). Totalization agreements essentially eliminate dual Social Security taxation and fill gaps in benefit protection for workers who have divided their careers between countries. They specify both taxes paid and benefits foreign citizens can receive when working in a treaty country. Since the late 1970s, the United States has entered into international social security agreements with 20 countries, all members of the Organization for Economic Cooperation and Development (OECD) with one exception, Chile. Most developing countries lack "comparable" social security systems.

SHARED VISA FEES/VISA AUCTION RECEIPTS. The foregoing compensation methods have placed the burden directly on destination-country governments. As

5. Developing countries are defined here as all countries except the OECD economies and the transition economies of Eastern Europe.

noted earlier, however, it is the emigrant who obtains much of the migration-related gain. The rich country could capture this gain and send the proceeds—or at least a share of those proceeds—to the source-country government. Possibilities for such capture and return include setting high fees for visas and sharing the proceeds with the source country, or even auctioning visas and sharing the auction revenues.

As an illustration of the spoils at issue, suppose (conservatively) that a move results in a $5,000 annual income gain after adjusting for purchasing power parity. At a discount rate of 10 percent, a 20-year work horizon, and no adjustment for wage inflation, the present value of the income gain is almost $47,000 dollars. The point here is not to argue for massive visa fees, but simply to note that the gains from long-term access to a rich-country labor market can be very large. If anything, this example greatly underestimates the size of the long-term gain. Others would place the average purchasing power parity adjusted income gain at more than $20,000.[6]

Creation: Invest More in Domestic Human Capital (and Use That from Poor Countries Wisely)

Rich-country demand for poor-country talent is often the result of the former's inadequate investment in needed skills. Governments laboring under large budget deficits tend to underinvest in the training of doctors, nurses, and teachers—especially when the benefits of these investments are not realized until years later. Hence there can be an almost perpetual shortage of professionals to staff key public services and an ongoing "crisis"-driven recruitment of foreign professionals. As countries get richer, it also becomes harder to entice young people to pursue demanding (and not always glamorous) careers in science and engineering. The resulting shortage—and cost—of technically skilled graduates fuels competitiveness-driven lobbying to ease immigration restrictions for foreign-trained scientists and engineers. Rich countries facing systemic shortages of key human capital defend their foreign recruitment by inevitably pointing to pressing domestic shortages. When such crises recur, however, the solution should be to increase investments in domestic capabilities, rather than simply poach from poor countries.

A common complaint of highly skilled immigrants is that their credentials are often not recognized when they arrive in rich countries. This indicates a large gap between skill-focused immigrant recruitment policies

---

6. Jasso, Rosenweig, and Smith (2002).

and policies regarding efficient use of those skills after arrival. It is often said that a "brain drain" is better than a "brain in the drain," alluding to the idea that staying behind would simply amount to wasting one's talents. While this is sometimes true, so is the converse: many skilled developing-country nationals find themselves shut out of the labor market because their credentials are not recognized abroad. Although it is obviously necessary to regulate credentials, a case can also be made for streamlining needlessly cumbersome procedures. With greater recognition, emigrants can expect higher incomes and the opportunity to work in their chosen occupations in destination countries—and thus to assimilate more easily.

As noted in chapter 5, the improved *prospect* of gaining a visa could increase the expected return to education and possibly the amount of human capital available to the source country. For this to happen, the loss of human capital through emigration would have to be outweighed by the emigration-prospect-induced increase in the human capital of those who ultimately do not get to (or choose not to) go. Greater recognition of foreign credentials by rich countries will increase the return on domestically acquired human capital, thus potentially strengthening this effect.[7] In any case, if rich countries are going to recruit poor-country talent to make up for domestic shortages, they should ensure that everything possible is done so that talent is not wasted when it arrives.

Connection: Remove Barriers to Temporary Migration and Leverage the Diaspora

Although losses that stem from absent talent are indeed a major concern, the diaspora can be a valuable asset to the source country, not only as a potential source and facilitator of international business but also as a potential incubator of returnee talent and enterprise. These international connections can be valuable to the destination country as well.

What might the destination countries do to increase the value of this asset? The two obvious answers are, enhance *temporary* skilled migration and, where it is permanent, decrease the emigrant's cost of interacting and transacting with the home country. In the latter case, immigration restrictions, such as requirements that new visas be issued to reenter the country after a trip home, clearly limit interactions.

7. Of course, it is also possible that the increased recognition of credentials will hurt TRBs. This will happen if the higher human capital levels of those who ultimately choose to stay do not offset the resulting higher emigration rate.

Although temporary skilled migration produces the most significant gains, this solution has two major drawbacks. First, it is not easy to make economic migrants return home. The cliché that there is nothing more permanent than a temporary migrant captures well the fact that foreign workers and their families are often loath to return once established in a community. Some would also question the fairness of forcing people to return home. Others would say there is nothing wrong with enforcing the terms of the initial contract if migrants know from the outset that they have permission to stay for only a temporary period.

While there are indeed numerous examples of temporary migration programs that have not worked, such arrangements are much more feasible in the case of skilled migrants. However, destination-country policies remain a large obstacle. Limits on the portability of social security entitlements can make it costly to return home permanently. If returnees have to give up hard-won permanent residency status, which can happen if they return to their country of origin for more than a year, they will be reluctant to take a chance on returning home. This is a severe deterrent even to skilled migrants who want to try to go back to the country of origin, since they would lose the "option value" of returning to the rich country if things do not work out back home. A year is simply too short a time to find out if things are working out. Of course a migrant who has obtained citizenship is in a better position to take the risk, although by that time roots in the new country are so much deeper that the likelihood of returning decreases correspondingly.

The need to encourage the return of talent is particularly obvious in the case of weak and so-called failed states. The fiscal challenge of rebuilding these states is enormous and the legitimacy of the enterprise questionable when done by outsiders. Returning talent would address some of these problems, but sharp differences between private and social returns are a severe damper. Policies that would offer stronger guarantees on return would ease such concerns.[8] One controversial way to increase the return flow is to make visas temporary and place limits on renewal. For example, a country might make it easy to obtain a student visa but hard to obtain a work visa after an individual's studies are

8. One option would be that proposed by Senator Joseph Biden, who in November 2003 introduced the "Return of Talent" Act (S. 1949), which would allow legal aliens resident in the United States to return temporarily to their country of citizenship if that country is engaged in postconflict reconstruction, and for other purposes. Immigrants would not be penalized for returning to the country of origin to help with reconstruction, and the time spent in their country of origin would apply toward their five-year residency requirement.

completed. Alternatively, the barriers to transition from a time-limited work visa to permanent residency could be made more onerous. The idea behind such a policy is to enable migrants to build skills, savings, and social networks while in the country, but eventually make them bring these different forms of capital home. Knowing that they will eventually have to return home, people will choose to form the kind of capital that is most productive there.[10]

Temporary migration has worked in practice, but mainly in countries with less liberal regimes, ranging from the Middle East to Malaysia. Furthermore, virtually all temporary migration programs have been designed to bring in *less*-skilled workers. Skilled workers are much less likely to stay on illegally, but such programs can work only if receiving countries themselves change their practices. Granting skilled workers on temporary work programs social security numbers of limited duration can make the program self-enforcing. Temporary skilled programs are undermined by expedient receiving country policies as much as anything. Recently, Canada began offering a new "contract" to temporary skilled workers, granting them permanent status in the country at the end of the three- to five-year contract if they agreed to restrict their mobility rights and settle somewhere other than Toronto, Vancouver, or Montreal. Any such contracts should also ensure that foreign labor is not driven underground through artificial distinctions between foreign and domestic workers. In 1993 South Korea, long an exporter of labor, allowed Korean employers to hire foreign workers through a trainee system (by 2002, admissions had increased to 85,000 a year). Trainees, however, receive only about half of the minimum wage and are bound to their assigned employer, with the result that many abandon their jobs because they can earn more money as illegal workers. Although there is a strong case to treat these trainees as guest workers with the same rights as Korean workers, so as to ensure that local Korean labor does not lose out because of the minimal pay at which their counterparts are willing to work, employers oppose it, as it would increase their labor costs.

In the 1970s, the United States created the J-1 visa program for skilled personnel, especially from developing countries. This allowed foreign doctors and scientists to come to the country, augment their human capital, contribute relatively low-cost labor, and return home. One participant in the program, the National Institutes of Health (NIH), provides postdoctoral opportunities for foreign scientists, on the understanding that the scientists will return and set up or work in laboratories in their country of origin. These programs permit the transfer of medical expertise, and they increase the number of developing-country institutions that can collaborate with U.S. scientists. The program's intent, however, was subverted when state and local governments, unable to persuade many U.S. physicians to work in underserved areas afflicted by physician shortages, began to turn to noncitizens who had just completed their graduate medical education in the United States. These physicians generally enter the United States under an exchange visitor program with J-1 visas, which require them to return to their home country (or to their country of last legal residence) for at least two years after completing their training. However, this requirement can be waived at the request of a federal agency or a state, usually on the condition that the physician practice for a specified period in an underserved area. A General Accounting Office study found that the number of such waivers for physicians rose from 70 in 1990 to more than 1,374 in 1995. By the mid-1990s (the most recent period for which data are available), the number of waivers processed equaled about one-third of the total identified need for physicians in the country. Here is a visa program created to pass advanced medical knowledge to other countries. Instead, "the use of waivers for physicians with J-1 visa requirements has become so extensive that this exception policy now resembles a full-fledged program for addressing medical underservice in the United States."[9]

Rather than rely on temporary visas that eventually force people to return home, it is more beneficial to create incentives that make them *want* to return home. Acquired pension benefits could be made portable, for example, and a part of them vested in the country of origin if the migrant did not return. Skilled temporary migrants in the United States are often tempted to stay on longer, knowing they will lose their Social Security contributions unless they have worked for 40 quarters. However, that period of time is so long that the migrant will inevitably develop deep roots locally and find it harder to return.

The Bush administration's recent proposals for a large temporary visa program include both a carrot (access to funds in accumulating accounts upon return) and a stick (time-limited visas). Parallels exist elsewhere. In South Africa, where nearly 50 percent of miners are migrants, mainly from Mozambique and Lesotho, they are required to participate in the Compulsory Deferred Pay system, which sends a portion of their wages to banks in their native countries. The sending and receiving countries

9. GAO (1996).

have a labor migration agreement in which the receiving country protects the rights of the legal migrant workers while the sending country takes steps to check illegal migration. However, the case of Mozambican guest workers in East Germany who were returned after 1990 shows that such arrangements are not without risks. Between 1982 and 1990, the East German government transferred $93 million, including $18 million in social insurance payments, to the Mozambican Labor Ministry. But the workers did not receive the money, possibly owing to the government's dire fiscal state. Similarly, the Mexican government did not pass on benefits accruing to temporary labor working in the United States during the 1950s.

A different tactic might be to make it easier to come to the (receiving) country legally, so that illegal immigrants already there (and who want to return) do not view leaving as giving up the option of living in the country. Return migration is often stymied because policies that raise barriers to circulatory migration also reduce return. Thus when the United States increased strict policing on the Mexican border in the 1980s, it increased permanent settlement in the country by sharply increasing the risk of going back and forth. Similarly, permanent residents ("green card" holders) who face the forfeiture of their status if they leave the country for more than one year are less likely to return to their countries of origin to try to work there. By taking away the option value of a green card, such a policy reduces the probability of migrants' returning. Lengthening that period from one to three years would increase circulatory migration as well as permanent return.

Policies of Poor (Source) Countries

What policies are open to developing countries seeking a better return on the various forms of capital carried by their nationals? The options again fall under the headings of control, compensation, creation, and connection. In this case, however, *control* means various barriers to exit. *Compensation* consists of a menu of obligations that emigrants might be seen to owe to their former homes in return for continuing citizenship or other privileges. *Creation* now refers broadly to policies to create and retain domestic human capital.[10] And *connection* pertains to home-country policies that help build an effective diaspora and entice return.

10. In an early discussion of the manuscript, these exhortations elicited the criticism that we were being utopian in our policy suggestions. Perhaps. But if institutional failures are compounded by an induced brain drain, then we hope that drawing attention to this added source of damage can induce policy change.

Control: Keeping Talent

It seems pernicious to prevent people from leaving a country in which they no longer wish to live. Although emigration barriers are now seen as constraints on a basic freedom—the freedom to live and work where one wishes, this has not always been the case. In the early nineteenth century, in an effort to thwart French and Russian efforts to recruit its skilled workers, Britain sharply limited their emigration. Emigrant workers who failed to return home within six months of warning could lose their land, property, and even citizenship.

More recent restrictions imposed by authoritarian governments to control emigration of their citizens have been protested by Western governments. When U.S. president Jimmy Carter met with Deng Xiaoping in 1979, he reminded the Chinese leader that U.S. law forbade granting most favored nation status to any country that did not embrace free-market principles and prevented its citizens from emigrating freely. Deng reportedly responded, "How many millions of Chinese does the United States want?" Liberal indignation at the idea and reality of a Berlin Wall reflects the belief that exit should be a matter of individual choice. But there is noticeable reticence when it comes to the "New Berlin Walls" and great irony in the fact that more people have died at the Mexican-U.S. border than did at the Berlin Wall. If nations have the right to limit *entry* because of its impact on the common national good and the preference of their citizens, why is that acceptable but the right to free *exit* is not? Both cases can be viewed as a tragedy of the commons—in that what is individually optimal may be socially suboptimal.

However, even if it could be argued that poor countries should have stronger control policies (whatever the precise mix), desirability is not the same as feasibility. The history of development is replete with examples of well-intentioned administrative controls degenerating into rent seeking. Barriers to movement infringe on both freedom and efficiency. Consequently, not much of a case can be made for explicit barriers to exit (other that those considered a security threat).

Compensation: Taking a Share of the Spoils

The control policies that we would dismiss are outright prohibitions on exit common under totalitarian systems. What about policies that impose financial burdens on exit or continuing financial obligations on emigrants, which also construct a barrier to leaving? Although ethical and practical problems exist here, too, these are *potentially* legitimate responses by poor-country governments insofar as they change incentives rather than impose outright prohibitions. Their appeal is threefold: they can curb the loss of talent without actually preventing people from leaving; they provide greater freedom in the design of the domestic tax and public sector compensation systems; and they create a fair system, in that when people actually do leave they share their private gains with TRBs to compensate for the investments of public resources.

Fiscal Options

Among the fiscal options that might reap considerable dividends in developing countries are taxation regimes.[11] Three such regimes are examined here: the American model, a cooperative regime for tax sharing, and an exit tax on accumulated human capital. Which regime is most desirable depends on implementation capacity, the implications for infringements on freedom of movement, the impact on TRBs, the revenue potential, and the ability to deal with flows of emigrants and pre-existing stocks of previous emigrants abroad.

THE AMERICAN MODEL. Under a tax system along the lines of the American model, the basis of taxation would have to change from residency to citizenship for most countries, and compliance would be required from citizens residing abroad. The American model has several advantages over other alternatives. It is the most comprehensive system for taxing the ongoing labor income of individuals with high human capital that are globally mobile. Given the obvious possibility of liquidity constraints at the time of emigration, ongoing taxation would better match the burden of taxation with the actual income streams of individuals. Moreover, the use of exclusions and credits would allow for those with lower human capital to be effectively exempt from the system. By matching the actual incomes with tax payments and by not creating a barrier at the time of emigration, such a system might also be politically appealing, in contrast to one-time departure taxes. Finally, for countries that already have large stocks of citizens abroad, only the American model offers the potential of tapping into those labor income streams. Effectively enforced, the American model may offer the largest ultimate gains to countries whose immigrants have high human capital.

Arguments against the American model typically center on its enforcement and compliance costs. For developing countries that find

11. This sections draws heavily on Desai, Kapur, and McHale (2004). We are indebted to Mihir Desai for his expertise on international taxation issues. Our understanding of the options of such taxation owes a great deal to the analysis and advocacy of Jagdish Bhagwati. See, for example, the papers in Bhagwati and Wilson (1989).

managing an individual tax base *domestically* problematic enough, the thought of enforcing the American model may be unimaginable. While the enforcement and compliance costs of the American model may be higher than for an exit tax, the technology now available to track citizens suggests that these costs may not be as overwhelming as previously thought.[12] Moreover, as American experience indicates, firms are sometimes willing to bear the vast majority of compliance costs under the American model. A similar practice could conceivably evolve with emigrants from developing countries if hiring firms could shield individuals from the tax differences and the compliance costs imposed by such a system. Indeed, many of the multinational firms hiring skilled workers from developing countries are already well versed in the complexities of the American model.[13]

Another problem in applying the American model is that it requires precise estimates of the distribution of earnings for citizens abroad; otherwise revenue might be limited by overly generous exemptions or credits. In addition, since many citizens of rich countries working overseas have the incentive to remain tax compliant because of their intention to return home, the trade-off for developing countries is that their nationals may give up their citizenship if the "price of citizenship" is set too high. According to one estimate of the revenue consequences of instituting the American model in India, even with quite conservative assumptions, India would gain about a half billion dollars annually.[14] This equals about 10 percent of the country's individual income tax base and a fifth of its tertiary education budget.

A COOPERATIVE REGIME FOR TAX SHARING. Under a cooperative regime, payroll and income taxes paid by a country's emigrants could be collected by host countries and shared with developing home countries. For example, a share of payroll taxes contributed by temporary migrants to a host country would be returned to the home country via a governmental

---

12. The GAO (1998, 2000) reviews noncompliance issues for citizens residing abroad and for expatriates. The U.S. experience suggests that compliance problems are much greater for expatriates than for citizens living abroad.

13. On the other hand, smaller firms hiring immigrant and nonimmigrant workers might be less willing to bear the compliance costs. A firm hiring workers from different parts of the world would have to deal with multiple taxing authorities without the informational advantage of having a presence in those countries. Moreover, many of the firms hiring migrants will be small compared with the multinationals that send nationals overseas and thus might have less administrative capacity to deal with complex international tax issues.

14. Desai, Kapur, and McHale (2003).

transfer. Such a regime has the potential to generate considerable and immediate revenue for developing countries. Efficient administration on the part of developed countries would increase its effectiveness. Furthermore, the system would have minimal repercussions on the behavior of the labor flows of developing countries and thus would not impinge on the free movement of labor.

Such a regime would, however, require a web of bilateral treaties or the creation of a multilateral institution to manage these transfers. Moreover, developed countries would have to voluntarily return some of the tax revenue from immigration just when they would be facing tremendous fiscal pressures from an aging population. OECD economies have found it difficult enough to reach an international agreement on how to deal with tax havens, let alone tax-sharing proposals. Two trends, however, suggest that tax sharing may eventually work. First, it is conceivable that increased competition for the world's supply of skilled labor, combined with greater reluctance to allow talented individuals of poor countries to leave without some form of compensation, will induce pairs of countries to enter into bilateral tax-sharing agreements. Second, the preference of industrialized countries for temporary immigrants means that tax-sharing arrangements can serve as an incentive to ensure that migrants return. Even objections to portable pensions may eventually subside, if a proposal by former senator Phil Gramm for Mexican workers in the United States is any indication. The Gramm proposal would allow them to work in the United States on an annual or seasonal basis, with enrollment flexibly adjusted to U.S. economic conditions. Recognizing that "the current 15.3 percent payroll tax paid by illegal aliens and their employers produces no benefits for the illegal workers," the proposal would allow the payroll tax to be used to fund emergency medical care for the temporary migrants and an IRA account owned by the individual worker, which could be withdrawn only when the worker leaves the program and returns to Mexico.[15] The Gramm proposal portends the importance of reconciling the social security needs of temporary migrants from developing countries with the domestic payroll tax provisions of developed countries.

AN EXIT TAX ON ACCUMULATED HUMAN CAPITAL. Current exit taxes on emigration or expatriation are almost all designed to prevent wealthy individuals from escaping capital gains or estate taxation. For developing countries, however, the issue is how to deal with individuals who have high human

15. See www.senate.gov/~gramm/press/guestprogram.html.

capital but may otherwise be liquidity constrained. Nonetheless, an appropriately administered exit tax might usefully raise significant amounts of revenue with a limited administrative burden.

An exit tax on human capital could take several forms. First, and most simply, any emigrant, or possibly the firm hiring that emigrant, could be forced to pay a flat sum to the home country. More complex variations of this mechanism would index that tax payment to some measure of human capital. Exit taxes could be considered the equivalent of headhunter fees and, assuming the deductibility of such payments, would translate into a modest after-tax cost to the hiring firm. Indeed, an analogue to this fee is the filing fees paid by firms sponsoring people for temporary work visas, with the fees used for scholarships for low-income individuals and for workforce training. A potential exit tax paid by a sponsoring firm to the source country would have the same distributional rationale.

Such an exit tax could also be seen as an unacceptable infringement on the freedom of international movement. A politically more palatable alternative would be to replace existing state funding of tertiary education with a system of forgivable loans. The loans would be forgiven on the condition that the individual works in the domestic economy after graduation but would become payable if the individual emigrated. To increase compliance, the issuance and renewal of a passport could be made conditional on loans being in good standing. To increase flexibility, such loans could be indexed to the duration of stay for graduates of institutions of higher learning so that those leaving immediately after graduation would pay the full amount while graduates who spent more time working in their home countries would pay less. Alternatively, more elaborate defeasance schemes could be designed to spur temporary stays abroad and encourage graduates to return, thereby maximizing the gains to the source country of work experience abroad.

While such a conditional exit charge does restrict freedom of movement, advance notice of it when education was initiated would seem to obviate concerns about the restriction of movement. Though politically appealing, a loan forgiveness scheme may be formidable to implement. Tracking individuals for repayment of loans to educational institutions could be extremely cumbersome, and in any case it might be possible to circumvent conditional charges through political connections. In addition, human capital flows often are associated with education and not employment, so taxing them at the initial exit stage could jeopardize a mechanism critical to augmenting human capital. Recent U.S.

experience with student loan defaults suggests that greater effort and increased use of information technology could significantly improve repayment rates and hence that such schemes are not completely quixotic.[16] The experience of Singapore is also instructive in this regard, though few countries have the administrative capacity and political will to replicate its experience.

The legitimacy of policies such as exit taxes or the taxing of foreign income can be established in different ways. Most obviously, foreign earnings may be considered partly a return on human capital that was funded by the source country government. Also, citizenship can be said to provide obligations as well as rights. It is arguably fair to impose tax obligations in return for continuing citizenship—although the strength of that claim depends on the precise rights that the overseas citizen actually has, not least the right to vote in domestic elections.

Putting aside questions of legitimacy and enforceability, is the potential emigrant tax base large enough to be of much practical significance? Clearly, considerable sums can be at stake, as is evident in the case of the Indian-born population residing in the United States. As discussed in chapter 2, this population is very well educated and is top-heavy with high earners. Although it applies to a little more than 2 percent of the tertiary-educated Indian stock and around 0.1 percent of the total Indian population, the total Indian-born income is roughly $40 billion, or about 10 percent of Indian GDP.[17] This income pool is huge because emigrants to the United States are positively selected (that is, graduates of the best Indian schools are heavily overrepresented), and the dollar income gains (nonpurchasing power parity adjusted) upon emigration are very large. Of course, in salivating about this income pool, one should not forget that these individuals must also pay U.S. taxes. Although they should not be made to bear an unjust burden, it does seem legitimate to ask if the home country is entitled to some share of the spoils, preferably in the context of tax forbearance by the destination-country government and recognized as explicit compensation for past investments or ongoing privileges.

In recognizing that legitimate and enforceable ongoing taxation must be a quid pro quo for privileges granted, one can also entertain the possibility of dual nationality. To retain links with their diasporas, many developing countries have already enacted policies on dual nationality

16. For a discussion of improved performance regarding default rates on federal student loans in the United States, see GAO (2003).

17. This analysis is based on 2000–01 data.

and dual citizenship (the latter allowing for greater political rights compared with the former).

Dual Nationality

In the past, countries were suspicious about dual nationality, on the grounds that this would lead to dual loyalties and conflict of interest. However, for a variety of reasons—the economic advantages, the sheer size of the migration, and the domestic political clout of households and social groups from which the diaspora is drawn—attitudes have changed over the past two decades. Liberal democracies around the globe are beginning to tolerate—though not yet embrace—dual nationality, for example, by not trying to reduce the incidence of dual citizenship through such means as sharing naturalization information.[18] However, immigrants and sending countries are more enthusiastic about the positive benefits of dual nationality than receiving countries are.

The rights and requirements of dual nationality vary across countries, although in general dual nationality does not necessarily entail access to all the rights and benefits of national citizenship (such as voting). Dual nationality regimes may be classified as open, tolerant, or restrictive. Open regimes (such as those of Canada, France, and the United Kingdom) follow *jus soli*—citizenship by place of birth—which confers dual nationality on children born in their territory whose parents are noncitizens. These systems do not require selection of one nationality; citizens may naturalize elsewhere without forfeiting citizenship, and naturalizing citizens do not renounce prior citizenships. Tolerant regimes also follow *jus soli*, permitting dual nationality at birth, with some but not all the characteristics of open regimes. Examples include Australia, Germany, Israel, Mexico, South Africa, and the United States. Restrictive regimes, on the other hand, follow *jus sanguinis,* wherein a person's citizenship is determined by that of his or her parents (that is, by blood ties), which limits the possibilities for dual nationality. These countries, including Austria and Japan, are quite strict about requirements and limitations of nationality.

There is as yet little systematic evidence on the implications of dual nationality for immigrants or for sending and receiving countries. Immigrants generally support their country of origin's recognition of dual nationality—it has an "option value" for them. Dual nationality makes

18. As of 2001, dual nationality was fully recognized by 27 percent of countries (of 159 countries for which data were available) and recognized under special circumstances by another 42 percent, while the remaining 31 percent of countries did not recognize it (Bertocchi and Strozzi, 2004).

it easier to remain in their new countries of residence and exercise political rights, while forfeiting little from their status in their home country. Indeed, by having rights in multiple jurisdictions but obligations in one, be it taxes or military service, dual nationality can make it possible for international migrants to have their cake and eat it too.

Sending countries have come around to viewing dual nationality in a positive light, believing that it helps foster ties between expatriates and countries of origin. These stronger ties, they hope, will pay off in terms of current remittances and future investments. Dual nationality also allows nationals to mobilize as a lobbying group in receiving countries around issues of concern to the sending country. If granted voting rights, it can imply representation without taxation, giving expatriates leverage in domestic politics without any de jure obligations. Receiving countries are understandably more suspicious of dual nationality, fearing it may undermine national sovereignty and singular loyalty. Regardless of these concerns, most countries are becoming less intolerant of dual nationality, and many allow citizens to passively retain citizenship rights in another country even if that country does not recognize, or is indifferent to, the new attachment.

Latin America clearly exemplifies the global movement toward acceptance of dual nationality. The acceleration of interest in dual nationality in the region had been instigated in part by country-of-origin governments (top-down) and in part by pressure from their overseas migrant communities (bottom-up). Dual nationality has existed for a while in El Salvador, Panama, Peru, and Uruguay, put into place through top-down policy changes. This has also been the case more recently in Brazil and Costa Rica. On the other hand, pressures from expatriate communities contributed to policy shifts in Colombia, the Dominican Republic, Ecuador, and Mexico. Three factors explain this policy shift: the sheer growth in the size of migrant communities abroad; the concomitant massive increase in remittance inflows (see chapter 8), along with recurrent balance of payments problems in the region (money does talk); and a shift in the attitude of the United States (where many of the migrants have concentrated), which has taken a "Don't ask, don't tell" policy stance that has made it easier for migrants to avoid binary choices.

The increasing political salience of dual nationality in domestic politics is clearly evident in the Dominican Republic. This Caribbean nation of about 8.5 million people has more than a million migrants in the United States, concentrated in New York and Miami. If born in the Dominican Republic, they retain dual citizenship and can vote in

Dominican elections. Before 2004, Dominicans could only vote within the country. This meant that only the wealthy expatriates who could afford to send money back to fund campaigns or fly home to vote could effectively take part in the political process. In 2004 the Dominican Republic introduced "remote voting," allowing Dominicans to vote overseas in "booths" in select restaurants, salons, even taxi companies. Now, citizens are simply required to bring their "cédula"—a photo ID issued in the Dominican Republic—to the "local" voting booths on election day, where their votes will be e-mailed back to the island. With the advent of remote voting, dual nationality has taken on a more significant role and is likely to encourage expatriates to maintain closer and more lasting ties with homeland politics.

Like developing countries, industrialized nations have begun constructing more expansive citizenship laws, in their case to address economic problems associated with demographic pressures. To this end, some have adopted a more liberal interpretation of *jus soli*. In January 2003, Spain, for example, approved a new law that allows Spanish women to claim citizenship for children over 21 years old born out of Spain and allows foreigners with Spanish relatives to apply to live in Spain without having a work visa. As a result, over a million foreigners, primarily in Latin America, are expected to apply to migrate to Spain, including 400,000 from Argentina.

Creating (and Retaining) Human Capital

It is far more important to try to address the reasons why talent leaves—be it a mismatch between supply and demand, a lengthy recruitment process to find a job, poor working conditions, low salaries, poor quality of life, or a lack of confidence in the country's future. In many developing countries, abject political management, which leads to the deep economic crises that spark an exodus of already scarce talent, is not uncommon. Countries such as Haiti or Zimbabwe epitomize this phenomenon.

As talent becomes more globally mobile, its bargaining power increases. Developing countries have little choice but to adapt to this reality. It would be easy to argue that simply stark differences in salaries and standards of living are what drive human capital to developed countries. Although certainly an important factor, this is but one of many. Weaknesses in higher education are critical too, especially because they affect the quality of training of future generations in these countries.

Most developing countries have put little effort into reforming higher education, which continues to be plagued by misguided attempts at equity, poor administration, and bureaucratization. Quantitative inputs are used to monitor education systems, with little more than lip service being paid to the quality of output. Substantial amounts of money are wasted on unviable institutions, while those that were once well run have atrophied. The lack of institutional autonomy and poor academic governance makes it difficult for higher education to attract talent, especially if that talent has other alternatives. As individuals at the upper end of human capital distribution leave, the quality of the remaining pool declines even further. This not only prompts the more talented to consider leaving but also discourages those who left earlier from returning, ensuring that mediocrity will become entrenched in these institutions.

It is not only salaries but also the environment that needs drastic change to instill the idea that performance rather than process matters, that appointments should be depoliticized, that higher education is a privilege rather than a right, and that institutions should adapt and change to reflect newer challenges. Although the scarcity of resources is an undoubted constraint, more flexible rules, access to modest research resources, and a work environment that encourages innovative practices and research—all within the capacity of many middle-income developing countries—could achieve much. What often stands in the way is the domestic political economy. A country like Pakistan, in which former army officers run universities, is unlikely to create an environment conducive to this kind of innovation.

The problems in higher education have been exacerbated by the analyses and actions of the international development community. Education expenditures were skewed in favor of higher education, and because elites were more likely to be enrolled in degree programs, this funding was rightly viewed as a regressive income transfer. However, and wrongly in our view, this was also seen as the reason for diverting much-needed resources for primary and secondary education for the masses. As resources for higher education were cut back, and costs rose even as quality deteriorated, elites began sending their children abroad. The exit of elites from higher education undoubtedly renders subsidies less regressive, but it also mutes the voice of those who had the power to pressurize the system and demand quality. The public cost savings have been much less than the substantially higher private expenditures abroad. Before jumping to the conclusion that there is a distinction between private and public sector expenditures, one must recognize that paying large amounts for the education of children is an easy way to launder ill-gotten wealth.

Higher education has seen the most limited reforms in most countries, reflecting the strength of entrenched interests in this sector. Fiscal pressures and growing demand-supply imbalances have led to an enormous growth in private sector higher education, more by default than by design. Even as countries rail against privatization and refuse to raise tuition in public institutions, mediocre commercial educational institutions have sprung up to meet pent-up demand. This has created a new set of problems, in that the latter often consist of little more than profit-maximizing operations, rather than institutions that can serve the public good and enhance public welfare.

Developing countries also inflict self-imposed costs by treating skilled workers coming in more strictly than developed countries do. Countries in East Africa, for instance, threw out talented ethnic minorities in the 1960s. Even as they wring their hands at the cost of producing a medical graduate, many developing countries do everything to block the entry of skilled immigrants who may want to work, on the grounds that they will take away local jobs. Instead of seeing skilled labor as a complementary input, they view it as a substitute. Prompted by a false sense of nationalism, many developing countries refuse to recognize foreign degrees of countries that do not engage in a reciprocal recognition. This is especially true for disciplines such as law, medicine, and accounting. There can be no doubt that a severe imbalance exists in the supply and demand of talented people wanting to work in developed countries compared with those wanting to work in developing countries. Developing countries, in particular, have to realize that skills are a global commodity, and wealthy countries will do whatever is necessary to maintain their national interests. Some countries insist that companies train local staff as the price for bringing in a skilled immigrant. This works in some cases, but in others, the skills required include advanced education and experience rather than a few months of in-house training. Of course, expatriate staff is much more expensive than locals are—and a competitive environment will do much more to persuade firms to hire locals than policies with domestic content.

However, programs to retain talent must be designed in such a way as to prevent the distortion of incentives among a country's citizens. For instance, Romania offers tax cuts for information technology (IT) workers who want to stay. But using tax incentives can sometimes backfire. This policy has had negative side effects, in that some engineers have reclassified themselves as IT workers, and as a consequence tensions have arisen between IT workers and other members of the workforce.

Connection: Staying in Touch

Until recently countries with substantial emigration rarely embraced their diasporas, owing to complex feelings of shame for not having provided better opportunities at home, irritation at seeing emigrants take the easy way out, and even envy of the emigrants' success. As we stressed in chapters 7 and 8, however, more and more countries are treating a diaspora as an economic asset. After all, it is a source of trade, investment, and remittances and is a facilitator of international business. It is also an incubator of potential returnee talent. Developing-country governments are attempting to leverage this asset.

In principle, it is possible to mobilize expatriates so that they can be better connected to the development of their country. Although expatriate specialists have always had some links with their countries of origin, the explosion in communication technologies has made it possible for multiple and dense links to develop, particularly among migrants of recent vintage. These diasporic networks are likely to be more successful when they link up with other forms of professional collaboration and knowledge transfer to developing countries. Although many such international networks focus on various technical areas, interest in diaspora networks linking expatriate specialists with their home countries is increasing.[19] The goals are broadly similar: connect members of the diaspora with each other and with their country of origin; promote the exchange of skills and knowledge through joint developmental projects with government agencies, businesses, and nongovernmental organizations in their countries of origin. As yet, however, these networks appear to be playing little more than a modest role.

International organizations have created programs to facilitate the return of expatriate talent. The UNDP's TOKTEN program (Transfer of Knowledge through Expatriate Nationals) is one such example, but it is limited in scope, and its effects are modest. In other cases, international organizations have sought to promote the return of qualified talent in states rebuilding after a collapse, by providing travel and living allowances and supplemental pay to persuade nationals of a country to return to assist development. A UNDP program for identifying skilled Somalis abroad for short missions in Somalia, and one by the International Organization for Migration (IOM) to help expatriate human

---

19. Examples include the Worldwide Indian Network (India), the Global Korean Network (South Korea), Brain Gain Network (Philippines), the Reverse Brain Drain Project (Thailand), and many others. See Meyer, Kaplan, and Charum (2001).

capital from Afghanistan to return, are examples in this regard. This is one area where the international community can do much more by way of financial and logistical support.

In general, return programs have proved to be expensive and difficult to implement, and few have succeeded in encouraging large-scale or sustained return of the highly skilled in particular. National programs work only in rare cases where the state itself has well-developed capabilities, which for the most part are confined to a few middle-income countries. However, they are unlikely to see a significant flight of human capital to begin with. Countries like China, South Korea, and Taiwan may have successful programs, but they will not work in source countries whose science and technology capabilities are not developed enough. Financial incentives are not the most important, or at least not the only factor that influences the migrant's decision to return. Return policies will be ineffective unless source countries are simultaneously assisted in developing and raising their scientific capabilities and favorable economic and political conditions.

International Cooperation

As global trade in services increases, the liberalization of the "temporary movement of individual service suppliers" being currently negotiated under the General Agreement on Trade in Services (GATS) will become more important. How is such liberalization best accomplished, in a way that benefits both home and host countries? Negotiations on this so-called Mode 4 of supplying services were launched during the Uruguay Round but have not proceeded far beyond facilitating exploratory business visits and the movement of high-level personnel within multinational firms.[20] Developing countries have pressed for more international movement of workers unrelated to commercial presence (tied in with foreign direct investment [FDI]), while many multinational firms would like greater ease in the transnational movement of their personnel.

---

20. Mode 1 is "cross-border supply," which is analogous to trade in goods; Mode 2 is "consumption abroad," as in the case of tourism or study abroad; and Mode 3 is "commercial presence," as in the supply of a service through a subsidiary or branch in another country. The Annex on Movement of Natural Persons Supplying Services under the GATS Agreement covers two categories of natural persons—Mode 4: those who are "service suppliers of a Member," that is, self-employed individuals who obtain their remuneration directly from customers, and those affecting natural persons of a member who are "employed by a service supplier of a Member in respect of the supply of a service."

Domestic regulations pertaining to technical standards and qualification requirements may imply additional costs for foreign services or service suppliers. Whether this is a form of protection or simply necessary to ensure a desired quality of the service is a thorny issue, however, and GATS does not appear to provide an unambiguous framework for resolving it. Perhaps, as some have suggested, one needs to distinguish between the universal (fixed) component of professional standards, which is identical between countries, and country-specific training (the variable component).[21] In fields like management and engineering, the former takes priority, whereas in accounting and law, the latter does. To address the problem of asymmetric information about foreign suppliers' abilities, the least costly and least arbitrary optimal instrument is a test of competence, similar to ones administered to domestic residents.

While global goods trade has seen a sharp decline in quotas, they continue to be pervasive in services. They are not inconsistent with GATS unless a member has undertaken not to use them. Furthermore, quotas under GATS restrict not only the quantity or value of services output but also the number of (foreign) service suppliers. Numerous barriers constrain the movement of individuals. The most obvious are explicit prohibitions or tight visa quotas on foreign service providers. There are various forms of economic needs tests—such as requirements that employers take steps to recruit and retain sufficient national workers before they can employ foreigners. Compounding the problem are the many formalities (for example, in obtaining a visa) that make the red tape related to FDI seem trivial by comparison. Finally, the entry of foreigners is impeded by a refusal to recognize their professional qualifications, by burdensome licensing requirements, and by the imposition of discriminatory standards. There are interesting parallels with developing-country policies in manufacturing, which long imposed local content requirements. Although developing countries have basically discarded these after years of pressure by developed countries, similar policies are becoming more prevalent in developed countries, though they are now concentrated in the services sector.[22]

Countries issue basically two types of visas: work visas for long-term stays and business visas for short-term business-related travel. There is, however, no sharp distinction between the two that would allow short-term business visits that are also related to work, such as support for a

---

21. Mattoo (1999).
22. This discussion draws heavily on Mattoo (2003).

software product. More important, delays in granting visas are the equivalent of nontariff barriers (NTBs), just as inspection delays (by the receiving country) can be lethal to the export of perishable goods. Delays in issuing visas are also very costly to the supplier firm. In today's business environment, suppliers who cannot service their product at short notice are unlikely to retain the customer. Either the supplier gets the work visas, which takes time, or runs into country quotas and then tries to find ways to cut corners, perhaps by stocking up on work visas or arranging intracompany transfers with the personnel located in the client company's offices. Although little research has been done on the tariff equivalent of NTBs in issuing visas for service sector professionals, it stands to reason that this barrier must be addressed in any future negotiations, particularly those involving Mode 4.

Considering the current stalemate in negotiations, however, this is unlikely to occur at the multilateral level. One is likely to see more movement at the bilateral level, where source and destination countries have already agreed on a large number of cooperative arrangements for managing circulation. Bilateral labor recruitment agreements are the most common. Spain, for instance, entered into such agreements with Romania, Poland, Ecuador, Morocco, and Bulgaria in 2004. The foreign workers participate in Spanish social security and health systems on the same basis as domestic workers. Portugal has a similar arrangement with Ukraine, thus allowing an estimated 200,000 unauthorized Ukrainians to become legal seasonal workers. The United States has been adding a sweetener of temporary skilled visa set-asides as part of its bilateral free trade agreements. As part of its free trade agreements with Chile and Singapore, the United States has aside nearly 7,000 H1-B visas for the two countries.

Multilateral agreements at the regional level appear to be most liberal among countries that enjoy geographic proximity and similar levels of development (such as the members of the European Union, European Free Trade Association, European Economic Area, or Trans-Tasman Travel Arrangement). Less liberal are agreements among countries that are geographically close but differ substantially in their incomes (such as those in the North American Free Trade Agreement). Least liberal are those whose members are geographically distant and at differing levels of development (as in Asia-Pacific Economic Cooperation and U.S.-Jordan). The Regional Migration Conference (referred to as the Puebla Group) that encompasses all of the governments of North and Central America and the Dominican Republic is a possible model for future collaboration among source, transit, and destination countries. Another important example is the French government's program of "co-development" linking cooperation in managing migration with enhanced development aid, which makes use of the diaspora communities in France. In addition, the Philippines and eight other Asian labor exporters—Bangladesh, India, Pakistan, Nepal, Sri Lanka, Indonesia, Thailand, and China—plan an organization aimed at reducing the cost of exporting workers. Another example is the Caribbean Single Market and Economy agreement of the Caribbean Community (CARICOM), which allows persons with a bachelor's or higher degree to move freely among member countries; there is a push to extend freedom of movement rights to all CARICOM nationals.[23]

The European Union is well versed in the problems of arriving at a common migration policy—it had an easier time adopting a common currency. In the end, it agreed on a two-track approach: first, establish a basic framework that sets out minimum standards in areas such as the treatment of asylum seekers; second, agree on common enforcement policies, particularly those surrounding visa issuance. By all accounts, it has been more successful in harmonizing asylum policies than migration policies. Its efforts continue, nonetheless, most recently in examining the link between its migration policies and its relations with developing countries. One option being considered is whether to offer more temporary work permits as an incentive to get countries to take back their illegal migrants. Another is whether to offer extra aid outside the normal development programs to reward cooperating countries. In June 2002 EU leaders meeting in Seville threatened to impose sanctions against "uncooperative countries in the fight against illegal immigration," but because French and Swedish leaders objected to this approach, a strategy to use work permits and increased aid as incentives has emerged instead.

Institutionalizing International Cooperation on Migration

Although the global community has institutionalized international cooperation on international capital flows and trade through the Bretton Woods institutions and the World Trade Organization (WTO), respectively, there is no comparable body to comprehensively address the wide

---

23. The 15 CARICOM member states are Antigua and Barbuda, the Bahamas, Barbados, Belize, Dominica, Grenada, Guyana, Haiti, Jamaica, Montserrat, Saint Lucia, St. Kitts and Nevis, St. Vincent and the Grenadines, Suriname, and Trinidad and Tobago.

range of issues surrounding international migration. Some of the major questions are how to protect the rights of migrants, how to stem international trafficking in women and children, and how to deal with labor mobility, human capital flows and the brain drain, refugee crises, asylum seekers, and law enforcement. These issues constitute "the last remaining gap in the institutional architecture that covers our interdependent world," perhaps reflecting the very different powers of capital and labor.[24]

There are few multilateral treaties on the subject, and even these are widely ignored. In 1990 the United Nations passed the International Convention on the Protection of the Rights of All Migrant Workers and Their Families, 11 years after it established a working group on the subject. By 2004 just 26 countries had ratified it, only one of which was from the OECD (Mexico). This is hardly surprising. A much older labor convention to protect migrants, the International Labor Organization (ILO) Convention adopted in 1947, is hardly enforced. That convention covered registered or legal workers while the 1990 UN convention established an even higher standard of migrants' rights and extended it to include undocumented migrants.

A plethora of agencies and conventions deal with different aspects of migration. The principal one, the IOM, was originally set up in 1951 to resettle the massive number of refugees in Europe after World War II. Although partly an intergovernmental body with 105 member states (as of June 2004), the IOM is neither a treaty organization nor a part of the UN system. Other international organizations include the UN High Commissioner for Refugees, which deals with forced migrants; the ILO, which is charged with protecting workers' rights; and the WTO, which under Mode 4 of GATS addresses issues related to temporary migration of professional workers.

Jagdish Bhagwati has forcefully argued for the creation of a treaty-defined World Migration Organization (WMO), similar to the WTO.[25] Rather than specify rules for member countries, the proposed WMO would mainly provide information of interest to the migrants' host and source countries, the migrants themselves, and civil society. Over time, these norms would evolve into ratified conventions. The new organization would also periodically review the migration policies of member

24. Bhagwati (2003).

25. Jagdish Bhagwati, "The World Needs a New Body to Monitor Migration," *Financial Times,* October 24, 2003, p. 24.

countries and push them to improve their practices, just as the WTO uses its trade policy review mechanism to influence member countries' trade policies. With global migration on the verge of transforming the international landscape, such an organization is needed now more than ever.

Concluding Thoughts

In the next half century the bulk of migration will take place within developing countries themselves, and the most notable will be rural-to-urban movements in the giants—China and India. The second largest migration flows will occur internationally, among developing countries, thus continuing the trend of recent years. And a considerable part of migration from the South to the North will be undertaken by semi-skilled labor. The last is likely to result in the largest total income gains, even if the movements of labor are modest.[26]

Given these empirical realities, the welfare of many migrants, both intra- and international, will require the attention of policymakers the world over, irrespective of the specific circumstances—income gaps, ethnic cleansing, economic instability, or human trafficking—that provoked their departure from their country of origin. Nonetheless, that small part of migration that is the focus of this book, namely skilled migration from developing to developed countries, will have a significant impact on sending countries for the many reasons that have been discussed in previous chapters. As we have argued, the implications are complex and defy any simple-minded, facile bottom lines.

The human dilemmas can be poignant. To return to the Jamaican woman who becomes a nanny in New York, she will have left her own children behind to take care of a stranger's family. Though her children will enjoy higher consumption because of remittances from their overseas resident mother, they will grow up without her physical presence. How does one weigh the long-term impact on children who have higher levels of material consumption but are being raised in the absence of their mother?

The movement of global sports talent epitomizes the analytical complexities that accompany an exodus of talent. Japan's most popular

---

26. For example, Winters (2003) estimates that an increase in developed countries' quotas on the inward movements of both skilled and unskilled temporary workers equivalent to 3 percent of their workforce would generate an estimated increase in world welfare of more than $US150 billion a year. Both developed and developing countries share in these gains, and they are largest if both low-skilled and high-skilled mobility is permitted.

sport, baseball, has lost thousands of ticket-buying fans and TV viewers in recent years "as the sport's dazzle is diminished by the defection of home-grown stars to the U.S. Major Leagues."[27] With Africa's best soccer talent migrating to European soccer leagues, fans prefer to watch them on TV rather than attend games of African soccer leagues, thus producing negative consequences for the latter. On the other hand, playing in the world's most competitive leagues (abroad) raises the quality of African soccer talent, thereby helping African national teams do much better in interstate competition.

The preceding chapters have dealt with the forces behind and the extent of international human capital flows. The range of development-related consequences merit even closer attention, especially in view of the changing attitude toward the migration of human capital from developing countries. While in earlier years this migration was viewed with alarm, the sentiment has become much more sanguine in recent years. As mentioned at the outset, this is typical of development thinking, which tends to swing from one extreme to another. We would urge a more moderate view, based on five important features of such migration.

1. International migration is poorly understood in comparison with other forms of international social and economic integration. It is impossible to arrive at a simple judgment about the desirability of talent flows from poor to rich nations. Sometimes the flows are beneficial. On balance, the Indian software industry benefited from the migration of Indian IT personnel abroad. At other times, the results are deleterious. It would be hard to deny that the exodus of Ghanaian doctors has had adverse health care consequences for those remaining behind.

2. When human capital exits at a high rate, this is invariably a signal of deep and significant problems in a country. In such cases, tackling the brain drain would simply be treating the symptoms of the problem rather than its root causes.

3. The idea that the migration of a significant fraction of a country's best and brightest is not particularly harmful and may even be beneficial to the country is simply unwarranted. As we have shown, although the effects are undoubtedly complex, the fundamental reality is that countries need talent to ensure innovation, build institutions, and implement programs—the key pillars of long-term development. The example of the Philippines is instructive. No other country has made the export of human capital such a fundamental part of its development strategy. The

27. Jagdish Bhagwati, "Strike Three," *Financial Times*, July 7, 2004, p. 12.

Philippines has not done badly, and Filipinos in general (including those within and outside the country) have done better than the country itself. Yet the performance of the Philippine economy pales by comparison with that of its East Asian counterparts, and this is unlikely to change in the foreseeable future.

4. The checkered history of foreign aid clearly illustrates the severe limitations of what outsiders can do. To the extent that the problems of a country are endogenous, the solutions are also likely to lie largely within. Like foreign aid, diasporas can facilitate (and sometimes harm) development, but they cannot by themselves fundamentally improve the development prospects of a country.

5. The maximum advantages of international human capital flows accrue to receiving countries and to those sending countries in which the flows are a relatively modest fraction of the stock. For receiving countries, studies that try to capture the effects through changes in the labor market fundamentally miss the point. Modern growth is about innovation. The fact that more than half of the science and technology Ph.D.s in the United States are foreign-born has significant implications for innovation in this country, and hence for long-term productivity and growth. And it is here, rather than in labor market effects, that the long-term gains and losses of human capital flows are probably most manifest. For sending countries, the positive impacts have focused on financial remittances. This again (as with earlier growth models) may be missing a more important point. The flows of ideas and business networks that are critical for economic dynamism and institutional change are likely to have the more significant long-term consequences. Although financial remittances are certainly playing an important role in augmenting scarce resources for poor households as well as countries, it would be a singular mistake to believe that they can address the development problems of poor countries.

We hope our analysis of international skilled migration will move policy discussions in constructive directions. If rich countries are to live up to their promise to be development-sensitive in their actions, they cannot avoid paying attention to the effects of their immigrant selection policies on developing countries. This need not mean that talented individuals must be denied emigration possibilities, rather that different mechanisms should be developed to help poor countries share in the considerable global gains that often attend such movements. To name a few, policies could entertain fiscal sharing, be more sensitive in targeting scarce skills, and encourage eventual return. Poorer countries also need to accept the loss of their talent as a wake-up call. Most important, they must remedy the institutional breakdowns that drive their scarcest resource away. The tragedy is that these are the very people often needed for institutional transformation. But even from a distance, the absent talents of the diaspora serve as a valuable economic asset when not thwarted by suspicious home-country governments.

With large income gaps across countries likely to persist over the foreseeable future, the international human capital dynamics discussed in this book will be a major development issue in the decades ahead. Although predictions are perilous, flows of talent from poor to rich countries are more likely to increase than decrease, as the rich-country demand for talent appears more powerful than any possible reduction in poor-country supply from the narrowing of income gaps. Our modest hope is that the issues raised here will help push this neglected phenomenon onto the development agenda.

Emigration Losses in a Model with Specialized Skills

There are two classes of inputs in our model: skilled and unskilled workers.[1] Unskilled workers (L) are perfectly substitutable for one another, but each skilled worker has a unique skill that differentiates him or her from peers. As a result, each skilled worker (indexed $i = 1$ to N) sells a level of skilled services, s^i, in monopolistically competitive skills markets to a competitive final goods industry. We do not explore how the number of specialists are determined before immigration but assume that there are fixed costs to becoming a specialist, thereby limiting their number.

The aggregate production function for competitively supplied final output is of the following form:[2]

$$(A\text{-}1) \qquad\qquad Y = L^{1-\alpha} \sum_{i=1}^{N} s_i^{\alpha},$$

where $0 < \alpha < 1$, and α is a measure of how easily one specialist can be substituted for another, with low values of α implying low degrees of substitutability.

---

1. In this appendix we adapt Romer's (1993) model of the welfare costs of trade restrictions on specialized intermediate capital inputs to explore the loss from the emigration of skilled specialists.
2. Introduced by Ethier (1982).

Differentiating (1) with respect to skill level i gives the inverse demand curve for that skill:

(A-2) $$\frac{\partial Y}{\partial s_i} = p(s_i) = \alpha L^{1-\alpha} s_i^{\alpha-1}.$$

Each skilled specialist chooses the price that maximizes profits given a constant cost, c, per unit of skill services provided. For simplicity, we think of c as being the monetary equivalent of the disutility of working, and thus it is not a source of income for any other actor in the economy. The optimal price and output for skill provider i are then given by

(A-3) $$p_i^* = \frac{c}{\alpha}$$

and

(A-4) $$s_i^* = \alpha^{\frac{2}{1-\alpha}} c^{\frac{-1}{1-\alpha}} L.$$

Since all skilled specialists face identical demands and costs, we can drop the i subscripts. And with each skill specialist supplying an identical skill level, s, we can rewrite the aggregate production function simply as

(A-5) $$Y = L^{1-\alpha} N s^{\alpha}.$$

We now conduct the standard experiment of removing a number of the skilled specialists, E, through emigration and observe what happens to the income of TRBs. Before the emigration takes place, TRBs receive that entire national output (Y_0) less the total revenue that is being paid to the soon-to-be emigrants. After the emigration, TRBs receive the entire national output (Y_1) that is produced with the now smaller skilled labor force. As usual, we measure the loss to TRBs as a fraction of the total skilled wage bill, which in this case is equal to the revenue of the entire set of skilled specialists $(N \times p \times s)$:

(A-6) $$\frac{Loss}{Nps} = \frac{Y_0 - Eps - Y_1}{Nps} = \frac{L^{1-\alpha} s^{1-\alpha}}{p} - \frac{E}{N} - \frac{L^{1-\alpha} s^{1-\alpha}}{p} \left(\frac{N-E}{N}\right).$$

If we substitute using (3) and (4) and rearrange, we obtain a very simple expression for the loss to TRBs as a fraction of the preemigration total wage bill:

(A-7)
$$\frac{Loss}{Nps} = \left(\frac{1}{\alpha} - 1\right)\frac{E}{N}.$$

The first term on the right-hand side is equal to the proportionate markup applied by each of the profit-maximizing skill specialists. The second term is the emigration rate. Suppose, for example, that α is equal to 0.5, so that firms apply a 100 percent markup to their unit costs, c. In this case, the loss as a fraction of the (preemigration) wage bill is exactly equal to the emigration rate. That is, a 10 percent emigration rate leads to an income loss to TRBs equal to 10 percent of the (preemigration) wage bill. Although the model is highly simplified and the chosen markup is just illustrative, this calculation does hint that the losses sustained could be much greater than in a competitive skill market.

Effects of the Brain Drain on Institutions of Higher Education

The institutional consequences of international human capital flows can be illustrated by their effects on institutions of higher education, the source of future human capital. To assess these effects, we posited a closed economy with a faculty-to-student ratio (akin to a capital-to-output ratio) of x:y where $t = 0$. The attrition rate in the faculty is $f(x)$, and a certain part of the student output, $F(y)$, becomes new faculty. In time period $t = 1$, the new stock of faculty, x^*, can be expressed as

$$x - f(x) + F(y) = x^*.$$

Assuming a constant faculty-to-student ratio, if

$$f(x) > F(y), y^* < y,$$
$$f(x) < F(y), y^* > y, \text{ and}$$
$$f(x) = F(y), y^* = y.$$

Note that y is a variable with both a quantity and quality dimension. Long-term growth for a developing country requires $y^* > y$ both in quantity and quality. If this is the case, then $F(y)$ cannot be a random draw from the pool of y; the average quality of $F(y)$ must be greater than the median quality of y.

In an open economy with out-migration of human capital, $f(x)$ would initially increase, and $F(y)$ would decline. The attrition rate, $f(x)$, would increase both because the opportunity cost of teaching would increase (since wage convergence is greater in tradables than in nontradables) and because international migration implies that the mobile factor may be able to secure greater rents. On the other hand, $F(y)$ would decline, inasmuch as a computer science graduate from an elite educational institution is much less likely to consider teaching as a career; his or her non-teaching salary is being set globally, but teaching salary is still being set locally. If $y^* > y$, but only on the quantity dimension, either the ratio $x{:}y$ must decline or the quality of the pool from which $F(y)$ is drawn must decline. In either case, y^* is likely to decline in quality. A society needs good teachers to produce even moderate quality in large numbers whether or not they are engaged in research.

C

Open Economy Effects

As noted in chapter 4, the most widely used framework for investigating how changes in factor endowments affect an open economy is the Heckscher-Ohlin model. In a small open economy facing given terms of trade and internationally equalized factor prices, and using the same technologies as its trading partners, the emigration of skilled workers will reallocate resources away from skill-intensive sectors. But in contrast to our closed-economy benchmark model, this one assumes no change in the skilled wage or any other factor price. Hence the model predicts that emigration shrinks a skill-intensive sector such as software but does not harm the welfare of TRBs as factor incomes are unchanged. The mechanism at work is that described in the famous Rybczynski theorem: output is reallocated away from the skill-intensive sector until the demand for skill is reduced to match the shrunken supply.

Few governments around the world would be sanguine about the shrinkage of skilled-labor pools even if they were convinced that current factor prices are not affected. Part of the reason may be that policymakers believe high-tech sectors such as software—especially at the more innovative end of the industry spectrum—generate ample opportunities for learning-by-doing and knowledge spillovers.[1] Thus our shift to an open economy setting moves attention away from current income losses

---

1. For arguments along these lines, see Lucas (1993).

incurred by those remaining behind (TRBs) to shifts in the allocation of remaining resources to industries with lower growth potentials.

Daniel Trefler's work with a variety of trade models challenging the myth of an immigration surplus may shed some light on the question of whether an emigration surplus exists in an open economy.[2] Trefler's results show that an emigration surplus loss is present in a specific factors trade model, whether skilled workers are the mobile factor or one of the specific factors. He also shows that Heckscher-Ohlin results change when technologies differ across countries. Interestingly, it does matter whether the technological (or productivity) differences are inherent in workers (hence any technological backwardness will travel with them) or in countries (which means an emigrating worker can leave the backwardness behind). When technology differences are inherent in workers, says Trefler, the standard Heckscher-Ohlin results are not affected as factor price equalization occurs for productivity-adjusted factor prices. This is not true when technology differences are specific to countries, as emigration leads to favorable movements in the terms of trade and an increase in the welfare of TRBs.

A recent assessment of how balanced flows of factors affect an economy with a superior CRS technology has come to the following conclusion: to the extent that the resulting increased size of the economy leads to a worsening of its terms of trade, the balanced inflow of productive factors leads to lower welfare.[3] The United States, it seems, has been made *worse off* because of its openness to foreign capital and workers. On the sending side, a balanced outflow of factors will lead to an improvement in welfare, provided it is large enough for its terms of trade to change. A welfare loss to the sending country could reemerge if the factor outflows (for example, all skilled workers) are unbalanced, or if there are adverse fiscal effects.

2. Trefler (1997).
3. Davis and Weinstein (2002); their work focuses mainly on the United States. See also Trefler (1997).

References

Acemoglu, Daron. 2002. "Technical Change, Inequality, and the Labor Market." *Journal of Economic Literature* 40 (March): 7–72.

Adams, Richard H., Jr. 2003. "International Migration, Remittances and the Brain Drain: A Study of 24 Labor-Exporting Countries." Policy Research Working Paper 3069. Washington: World Bank.

Adams, Richard H., Jr., and John Page. 2003. "International Migration, Remittances, and Poverty in Developing Countries." Policy Research Working Paper 3179. Washington: World Bank.

Agrawal, Ajay, Iain M. Cockburn, and John McHale. 2003. "Gone but Not Forgotten: Labor Flows, Knowledge Spillovers, and Enduring Social Capital." Working Paper 9950. Cambridge, Mass.: National Bureau of Economic Research.

Alarcon, Rafael. 2002. "The Development of Hometown Associations in the United States and the Use of Social Remittances in Mexico." In *Sending Money Home: Hispanic Remittances and Community Development,* edited by Rodolfo de la Garza and Briant Lindsay Lowell. Lanham, Md.: Rowman and Littlefield.

Altonji, Joseph, and David Card. 1991. "The Effects of Immigration on the Labor Market Outcomes of Less-Skilled Natives." In *Immigration, Trade, and the Labor Market,* edited by John Abowd and Richard Freeman. University of Chicago Press.

Ammassari, Savina. 2003. "From Nation-Building to Entrepreneurship: The Impact of Elite Return Migrants in Côte d'Ivoire and Ghana." International Workshop on Migration and Poverty in West Africa, University of Sussex.

Armstrong, Gary, and Richard Guilianotti, eds. 2004. *Football in Africa, Conflict, Conciliation, and Community.* Basingstoke: Palgrave Macmillan.

Australian Bureau of Statistics. 2001. *Census of Population and Housing: 2001.* AusStats.

Autor, David H., Lawrence F. Katz, and Alan B. Krueger. 1998. "Computing Inequality: Have Computers Changed the Labor Market?" *Quarterly Journal of Economics* 113, no. 4: 1169–13.

Banerjee, Abhijit V., and Esther Duflo. 2000. "Reputation Effects and the Limits of Contracting: A Study of the Indian Software Industry." *Quarterly Journal of Economics* 115 (August): 989–1017.

Bardhan, Pranab. 2000. "Social Justice in a Global Economy." Social Policy Lecture. Geneva: International Labor Organization.

Barrett, Alan, and Philip J. O'Connell. 2001. "Is There a Wage Premium for Returning Irish Migrants?" *Economic and Social Review* 32 (January): 1–21.

Barrett, Alan, Tim Callan, Aedin Doris, Donal O'Neill, Helen Russell, Olive Sweetman, and James McBride, eds. 2000. *How Unequal? Men and Women in the Irish Labour Market.* Dublin: Oaktree Press.

Barro, Robert J. 1991. "Economic Growth in a Cross-Section of Countries." *Quarterly Journal of Economics* 106 (May): 407–43.

Barro, Robert J., and Jong-Wha Lee. 1993. "International Comparisons of Educational Attainment." *Journal of Monetary Economics* 32 (March): 363–94.

———. 2000. "International Data on Educational Attainment Updates and Implications." Working Paper 7911. Cambridge, Mass.: National Bureau of Economic Research.

Beine, Michael, Frédéric Docquier, and Hillel Rapoport. 2001. "Brain Drain and Economic Growth: Theory and Evidence." *Journal of Development Economics* 64, no. 1: 275–89.

———. 2002. "Brain Drain and LDCs' Growth: Winners and Losers." Working Paper 129. Stanford University, Center for Research on Economic Development and Policy Reform.

Berman, Eli, John Bound, and Zvi Griliches. 1994. "Changes in the Demand of Skilled Labor within U.S. Manufacturing: Evidence from the Annual Survey of Manufacturers." *Quarterly Journal of Economics* 109 (May): 367–97.

Berman, Eli, John Bound, and Stephen Machin. 1998. "Implications of Skill-Biased Technical Change: International Evidence." *Quarterly Journal of Economics* 113 (November): 1245–80.

Bertocchi, Graziella, and Chiara Strozzi. 2004. "Citizenship Laws and International Migration in Historical Perspective." CEPR Discussion Paper 4737. Center for Economic Policy Research. November.

Bhagwati, Jagdish. 1982. "Introduction [Symposium on taxation and international mobility]." *Journal of Public Economics* 18 (August): 285–89.

———. 1991. "International Migration and Income Taxation." In *Political Economy and International Economics*, edited by Douglas Irwin. MIT Press.

Bhagwati, Jagdish, and John Douglas Wilson. 1989. *Income Taxation and International Mobility.* MIT Press.

Bhattacharjee, Debashis, Karthik Krishna, and Amol Karve. 2001. "Signalling, Work Experience, and MBA Starting Salaries." *Economic and Political Weekly, Review of Management and Industry* 36 (November 24): 46–47.

Borjas, George J. 1987. "Self-Selection and the Earnings of Immigrants." *American Economic Review* 77 (September): 531–53.

———. 1990. *Friends or Strangers.* New York: Basic Books.

———. 1994. "The Economics of Immigration." *Journal of Economic Literature* 32 (December): 1667–1717.

———. 1995. "The Economics Benefits of Immigration." *Journal of Economic Perspectives* 9, no. 2: 3–22.

Borjas, George J., and Bernt Bratsberg. 1996. "Who Leaves? The Outmigration of the Foreign-Born." *Review of Economics and Statistics* 78 (February): 165–76.

Borjas, George J., Richard B. Freeman, and Lawrence F. Katz. 1996. "Searching for the Effect of Immigration on the Labor Market." *American Economic Review* 86, no. 2: 246–51.

Bresnahan, Timothy F., Erik Brynjolfsson, and Lorin M. Hitt. 1999. "Information Technology, Workplace Organization and the Demand for Skilled Labor: Firm-Level Evidence." Working Paper 7136. Cambridge, Mass.: National Bureau of Economic Research.

Brown, Enos. 2003. "The Jamaican Experience with the Movement of Natural Persons in the Provision of Services." In *Moving People to Deliver Services*, edited by Aaditya Mattoo and Antonia Carzaniga. Oxford University Press.

Buchan, J., and M. Dal Poz. 2002. "Skill Mix in the Health Care Workforce." *Bulletin of the World Health Organization* 80, no. 7.

Buchan J., T. Parkin, and J. Sochalski. 2003. *International Nurse Mobility: Trends and Policy Implications.* Geneva: World Health Organization.

Buencamino, Leonides, and Sergei Gorbunov. 2002. *Informal Money Transfer Systems: Opportunities and Challenges for Development Finance.* DESA Discussion Paper 26, ST/ESA/2002/DP/26. United Nations.

Card, David. 1990. "The Impact of the Mariel Boatlift on the Miami Labor Market." *Industrial and Labor Relations Review* 43 (January): 245–57.

Carrington, William J., and Enrica Detragiache. 1998. "How Big Is the Brain Drain?" Working Paper 98/102. Washington: International Monetary Fund.

Chiquiar, Daniel, and Gordon H. Hanson. 2002. "International Migration, Self-Selection, and the Distribution of Wages: Evidence from Mexico and the United States." Working Paper 9242. Cambridge, Mass.: National Bureau of Economic Development.

Citizenship and Immigration Canada. 2000a. *Planning Now for Canada's Future: Introducing a Multi-Year Planning Process and the Immigration Plan for 2001 and 2002.* Ottawa.

———. 2000b. *Facts and Figures 2000: Immigration Overview.* Ottawa.

———. 2002. *Facts and Figures 2002: Temporary Resident and Refugee Claimant Population.* Ottawa.

Clancy, P. 2001. *College Entry in Focus: A Fourth National Survey of Access to Higher Education.* Dublin: Government Publications Office.

Collier, Paul, and Anke Hoeffler. 2000. *Greed and Grievance in Civil War.* Working Paper 128. Washington: World Bank.

Collins, Susan M. 1998. "Economic Integration and the American Worker: An Overview." In *Imports, Exports, and the American Worker,* edited by Susan M. Collins. Brookings.

Commander, Simon, Mari Kangasniemi, and L. Alan Winters. 2002. "The Brain Drain: Curse or Boon? A Survey of the Literature." International Seminar on International Trade: Challenges to Globalization, National Bureau of Economic Research, Höberge Gård, Stockholm, May 24–25.

Cornwell, John. 2003. *Hitler's Scientists: Science, War, and the Devil's Pact.* New York: Viking.

Courbage, Youseff. 1995. "Fertility Transition in the Mashriq and the Maghreb." In *Family, Gender, and Population in the Middle-East,* edited by Carol Obermeyer. American University in Cairo Press.

Davis, Donald, and David E. Weinstein. 2002. "Technological Superiority and the Losses from Migration." Working Paper 8971. Cambridge, Mass.: National Bureau of Economic Research.

De Castro, Rafael Fernández, and Carlos Rosales. 1999. "Migration Issues: Raising the Stakes in U.S.-Latin American Relations." In *The Future of Inter-American Relations,* edited by Jorge Dominguez. New York: Routledge.

Desai, Mihir A., Devesh Kapur, and John McHale. 2003. "The Fiscal Impact of High Skilled Emigration: Flows of Indians to the U.S." Working Paper 03-01. Harvard University, Center for International Affairs.

Dixit, Avinash K. 2001. "On Modes of Economic Governance." Working Paper 589. Munich, Germany: Center for Economic Studies and IFO Institute for Economic Research.

Dobson, Janet, Khalid Koser, Gail McLaughlan, and John Salt. 2001. *International Migration to the United Kingdom: Recent Patterns and Trends, Research.* Occasional Paper 75. United Kingdom: Home Office, Development and Statistics Division.

Docquier, Frédéric, and Abdeslam Marfouk. 2004. "Measuring the International Mobility of Skilled Workers (1990–2000)." Policy Research Working Paper 3381. Washington: World Bank.

Domhoff, G. W. 1988. "The Policy Formation Network." In *Who Rules America?* edited by G. William Domhoff. Mountain View, Calif.: Mayfield.

Dominguez, Jorge, ed. 2000. *The Future of Inter-American Relations.* New York: Routledge.

Dovlo, Delanyo, and Frank Nyonator. 1999. "Migration by Graduates of the University of Ghana Medical School." *Human Resources for Health Development Journal* 3, no.1: 40–51.

Dustmann, Christian. 1996. "Temporary Migration, Human Capital, and Language Fluency of Migrants." Discussion Papers 96-21. London, England: University College London, Department of Economics.

———. 2001. "Return Migration, Wage Differentials, and the Optimal Migration Duration." IZA Discussion Papers. Bonn, Germany: Institute for the Study of Labor.

Eckstein, Susan. 2003. "Diasporas and Dollars: Transnational Ties and the Transformation of Cuba." Rosemarie Rogers Working Paper 16. MIT.

Ethier, William. 1982. "National and International Returns to Scale in the Modern Theory of International Trade." *American Economic Review* 72, no. 3: 399–405.

Ewald, Janet J. 1992. "African Slavery and the African Slave Trade." *American Historical Review* 97, no. 2: 465–85.

Feleciano, Cynthia. 2003. "Educational Selectivity and U.S. Immigration: How Do Immigrants Compare to Those Left Behind?" Draft, University of California, Irvine.

Foer, Franklin. 2004. "Soccer vs. McWorld." *Foreign Policy* 140 (January/February): 32–40.

Foster, Andrew, and Mark Rosenzweig. 2001. "Imperfect Commitment, Altruism and Family: Evidence from Transfer Behavior in Low-Income Rural Areas." *Review of Economics and Statistics* (August): 389–407.

Friedberg Rachel. 2000. "You Can't Take It with You? Immigrant Assimilation and the Portability of Human Capital." *Journal of Labor Economics* 18 (April): 221–51.

Friedberg, Rachel, and Jennifer Hunt. 1995. "The Impact of Immigrants on Host Country Wages, Employment and Growth." *Journal of Economic Perspectives* 9, no. 2: 23–44.

General Accounting Office (GAO). 1996. *Foreign Physicians: Exchange Visitor Program Becoming Major Route to Practicing in U.S. Underserved Areas.* Letter Report, 12/30/96, GAO/HEHS-97-26. Washington.

———. 1998. *Non-Filing among U.S. Citizens Abroad.* GAO Report No. 98-106. Washington: Government Printing Office.

———. 2000. *Information Concerning Tax Motivated Expatriation.* GAO Report No. 00-110R. Washington: Government Printing Office.

Global Development Finance. 2003. Washington: World Bank.

———. 2005. Washington: World Bank.

Gould, David M. 1994. "Immigrant Links to the Home Country: Empirical Implications for U.S. Bilateral Trade Flows." *Review of Economics and Statistics* 76 (May): 302–16.

Green, Alan, and David Green. 1999. "Economic Goals of Canada's Immigration Policy: Past and Present." *Canadian Public Policy* 25, no. 4: 425–51.

Grossman, Gene M., and Elhanan Helpman. 2002. "Outsourcing in a Global

Economy." Working Paper 8728. Cambridge, Mass.: National Bureau of Economic Research.

Hall, Robert E., and Charles I. Jones. 1999. "Why Do Some Countries Produce So Much More Output per Worker than Others?" *Quarterly Journal of Economics* 114, no. 1: 83–116.

Haque, N. U., and S. J. Kim. 1995. "Human Capital Flight: Impact of Migration on Income and Growth." *IMF Staff Papers* 42, no. 3: 577–607.

Hausman, Ricardo, and Dani Rodrik. 2002. *Economic Development as Self-Discovery*. Working Paper 8952. Cambridge, Mass.: National Bureau of Economic Research.

Head, K., and J. Reis. 1998. "Immigration and Trade Creation: Econometric Evidence from Canada." *Canadian Journal of Economics* 31 (February): 47–62.

Hirschman, Albert O. 1970. *Exit, Voice, and Loyalty: Responses to Decline in Firms, Organization, and States*. Harvard University Press.

Hugo, Grame. 2001. "Migration Policies Designed to Facilitate the Recruitment of Skilled Workers in Australia." In *International Mobility of the Highly Skilled*. Paris: Organization for Economic Cooperation and Development.

Humphreys, Macartan. 2000. "How Much Can Gerrymander?" Working Paper. Harvard University.

———. 2003. "Natural Resources, Conflict, and Conflict Resolution." Paper prepared for the Santa Fe Institute/Javeriana University "Obstacles to Robust Negotiated Settlement" Workshop. Bogota, Colombia, May 29–31.

Humphreys, Macartan, and John Garry. 2000. "Salience: the Electoral Importance of the Politics of Emphasis." Paper presented at the Oxford University Annual Political Sociology Workshop, April.

Husted, Leif, Helena Skyt Nielson, Michael Rosholm, and Nina Smith. 2000. "Employment and Wage Assimilation of Male First Generation Immigrants in Denmark." IZA Working Paper 101. Bonn, Germany: Institute for the Study of Labor.

Iliffe, John. 1995. *Africans: The History of a Continent*. Cambridge University Press.

Independent Commission on Migration to Germany. 2001. *Structuring Immigration, Fostering Integration*. Working Paper 8728. Berlin.

Inikori, J. E. 1982. *Forced Migration: The Impact of the Export Slave Trade on African Societies*. London: Holmes & Meier.

International Bank for Reconstuction and Development. 2000. *Higher Education in Developing Countries: Peril and Promise*. Report of the Task Force on Higher Education and Society. Washington: World Bank.

International Organization of Migration (IOM). 1999. *Percentage of Nationals with University Education Living Abroad*. Geneva.

Jaffe, Adam B., Manuel Trajtenberg, and Rebecca Henderson. 1993. "Geographic Localization of Knowledge Spillovers as Evidenced by Patent Citations." *Quarterly Journal of Economics* 108 (3): 577–98.

Jasso, Guillermina, Mark Rosenweig, and James Smith. 2002. "The Earnings of U.S. Immigrants: World Skill Prices, Skill Transferability, and Selectivity." New York University, University of Pennsylvania, and Rand Corporation. Photocopy.

Jokisch, Brad, and Jason Pribilsky. 2002. "The Panic to Leave: Economic Crisis and the 'New Emigration' from Ecuador." *International Migration* 40, no. 4: 75–101.

Kapur, Devesh. 2001. "Diasporas and Technology Transfer." *Journal of Human Development* 2 (July): 265–86.

Kapur, Devesh, and John McHale. 2003. "Migration's New Payoff." *Foreign Policy* 48 (November/December): 49–57.

———. 2004. "Sharing the Spoils: International Human Capital Flows and Developing Countries." Washington: Center for Global Development. Photocopy.

Kapur, Devesh, and Urjit Patel. 2003. "Large Foreign Currency Reserves: Insurance for Domestic Weakness and External Uncertainties?" *Economic and Political Weekly* 38 (March): 1047–53.

Katz, Lawrence. 1999. "Technological Change, Computerization, and the Wage Structure." Harvard University. Photocopy.

Ketkar, Suhas, and Dilip Rath. 2001. "Development Financing during a Crisis: Securitization of Future Receivables." Policy Research Working Paper 2582. Washington: World Bank.

Khadria, Binod. 1999. *The Migration of Knowledge Workers*. New Delhi: Sage Publications.

Klinthall, Martin. 2003. *Return Migration from Sweden 1968–1996: A Longitudinal Analysis*. Stockholm: Almqvist & Wiksell International.

Kremer, Michael. 1993. "The O-Ring Theory of Economic Development." *Quarterly Journal of Economics* 108 (August): 551–76.

Kruger, Alan. 1993. "How Computers Have Changed the Wage Structure: Evidence from Microdata, 1984–1989." *Quarterly Journal of Economics* 108 (1): 33–60.

Krugman, Paul. 1991. *Geography and Trade*. MIT Press.

Lanfranchi, Pierre, and Matthew Taylor. 2001. *Moving with the Ball: The Migration of Professional Footballers*. Oxford: Berg Publishers.

Law, Robin. *The Slave Coast of West Africa 1550–1750*. Oxford University Press.

Layard, Richard, Stephen Nickell, and Richard Jackman. 1991. *Unemployment: Macroeconomic Performance and the Labour Market*. Oxford University Press.

Levy, Frank, and Richard J. Murnane. 1996. *The New Division of Labor: How Computers Are Creating the Next Job Market*. Princeton University Press.

Longva, Anh Nga. 2001. "Apostasy and the Liberal Predicament." *ISIM Newsletter* 14. University of Bergen: Center for Middle Eastern and Islamic Studies.

Lowell, L. B. 2000. "H-1B Temporary Workers: Estimating the Population." Washington: Georgetown University, Institute for the Study of International Migration.

Lucas, Robert E. 1988. "On the Mechanics of Economic Development." *Journal of Monetary Economics* 22: 3–42.

———. 1993. "Making a Miracle." *Econometrica* 61(2): 251–72.

Lydon, Reamonn. 1999. "Aspects of the Labour Market for New Graduates in Ireland: 1982–1997." *Economic and Social Review* 30 (July): 227–48.

Martin, Philip, and Jonas Widgren. 2002. "International Migration: Facing the Challenge." *Population Bulletin* 57 (1). Population Reference Bureau.

Mattoo, Aaditya. 1999. "MFN and the GATS." Paper presented at the World Trade Forum Conference, "Most-Favoured Nation (MFN): Past and Present," Neuchâtel, August 28–29.

———. 2003. "Introduction and Overview." In *Moving People to Deliver Services*, edited by Aaditya Mattoo and Antonia Carzaniga. Washington: World Bank.

McCormick, Barry, and Jackline Wahba. 2003. "Return International Migration and Geographical Inequality." *Journal of African Economies* 12, no. 4: 500–32.

McHale, John. 2002. "Importing Taxpayers: Immigration and the Politics of Social Security Reform." Kingston: Queen's University. Photocopy.

———. 2003. "Canadian Immigration Policy in Comparative Perspective." In *Canadian Immigration Policy for the 21st Century*, edited by Charles M. Beach, Alan G. Green, and Jeffrey Reitz. McGill-Queen's University Press.

McLaughlan, Gail, and John Salt. 2002. *Migration Policies towards Highly Skilled Foreign Workers*. University College London, Migration Research Unit, Geography Deparment.

Meyer, Jean-Baptiste, David E. Kaplan, and Jorge Charum. 2001. "Scientific Nomadism and the New Geopolitics of Knowledge." *International Social Sciences Journal*, no. 168 (June): 309–22.

Mincer, Jacob. 1958. "Investment in Human Capital and Personal Income Distribution." *Journal of Political Economy* 66 (no. 4): 281–302.

Mitchell, Christopher 1999. "The Future of Migration as an Issue in Inter-American Relations." In *The Future of Inter-American Relations*, edited by Jorge Dominguez. New York: Routledge.

Mountford, Andrew. 1997. "Can a Brain Drain Be Good for Growth in the Source Economy?" *Journal of Development Economics* 53 (2): 287–303.

Mundell, Robert. 1957. "International Trade and Factor Mobility." *American Economic Review* 47 (June): 321–35.

Murphy, Kevin, W. Craig Riddle, and Paul Romer. 1998. "Wages, Skills, and Technology in the United States and Canada." In *General Purpose Technologies and Economic Growth,* edited by Elhanan Helpman. MIT Press.

National Research Council. 1997. *The New Americans: Economic, Demographic, and Fiscal Effects of Immigration*. Washington: National Academies Press.

National Science Board. 2004. *A Companion to Science and Engineering Indicators: An Emerging Critical Problem of the Science and Engineering Workforce* (available at www.nsf.gov/sbe/srs/nsb0407/start.htm).

National Science Foundation, Division of Science Resources Statistics. 2001. "Survey of Earned Doctorates." Unpublished tabulations.

Noorbakhsh, Farhad, Alberto Paloni, and Ali Youssef. 2001. "Human Capital and FDI Flows to Developing Counties." *World Development* 29 (September): 1593–1610.

Organization for Economic Cooperation and Development (OECD). 2000. *Trends in International Migration*. Paris.

———. 2001. *Trends in International Migration*. Paris.

———. 2002. *Estimates for Foreign Populations*. Paris.

Orozco, Manuel. 2003a. "The Impact of Migration in the Caribbean and Central American Region." FPP-03-03. Canadian Foundation for the Americas.

———. 2003b. "Worker Remittances in an International Scope." *Inter-American Dialogue* (March).

Parente, Stephen L., and Edward C. Prescott. 2000. *Barriers to Riches*. MIT Press.

Passas, Nikos. 1999. "Informal Value Transfer Systems and Criminal Organizations: A Study into So-called Underground Banking Networks." Report prepared for Netherlands Ministry of Justice.

Physicians for Human Rights. 2004. *An Action Plan to Prevent Brain Drain: Building Equitable Health Systems in Africa*. Boston.

Ramachandran, Vijaya, and Manju Kedia Shah. 1998. *Entrepreneurial Characteristics and Private Sector Growth in Sub-Saharan Africa*. Regional Program on Enterprise Development Paper 86. Washington: World Bank.

Rath, Dilip. 2003. "Workers' Remittances: An Important and Stable Source of External Development Finance." In *Global Development Finance, 2003*. Washington: World Bank.

Rauch, James E., and Joel Watson. 2002. *Entrepreneurship in International Trade*. Working Paper 8708. Cambridge, Mass.: National Bureau of Economic Research.

Reimer, Jeffrey J. 2002. "Estimating the Poverty Impacts of Trade Liberalization." Working Paper 20. Purdue University, Center for Global Trade Analysis, Department of Agricultural Economics.

Rodney, Walter. 1981. *How Europe Underdeveloped Africa*. Howard University Press.

Romer, Paul. 1993. "Idea Gaps and Object Gaps in Economic Development." *Journal of Monetary Economics* 32 (December): 543–73.

Rueschemeyer, Dietrich, and Theda Skocpol. 1996. *States, Social Knowledge, and the Origins of Modern Social Policies*. Princeton University Press.

Saxenian, AnnaLee. 1999. *Silicon Valley's New Immigrant Entrepreneurs*. San Francisco: Public Policy Institute of California.

———. 2002. *Local and Global Networks of Immigrant Professionals in Silicon Valley*. San Francisco: Public Policy Institute of California.

Sawada, Yasuyuki. 2003. "Income Risks, Gender, and Human Capital Investment in a Developing Country." Working Paper CIRJE-F-198. University of Tokyo, Faculty of Economics.

Skowronek, Stephen. 1982. *Building a New American State*. Cambridge University Press.

Spear, Thomas. 1996. "Africa's Population History." *Journal of African History* 37: 479–85.

Staiger, Douglas, Joanne Spetz, and Ciaran Phibbs. 1999. "Is There Monopsony in the Labor Market? Evidence from a Natural Experiment." Working Paper 7258. Cambridge, Mass.: National Bureau of Economic Research.

Stark, Oded, and Nancy H. Chau. 1998. "Human Capital Formation, Asymmetric Information, and the Dynamics of International Migration." IHS Working Paper 52e. Vienna, Austria: Institute of Advanced Studies, Department of Economics.

Stark, Oded, Christian Helmenstein, and Yury Yegorov. 1997. "Migrants' Savings, Purchasing Power Parity, and the Optimal Duration of Migration." *International Tax and Public Finance* 4, no. 3: 307–24.

Stark, Oded, and Yong Wang. 2001. *Inducing Human Capital Formation: Migration as a Substitute for Subsidies*. IHS Working Paper 100. Vienna, Austria: Institute for Advanced Studies.

Statistics Canada. 2004. *2001 Census of Canada: Profile of Census Divisions and Subdivisions*. Ottawa: Industry Canada.

Stilwell, Barbara, Khassoum Diallo, Pascal Zurn, Marko Vujicic, Orvill Adams, and Mario Dal Poz. 2004. "Migration of Health-Care Workers from Developing Countries: Strategic Approaches to Its Management." *Bulletin of the World Health Organization* 82 (August).

Sukhatme, S. P. 1994. *The Real Brain Drain*. Bombay: Orient Longman.

Taylor, Margaret, and T. Alexander Aleinikoff. 1998. *Deportation of Criminal Aliens: A Geopolitical Perspective*. Washington: Inter-American Dialogue.

Thomas, V., Y. Wang, and X. Fan. 2000. *Measuring Educational Inequality: Gini Coefficients of Education*. Working Paper 2525. Washington: World Bank.

Thornton, John. *Africa and Africans in the Making of the Atlantic World, 1400–1800*. Cambridge University Press.

Trefler, Daniel. 1993. "International Factor Price Differences: Leontief Was Right." *Journal of Political Economy* 101, no. 6: 961–98.

————. 1997. "Immigrants and Natives in General Equilibrium Trade Models." Working Paper 6209. Cambridge, Mass.: National Bureau of Economic Research.

Tseng, Wanda, and Harm Zebregs. 2002. *Foreign Direct Investment in China: Some Lessons for Other Countries.* Policy Discussion Paper, PDP/02/03. Washington: International Monetary Fund.

United Nations Population Division (UNPD). 2002. *International Migration 2002.* New York.

U.S. Census Bureau. 1990. Integrated Public Use Microdata Series. Washington.

U.S. Department of Homeland Security. 2003. "H-1B Petitions Received and Approved in Fiscal Year 2003" (Fact Sheet). Washington.

U.S. Immigration and Naturalization Service (INS). 2002. *Report on the Characteristics of Specialty Occupation Workers (H-1B): Fiscal Year 2001.* Washington.

Usdansky, Margaret L., and Thomas J. Espenshade. 2000. "The H-1B Visa Debate in Historical Perspective: The Evolution of U.S. Policy toward Foreign-Born Workers." Working Paper 11. San Diego: Center for Comparative Immigration Studies.

Vidal, Jean-Pierre. 1998. "The Effect of Emigration on Human Capital Formation." *Journal of Population Economics* 11, no. 4: 589–600.

Warner, R. Stephen. 2000. "Religion and New (Post-1965) Immigrants: Some Principles Drawn from Field Research." *American Studies* 41(2/3): 267–87.

Wibulpolparsert, Suwit. 2003. "International Trade and Migration of Health Care Workers: The Case of Thailand." In *Moving People to Deliver Services,* edited by Aaditya Mattoo and Antonia Carzaniga. Oxford University Press.

Winters, L. Alan. 2000. "Trade, Trade Policy and Poverty: What Are the Links?" Research Paper 2382. Washington: Center for Economic Policy Research.

————. 2003. "Going Alone: The Case for Relaxed Reciprocity in Freeing Trade." *Economic Journal* 113 (November): F656–58.

Wolf, Martin. 2004. *Why Globalization Works.* Yale University Press.

Woodruff, Christopher, and Rene Zenteno. 2001. "Remittances and Microenterprises in Mexico." Unpublished paper. University of California, San Diego.

World Bank. 2000. *Scientific and Technical Manpower Development in India.* Report 20416-IN. Washington.

World Health Organization (WHO). 2002. *Estimates of Population per Health Professional.* Geneva.

Yale, Richmond. 2003. *Cultural Exchange and the Cold War: Raising the Iron Curtain.* Pennsylvania State University Press.

Index